Pick of the Crop

Pick of the Crop

Cooking with vegetables

Gail Duff

Elm Tree Books: *London*

First published in Great Britain 1979
by Elm Tree Books/Hamish Hamilton Ltd,
Garden House, 57/59 Long Acre, London
WC2E 9JZ. Published in the United States
of America by Elm Tree Books in association
with David & Charles Inc, North Pomfret,
Vermont 05053, USA.

British Library Cataloguing in Publication Data
Duff, Gail
  Pick of the crop.
  1. Vegetables   2. Fruit   3. Cookery
  (Vegetables)   4. Cookery (Fruit)
  I. Title
  635   SB322   79-40441
  ISBN 0-241-10175-1

Typeset by Pioneer Associates
Printed & Bound in Great Britain by Redwood Burn

Acknowledgements

For every British farmer and grower

This book could never have been written without all the help and co-operation I have received from innumerable farmers and market gardeners. Many have spared valuable time to show me their vegetables being sown, planted, grown, harvested and packed, and others have supplied me with helpful information over the telephone.

In particular I should like to thank:
Paddy Rattray of Growers and Saphir (Kent) Ltd.
Vernon Groves of Home Grown Fruits, Canterbury
Frederick Barker and John Tremlett of J.J. Barker, Hook Place Farm, Southfleet
Ken Crundwell of J.J. Kemsley, Northend Farm, Betsham
John Gorf of Darland Farm, Hempstead
Ralph Stevens of Siloam Farm, Rainham
John Ackock of Fourayes Farm Ltd., Bicknor
Tim Long of Marshgate Farm, Cooling
Alan Osenton of Home Farm, Grain
Gerald Lane of Quichrells Farm, Cliffe
Roger Gedney of Dairy Farm, Chainhurst
Major Perrott of Garrington Watercress, Littlebourne
George Allen of Bilting Nurseries Ltd., Wye
Rodney Derrick of Westland Nurseries Ltd., Ash
Ken Hutchinson of Meresborough Nursery, Rainham
W. Ward of the British Land Settlement Association, Strawberry Hill, Newent, Gloucestershire
Market gardeners Ronald Sedge, Peter Witherden, Captain and Mrs Chester
Eric Humphrey of the British Farm Produce Council
Tom Penryth of the N.F.U., Maidstone
Eric Bate of the Ministry of Agriculture, Canterbury

Introduction

Fresh vegetables and fruit to me are one of the pleasures of life, not only eating them, but buying them, looking at colourful mounds of them in shop windows, talking about them and watching them grow. The more you work with them the more fascinating they become and the more you wish to make use of their every property. Vegetables can be prepared and cooked in innumerable ways to bring out their flavour and make the most of their goodness. Most have a long history in Britain and all sorts of recipes have been made with them over the years which can still be a form of inspiration to the modern cook. It's worth looking into history to discover forgotten uses and to see if they can be adapted today. We can take spices from one century and a method from another and blend them all together to make something completely new and exciting to be cooked quickly and easily on a new electric or gas stove.

When this, my second vegetable book, was planned, I intended simply to tie all the recipes together with snippets of interesting historical detail, to kindle people's interest and to share my fascination, but this was all changed one cold and windy spring day. I was driving along with my husband through the flat, bleak fields of the Isle of Thanet in Kent when we suddenly noticed some women crouching down in a field full of green pulling something up. From a distance we couldn't make out what it was, so we drove the Landrover down the track to investigate. It was salad onions — several acres of them! I don't think any thing has made such an impression before or since. I must have bought hundreds of bunches of salad onions in my time, but never had I actually looked past the shop window and thought how they had arrived there. I had been buying, cooking and singing the praises of fresh vegetables for years, but this small experience made me realize that there was so much I didn't know about them.

So, since the salad onion experience, I have skidded over muddy tracks in various farm vehicles, waded through seas of cauliflowers and curly kale, and followed along behind a seed drill up a stony field. In my searches I have been helped by many people and in the process made a good many friends. I have phoned shops who have recommended warehouses, who in their turn have given me the name of

1

farmers and growers. And when no information could be gathered this way I have turned to the Ministry of Agriculture, the local NFU and the British Farm Produce Council.

Wherever I have visited, I have found nothing but enthusiasm about their produce from farmers, farm managers and workers alike, and have been impressed by the way in which they all work together and the pride that they take in sending out nothing but the best.

In this book, I have tried to show just how much time, effort and loving care is involved in providing us all with fresh vegetables and fruit of all kinds right through the year. It isn't supposed to be a technical journal (although I hope all the information is correct!) — it is more a collection of facts gathered from present day farms and from a few history books, that I hope will kindle interest and spark off culinary enthusiasm.

One farm I have visited on several occasions has the motto 'Grown well to be cooked well' and I think that just about sums it up. We, the housewives and cooks, are the final ones in a chain of people all employed in producing the best possible vegetable dishes for our family and friends. These histories, accounts and recipes are intended to help us to do so.

Herbs

In this book I have used quantities for fresh herbs. Should these be unobtainable then substitute with dried but halve the quantities.

Roots

Parsnips

Think of root vegetables and parsnips probably come to mind first for they are classic roots in both shape and colour.

They have a long history in Britain being introduced first by the Romans and flourishing here as our climate is perfect for parsnips. They have the warm summer sun in which to grow and then, in the late autumn, sharp frosts to soften the roots and turn them mellow and sweet.

For many years the parsnip was a homely garden vegetable and not a widely-grown field crop. During Medieval times they were, like so many other vegetables, boiled up in the pot to make the thick soupy stew known as pottage. The earliest written recipe for parsnips tells you to boil them in broth, add some minced onions and saffron, and serve the result strewn with cinnamon and sugar.

It was common at the time to mix both sweet and savoury in the same dish. The rich could intensify the sweetness with both sugar and honey, but the poor could afford no such luxuries and so valued highly the natural sweetness of the parsnip. During Lent and on fasting days parsnips were boiled up with salt fish to make it more palatable, and very often they were mixed with spices and dried fruits and made into sweet pies. Parsnip fritters were a favourite in Elizabethan times, dipped in batter, deep-fried, and served with sugar or honey.

These ways with parsnips may sound a little incongruous for the present day when we have so many sweeteners and flavourers readily available; but if you boil parsnips without salt, mash them up, mix in some honey, cinnamon and nutmeg or perhaps a little ginger and some sultanas you have a perfect filling for a sweet pie. Make it a little richer by mixing in some beaten egg and bake it, uncovered, in a pastry-lined flan ring. It makes a traditional-tasting, relatively low-caloried sweet and usually no-one can guess its main ingredient.

In the eighteenth and nineteenth centuries these sweet dishes disappeared and parsnips were mostly boiled and buttered or mashed with cream or milk. They were still served with salt fish and sometimes with boiled pork or salt beef. Mrs Beeton recommends what we would now probably call sauteed parsnips — boiling them, slicing them thickly and frying them 'a good pale brown' in butter to be served with roast beef.

One other use for parsnips which certainly must not be forgotten is wine. The sweetness of the vegetable itself makes the brew mellow without being too pungent like some of the flower wines can be, and, with keeping, it becomes a golden colour, like the colour of the root when it is as its best.

Parsnips have been grown as a field crop since the end of the seventeenth century and they grow best on fine sandy soils. They are sown in March so the first ones will be ready in the autumn, and they are not all harvested at once, but stay in the ground until they are needed, sometimes right round until the following May. From August to October they have big, leafy, bright green tops but the leaves die down later on.

There are many machines for actually getting root vegetables out of

4

the ground, but once they are up most of the work is manual. The workers, usually women, come along the rows, snap off any leaves and load the parsnips into sacks to be carried off to be washed and sorted. The leaves are ploughed in now to enrich the soil, but until the nineteenth century they were fed to cattle and according to an agricultural manual of 1858 gave 'much richness to the milk'.

The extent to which root vegetables are washed or scrubbed usually depends on the size of the grower and their eventual market. A market gardener supplying local shops for example, may just brush off the worst of the dirt or perhaps scrub them manually in a big tank or bath. But for the supermarkets and big wholesale markets the process is more complicated with several stages of washing and trimming.

The clean parsnips are either boxed and sent to market as they are or put into polythene bags, check-weighed and sent off to supermarkets usually on the same day.

As with most vegetables, much of the goodness of parsnips is just under the surface, so for most of their season it is only necessary to give them a quick wash or scrub, depending on how you buy them and remove any brown pieces. Later in the season, however, you may find that the outside layer becomes tough, so scrape them or peel them as thinly as possible. Whatever the final dish is to be, the woody core should always be removed. If your parsnips are small you can boil them whole and remove the core after cooking; or alternatively, if they are large, cut them in half lengthways first and scoop out the core with a small, sharp knife.

There are all sorts of ways of cooking parsnips. You can fry them to make them golden and crisp on the outside and melt-in-the-mouth in the centre. Use them instead of potatoes, or use equal parts of both vegetables together.

You can cut parsnips into chunks and roast them in the oven in butter or dripping like potatoes. They are even better put round the joint so they pick up all the flavour. Beef is the best meat for putting with roast parsnips.

Stuffed with breadcrumbs, they can make a crispy and good-looking accompaniment to roast beef or chicken, the sage here providing a good savoury contrast to the vegetable's slight sweetness.

Stuffed Parsnip Rings

3 large parsnips, each weighing about 350g (12 oz) before coring
75g (3 oz) butter
1 medium onion, finely chopped

175g (6 oz) granary bread crumbs (or wholemeal)
15ml (1 tablespoon) chopped sage
fine sea salt and freshly ground black pepper to taste

Preheat the oven to 200°C (400°F)/Gas 6.

Cut the slightly knobbly stalk ends and any really narrow ends from the parsnips and cut each one into slices 3cm (1 in) thick. Cut the cores from the rings. (If they are small, use an apple corer; if not, then a small sharp knife.) Put half the butter into a large, flat, oven-proof dish and put it into the oven to melt. Melt the remaining butter in a frying pan on a low heat. Put in the onion and let it soften. Take the pan from the heat and work in the breadcrumbs, sage and seasoning. Take the dish of melted butter from the oven and turn the parsnip rings in it to make sure they are well-coated. Lay them all in the dish and pack the stuffing in the middles. Put the dish into the centre of the oven for 50 minutes.

The parsnips are brown on the outside and soft and succulent in the middle and the outside crumbs go brown and crisp.

Parsnips and potatoes can be pureed or braised together.

Potato and Parsnip Purée

450g (1 lb) potatoes
675g (1½ lb) parsnips weighed before removing the cores
40g (1½ oz) butter
90ml (6 tablespoons) milk
30ml (2 tablespoons) chopped parsley
30ml (2 tablespoons) chopped chives or scallions
15ml (1 tablespoon) grated Parmesan cheese

Boil the potatoes in their skins. Boil the parsnips separately until they are tender. Peel the potatoes whilst they are still warm. Put the potatoes and parsnips together through a sieve or mash them well together. Beat in the butter, milk and herbs and pile the mixture into a heatproof serving dish. Arrange it so it stands up in peaks and scatter the cheese over the top. Put it under a high grill to brown.

Braised Potatoes and Parsnips

450g (1 lb) potatoes
675g (1½ lb) parsnips (weighed before coring)
25g (1 oz) dripping
1 large onion, thinly sliced
30ml (2 tablespoons) chopped
parsley or 10 chopped sage leaves
275ml (½ pt) stock
fine sea salt and freshly ground black pepper

Preheat the oven to 180°C (350°F)/Gas 4.

Scrub the potatoes and parsnips, leaving their skins intact. Chop them into 2cm (¾ in) dice. Melt the dripping in a flameproof casserole on a low heat. Put in the onion and cook it until it is golden. Stir in the parsnips and potatoes and the parsley or sage. Pour in the stock, season well, and bring it to the boil. Cover the casserole and put it into the centre of the oven for one hour, by which time all the stock should be absorbed and the vegetables tender and tasty.

It is fairly hard to track down salt fish these days, but you can still use parsnips to make an unusual fish pie which is very cheap but delicious and attractive enough to be served at a dinner party besides being a good every-day meal for a family.

Parsnip Fish Pie

675g (1½ lb) parsnips
1 small onion thinly sliced
15ml (1 tablespoon) chopped thyme
15ml (1 tablespoon) chopped parsley
675g (1½ lb) whiting fillets

225g (½ lb) cockles
30ml (2 tablespoons) seasoned wholemeal flour
25g (1 oz) butter
1 large onion, thinly sliced
150ml (¼ pt) dry white wine
15g (½ oz) butter

Preheat the oven to 180°C (350°F)/Gas 4.

Core the parsnips, peel them if necessary, and slice the small onion. Boil them together in salted water until the parsnips are tender. Drain and mash them together and mix in half the parsley and thyme. Skin the whiting fillets and remove any fine bones that may still be left on. Cut the fish into small pieces about 3cm (1 in) square. Toss the whiting and the cockles in the flour and put them with the remaining herbs into a pie dish. Melt 25g (1 oz) of butter in a small frying pan on a low heat. Put in the large onion and cook it until it is soft. Pour in the wine and bring it to the boil and pour all the contents of the pan into the pie dish. Mix everything in the dish together. Spread the mashed parsnips over the top and make patterns on it with a fork. Dot the top with 15g (½ oz) butter and bake for 45 minutes so it browns on the top.

Parsnips and eggs here make a cheap lunch or supper dish. Although there are only four eggs the amounts here are quite enough for four people as the parsnips are so substantial.

Serve it hot immediately or cold and cut into wedges as a snack for parties or for a winter picnic.

For a vegetarian meal you could leave out the bacon and mix in 50g (2 oz) grated Farmhouse Cheddar cheese.

7

Parsnip and Egg Bake

450g (1 lb) parsnips
25g (1 oz) butter
1 large onion, finely chopped
100g (4 oz) lean bacon, finely
  chopped
4 eggs
freshly ground black pepper

15ml (1 tablespoon) mixed
  chopped thyme, sage and
  parsley
butter for greasing 18cm (7 in)
  enamel skillet, paella pan or
  cake tin

Cut the parsnips in half lengthways and remove their cores. Chop them into very thin slices. Melt the butter in a heavy saucepan on a low heat, put in the onion and bacon and cook them until they are on the point of browning. Stir in the prepared parsnips, cover with a butter paper and a lid and let them sweat for ten minutes. Take the pan from the heat and mash all the contents together with a fork (A potato masher will get blocked.) Stir in the eggs, pepper and herbs. Pour the mixture into the well-buttered skillet or tin and bake it for 20 minutes. It should be set, slightly risen and golden brown.

Cook parsnips and chicken together for an unusual winter meal which, although warming and tasty, has no thick sauce to make it too heavy. The slight saltiness of the bacon makes a good contrast to the sweetness of the parsnips and ale.

Chicken and Parsnips in Brown Ale

One 1.5kg (3-3½ lb) roasting
  chicken
100g (4 oz) streaky bacon
350g (12 oz) parsnips (weighed
  before coring)

1 large onion, thinly sliced
275ml (½ pt) brown ale
10 chopped sage leaves
freshly ground black pepper
a little grated nutmeg

Joint the chicken. Cut the rinds from the bacon and keep them. Dice the rashers. Core the parsnips and cut them into 1.5cm (½ in) dice. Put the bacon and bacon rinds into a large sauté pan or heavy frying pan and set it on a low heat. When the fat begins to run and the bacon has cooked a little, raise the heat to moderate. Put in the chicken joints, skin-side down first, and cook them until they are golden brown. Remove the chicken and bacon and discard the rinds. Lower the heat, put in the onion and let it soften. Stir in the diced parsnips. Pour in the ale and add the sage, pepper and nutmeg. Bring the ale to the boil and replace the chicken and bacon. Cover, and cook on a very low heat for 30 minutes, turning the chicken once. Serve the chicken smothered with the parsnips and bacon.

8

Parsnips make good thick soups which need no flour or cream. Savory is an ideal herb for this one as it is a good perennial and you will have no trouble in finding some in the herb garden all through winter. In this soup it takes away any sweetness in the parsnips and sharpens up the tomato flavour.

Parsnip and Tomato Soup

225g (½ lb) parsnips (weighed
   before coring)
225g (½ lb) tomatoes
25g (1 oz) butter
1 large onion, thinly sliced
725ml (1¼ pt) stock

bouquet garni
15ml (1 tablespoon) chopped
   winter savory
15ml (1 tablespoon) chopped
   parsley

Scrub the parsnips and remove the cores. Cut them into small, thin pieces. Scald, skin and chop the tomatoes. Melt the butter in a heavy saucepan on a low heat. Stir in the parsnips and onion, cover and let them sweat for ten minutes. Stir in the tomatoes, cover again, and cook for two minutes more. Add the stock and bring it to the boil. Put in the bouquet garni, cover again and simmer for ten minutes. Remove the bouquet garni. Cool the soup and work it in a blender until it is smooth. Return it to the saucepan, stir in the chopped herbs and reheat.

If you hate throwing anything away, use the cores and trimmings of parsnips to make a brown gravy to serve with plain vegetables or for mixing with the pan residue to make a sauce for roast beef.

A Good Brown Gravy

25g (1 oz) dripping
45ml (3 tablespoons) chopped
   parsnip trimmings
1 small onion, finely chopped
1 small piece celery finely
   chopped

15ml (1 tablespoon) wholemeal
   flour
425ml (¾ pt) stock
sea salt and freshly ground black
   pepper
1 bayleaf
bouquet garni

Melt the dripping in a fairly small saucepan on a low heat. Stir in the diced vegetables and let them brown. Stir in the flour and brown that too. Add the stock, season and put in the bouquet garni and bayleaf. Bring it to the boil and skim. Cover and simmer for three quarters of an hour. Strain the sauce through a nylon sieve or conical strainer, pressing down hard to extract as much liquid as possible. Return it to the rinsed-out pan, reheat it and simmer for two minutes.

Turnips

Turnips, with their smooth outer surface, even round shape, fresh green and white colouring and crisp crunchy texture also have an established place in both cooking and farming history.

They were first grown in Britain by the Romans who put them into a sauce flavoured with cumin, and also pickled them and used them as a substitute for anchovies. They were grown alongside parsnips in Anglo-Saxon gardens and both the leaves and roots were put into the pottage pot. Later the young leaves were chopped and put into salads.

Right from the beginning, the most common way with turnips seems to have been to boil them, either with the meat or poultry, or separately to be served as an accompaniment. Even the Romans, who rarely served up anything unless it was heavily disguised, served plain boiled turnips with roasted crane. In Elizabethan times they were boiled with duck and flavoured with onions and spices; and in the seventeenth and eighteenth centuries they were boiled with salt beef and served with plenty of pepper and butter. Occasionally, turnips were roasted whole in the hot ashes of the fire, and Eliza Acton in 1845 recommended boiling them whole in their skins, peeling them and making them into a purée with cream and milk. Most of the other recipes around this time are variations of the boiling and buttering method or boiling and coating them with a thick white sauce.

Like parsnips, turnips in early years were grown mostly in gardens and small plots and it was not until the seventeenth century that turnips were grown increasingly as a field crop, rotating very effectively with cereals and clover and being used primarily as animal fodder.

Turnips are still a dual-purpose crop and it is usually the ones that are grown on the smaller market gardens and on small areas of land that find their way into the shops. They are dug mechanically in the same way as parsnips, lifted by hand, and then washed and trimmed. They are sent out to markets in sacks and crates, and for supermarkets they are weighed and put into bags.

All you need to do to prepare turnips for cooking is to give them a quick wash or scrub. Keep in their flavour and goodness by leaving them unpeeled. Although boiling turnips has been the fashion for years, there are many more ways of cooking them to bring out a variety of flavours and textures.

I don't suppose you will be able to roast them in hot ashes, but whole, baked turnips can make an attractive garnish for roast chicken or duck. You can either put them into the same roasting pan or cook them separately in butter or dripping. Baste them well, and give them 1¼ hours in a moderate oven. Cooked in an open roasting dish they have a strong flavour and a brown, firm skin, but for a milder flavour and softer skin you can wrap them in lightly greased foil and cook them for the same amount of time.

Turnips can also be fried in shallow fat to give them a texture that is soft and melty. Use either butter or beef dripping and cook them on a moderate heat for 20 minutes, moving them around fairly frequently so they brown evenly.

Turnips can be simmered with a little liquid and different flavourings on top of the stove, or they can be braised in the oven to bring out a really savoury, rooty flavour.

Braised Turnips with Tomato Purée and Horseradish

450g (1 lb) small white turnips   15ml (1 tablespoon) tomato purée
25g (1 oz) beef dripping or butter   15ml (1 tablespoon) grated
150ml (¼ pt) stock   horseradish

Preheat the oven to 180°C (350°F)/Gas 4.

Cut the turnips into 2cm (¾ in) dice without peeling. Melt the dripping or butter in a small casserole on a moderate heat. Put in the turnips and let them brown, stirring them around occasionally. Pour in

11

the stock and bring it to the boil. Stir in the tomato purée and horseradish. Cover and put the casserole into the oven for half an hour.

Serve turnips cooked like this with plain roast beef.

Turnips can take on a light, fluffy texture when they are grated and steamed. If you do not have a steamer, put them in a colander over a saucepan of simmering water and cover them with foil.

Steamed Turnips with Lemon

450g (1 lb) white turnips
 (although you are grating
 them, choose the smaller ones
 if you can as they are firmer
 textured)
25g (1 oz) butter

juice 1 lemon
15ml (1 tablespoon) chopped
 lemon thyme (or ordinary
 thyme)
15ml (1 tablespoon) chopped
 parsley

Grate the turnips fairly finely. Put them in a vegetable steamer and cook them over lightly simmering water for 20 minutes, turning them over once for even cooking. Heat the butter in a saucepan on a moderate heat and let it brown. Pour in the lemon juice and add the herbs. Let the lemon bubble for a few seconds and stir in the turnips. Remove the pan from the heat and make sure everything is thoroughly mixed together.

Grated turnips can also make winter salads, sometimes alone and sometimes with apples or other root vegetables. This one includes tomatoes for a contrast in flavour, texture and appearance. Mixing them in at the last minute keeps them nice and firm.

Turnip, Carrot and Tomato Salad

2 small white turnips, grated
2 large carrots, grated
225g (½ lb) firm tomatoes,
 roughly chopped
1 carton (5 fl oz) natural yoghurt

30ml (2 tablespoons) cider
 vinegar
15ml (1 tablespoon) tomato
 purée

Mix the turnips and carrots together in a bowl. Blend the yoghurt, vinegar and tomato purée together and mix them into the grated vegetables. Let them stand for 15 minutes and mix in the tomatoes just before serving.

This turnip and ham soup is a good way of using the stock and any left-overs from a joint of boiled ham.

Turnip and Ham Soup

350g (12 oz) small white turnips
850ml (1½ pt) ham stock
15ml (1 tablespoon) Dijon
mustard

50g (2 oz) lean ham, very finely
diced
30ml (2 tablespoons) chopped
parsley

Dice the turnips and put them into a saucepan with the stock. Bring them to the boil, cover, and simmer for 20 minutes. Cool them slightly and then work them in a blender until they are smooth. Put the mustard into the saucepan and gradually stir in the soup. Mix in the ham and parsley and reheat.

Although turnips have their own characteristic flavour it is very adaptable and seems to go with most kinds of meat. They have always been popular in the low countries, so I have used lager, one of their favourite drinks, for this pork recipe.

Pork and Turnips in Lager

900g (2 lb) lean boneless pork
either from the lean end of
the belly or spare rib chops
450g (1 lb) small white turnips
30ml (2 tablespoons) of rendered
pork fat or 25g (1 oz) butter

1 large onion, thinly sliced
15ml (1 tablespoon) carraway
seeds
275ml (½ pt) lager
10 chopped sage leaves

Dice the pork and the turnips into 2cm (¾ in) cubes. Heat the fat in a large flameproof casserole on a high heat. Put in the pork pieces and brown them well. Remove them and set them aside. Lower the heat and cool the pan a little. Put in the onion, turnips, and carraway seeds and cook them until the onion is soft, moving them around occasionally. Pour in the lager and bring it to the boil. Replace the pork and add the sage. Cover, and set the casserole on a low heat on top of the stove for one hour.

Here is another recipe using beer with scones on the top which are deliciously light in texture and quite lemony. They make a beautiful contrast to the savoury turnip-flavoured stew.

13

Beef, Turnip and Lemon Cobblers

900g (2 lb) stewing beef
450g (1 lb) small white turnips
25g (1 oz) beef dripping
1 large onion, thinly sliced
275ml (½ pt) light ale less 45ml
  (3 tablespoons) that you take
  away for the scones

15ml (1 tablespoon) chopped
  parsley
15ml (1 tablespoon) chopped
  lemon thyme
juice ½ lemon
1 bay leaf

For the scones:

175g (6 oz) 85 or 81% wholemeal
  self-raising flour
pinch fine sea salt
freshly ground black pepper
5ml (1 teaspoon) mustard
  powder
grated rind 1 lemon

15ml (1 tablespoon) chopped
  lemon thyme
15ml (1 tablespoon) chopped
  parsley
50g (2 oz) butter
1 egg, beaten
45ml (3 tablespoons) light ale

Preheat the oven to 150°C (300°F)/Gas 2.

Dice the beef and turnips into 2cm (¾ in) cubes. Melt the dripping in a heavy flameproof casserole on a high heat. Put in the beef and brown it. Do this in two batches so as not to overcrowd the bottom of the pan. Remove the beef and set it aside. Lower the heat, put in the onion and turnips and cook them gently until the onion is soft. Pour in the ale and bring it to the boil. Add the lemon juice, parsley, lemon thyme and bayleaf and replace the beef. Cover and put the casserole into the oven for 1½ hours.

Make the scones while the beef is cooking. Put the flour into a bowl with the salt, pepper, mustard, lemon rind and herbs. Rub in the butter with your fingers. Make a well in the centre and gradually mix in the beaten egg and the beer, so you have a stiff dough. Divide it into eight and make round flat scones about 1.5-2cm (½-¾ in) thick. Take the casserole from the oven and raise the temperature to 200°C (400°F)/Gas 6. Put the beef into an oven-to-table casserole dish and remove the bayleaf. Put the scones on top of the beef and put the dish into the oven for 45 minutes so the scones are golden brown.

N.B. If you haven't an oven-to-table dish, put the scones on top of the beef in the original casserole and when you serve it, carefully lift the scones out first, put the beef into a serving dish and put the scones back on top.

The turnips in the next recipe turn out with a delicate flavour to go with that of the calves liver. The cream adds a special touch of richness, but you could just as easily leave it out.

Calves Liver and Turnips

350g (1½ lb) calves liver
450g (1 lb) small white turnips
50g (2 oz) butter
1 large onion, thinly sliced

150ml (¼ pt) dry white wine
5ml (1 teaspoon) dried sage
60ml (4 tablespoons) double
  cream

Cut the liver into small thin pieces. Scrub the turnips. Cut each one in half lengthways and then into thin slices. Melt half the butter in a large frying pan or sauté pan on a high heat. Taking half at a time, brown the pieces of liver on both sides. Remove them and set them aside. Lower the heat, cool the pan a little and put in the remaining butter. Stir in the turnips and onion, cover, and cook on a very low heat for ten minutes. Pour in the wine and bring it to the boil. Replace the liver and add the sage. Cover again, and continue cooking for a further five minutes. Stir in the cream, let the sauce bubble and serve.

A green salad and brown rice are ideal accompaniments.

Turnips provide the main flavouring for a chicken casserole.

Chicken with Turnips and Apples

one 1.5kg (3-3½ lb) roasting
  chicken
30ml (2 tablespoons) rendered
  chicken fat or 15g (½ oz)
  butter
4 small white turnips

3 small cooking apples
1 large onion, thinly sliced
275ml (½ pt) dry cider
large bouquet garni
30ml (2 tablespoons) chopped
  parsley

Preheat the oven to 150°C (325°F)/Gas 3.

Joint the chicken. Quarter the turnips. Peel, quarter and core the apples and cut each quarter in half lengthways. Melt the butter in a flameproof casserole on a moderate heat. Put in the chicken pieces, skin-side down first, and brown them. Lower the heat, put in the turnips, apples and onions and cook them until they are beginning to brown. Pour in the cider and bring it to the boil. Tuck in the bouquet garni, cover the casserole and put it into the oven for 50 minutes. Take out the chicken pieces, arrange them on a serving dish and keep them warm. Skim the juices in the casserole if necessary, bring everything in the casserole to the boil, add the parsley and simmer for one minute. Spoon all the juices and pieces of turnip and apple over the chicken to serve.

For a good contrast in colour, serve it with watercress or a green salad.

Swede

Swede, with their warm red colour and earthy flavour are the ideal winter vegetable. They were a late arrival to Britain coming, as their name implies, from Sweden in the late eighteenth century. At first they were called 'Swedish Turnips' and also by their original delightful name of 'Rutabagas', but this required a fair bit of tongue twisting, so swedes they became and swedes they stayed.

Whatever their name, they are a hardier vegetable than white turnips and it was soon found that they could be grown all through the cold winters in the north of England and in Scotland. Soon they were readily accepted as a fodder-crop all over the country.

Early recipes for swede are few and far between, and I have not been able to find out exactly when they were first used for cooking. They were put into pasties in Cornwall in the nineteenth century to make a substantial meal for the hard-working tin-miners and at around the same time they were put into mutton broths in Scotland.

Now most of those destined for the pot are grown in Devon although they are still grown in most counties for fodder. They are mechanically dug when they are needed, lifted by hand and put into crates and sacks and sent all over the country. They can be sold in the wholesale markets by the crate, still with the rich, red Devon earth clinging to them, or they can be sent to packhouses where they are washed and wrapped before going on to the big supermarket depots.

Washing swedes in bulk is a messy job. Often it is done outside the packhouse to prevent the puddles of red mud from being trodden everywhere. Then the clean vegetables trundle along on a conveyor belt to be trimmed, sorted and weighed. The large ones are wrapped alone and the smaller ones are put into packs, all usually within a day of their being lifted in the field.

The outer surface of swedes can be tough and stringy, and sometimes they can have a few knobbly pieces of root attached, and if this is the case, peel and trim them before cooking. Where the skins are fairly thin, keep them on to give a good earthy flavour, particularly for stews and for braising.

If swedes are small, they can be cut in half and roasted in butter or round the joint, and if they are large you can cut them into chunks 3cm (1 in) thick and 6cm (2 in) long, and treat them in the same way. Scatter some herbs over them for the last few minutes to make them really tasty. Use thyme if they are to be served with lamb, rosemary for pork, and parsley or sage for beef.

Grating and steaming swede gives a fresh-tasting, firm-textured purée, without the lumps or stringy pieces you sometimes get with boiling and mashing.

Steamed Swede

450g (1 lb) swede	*pinch sea salt*
bouquet garni	*freshly ground black pepper*
25g (1 oz) butter	*grated nutmeg to taste*

Peel the swede if necessary and grate it fairly finely. Put it into a vegetable steamer or colander covered with foil. Put in the bouquet garni and steam for 20 minutes, turning the swede over once for even cooking. Melt the butter in a saucepan on a moderate heat and, using a wooden spoon, stir in the swede. Lower the heat and stir in the salt, lots of pepper and freshly grated nutmeg to taste. Keep the pan on the low heat for five minutes, stirring fairly frequently.

Root vegetables always taste good cooked in beer. Try braising swede in the oven in barley wine. This is the basic method for braising swede. You can also use stock instead of beer and different herbs for flavouring.

Braised Swede in Barley Wine.

675g (1½ lb) swede
25g (1 oz) beef dripping or
* butter*
1 medium onion, thinly sliced

freshly ground black pepper
one 175ml (7 fl oz) bottle barley
* wine*

Preheat the oven to 180°C (350°F)/Gas 4.

Scrub the swede but do not peel it. Cut it into 2cm (¾ in) dice. Melt the dripping in a flameproof casserole on a low heat. Put in the onion and cook it until it is soft. Stir in the swede and season it well with the pepper. Pour in the barley wine and bring it to the boil. Cover the casserole and put it into the oven for 45 minutes.

Swede and bacon are another perfect combination, and the following recipe makes use of the fluffy but firm texture of grated swede.

Braised Grated Swede and Bacon

100g (4 oz) streaky bacon
1 medium onion, finely chopped
450g (1 lb) swede, grated

15ml (1 tablespoon) chopped
* thyme*
150ml (¼ pt) stock
freshly ground black pepper

Preheat the oven to 180°C (350°F)/Gas 4.

Dice the bacon and put it in a flameproof casserole with no fat. Set it on a low heat on top of the stove. When the fat begins to run, add the onion and cook it until it is just turning brown. Stir in the swede and thyme and pour in the stock. Season with lots of pepper. Cover the casserole and put it into the oven for 45 minutes.

Again, this is a basic method for braising. You could vary it by using butter or dripping instead of bacon; or by using beer or even white wine instead of stock. You can add nutmeg as well as pepper and a different herb such as parsley or savory.

And now for some really substantial pasties. All you need to go with them is a green salad, no potatoes as you have all the pastry instead.

Lamb and Swede Pasties

For four pasties

For the pastry:

450g (1 lb) wholemeal flour
225g (8 oz) good beef dripping
pinch fine sea salt

freshly ground black pepper
water to mix
beaten egg to brush it with

For the filling:

675g (1½ lb) lean boneless lamb,
   cut from the shoulder
225g (8 oz) swede
1 medium onion
30ml (2 tablespoons) chopped
   rosemary

30ml (2 tablespoons) chopped
   thyme
little fine sea salt
freshly ground black pepper
little freshly grated nutmeg

For the sauce:

15ml (1 tablespoon) dripping
1 small onion, finely chopped
1 small carrot, finely chopped
small piece celery stick, finely
   chopped
all the peelings from the swede,
   finely chopped

any trimmings from the lamb
   (not fatty ones), chopped
15ml (1 tablespoon) wholemeal
   flour
5ml (1 teaspoon) tomato purée
425ml (¾ pt) stock
bouquet garni

Preheat the oven to 160°C (325°F)/Gas 3.

For the pastry, rub the dripping into the flour, salt and pepper.

Bind the pastry with water and set it aside in a cool place while you prepare the rest. Dice the lamb into very small pieces. Peel the swede and reserve the peel. Chop the swede into dice the same size as the lamb. Mix the lamb with the herbs, salt and pepper. Divide the pastry into four and roll each one into a round. Put a quarter of the lamb across the centre of each one. Finely chop the onion and mix it with the swede. Scatter evenly over the lamb and grate over a little nutmeg. Bring the sides of the pastry rounds together and make them into Cornish Pasty shapes with the ridge of joined pastry down the top. Lay them on a large, floured baking sheet and brush them well with the beaten egg. Bake in the centre of the oven for 1½ hours.

Sauce. Melt the dripping in a saucepan on a low heat. Stir in the chopped vegetables, peel and trimmings and cook them until they brown. Stir in the flour and let it brown slightly. Take the pan from the heat and blend in the tomato purée and then the stock. Put the pan back on the heat and bring the sauce to the boil, stirring. Add the bouquet garni, cover and simmer for 45 minutes. Strain the sauce through a sieve or a conical strainer, pressing down hard to extract as much as possible. Return it to the rinsed-out pan and simmer for two minutes more. Serve the sauce and the pasties separately. When you eat the pasties, cut them open and pour the hot sauce inside.

Special note for slimmers: If you don't allow yourself pastry, put the same filling ingredients into a ring of foil and fold it into the same shape as the pastry. This way you won't miss out on the meal altogether. The

19

lamb and the vegetables will cook deliciously and will be just a little moist with all the aromas sealed in.

Nutmeg and cinnamon are perfect spices for swede and in this recipe all the flavours together penetrate the beef.

Rolled Skirt and Swede

900g (2 lb) beef skirt (choose two flat pieces rather than one thick one and make two separate rolls)
500-550g (1¼-1½ lb) swede
freshly grated nutmeg
5ml (1 teaspoon) ground cinnamon

15ml (1 tablespoon) chopped parsley
25g (1 oz) butter
1 large onion, thinly sliced
275ml (½ pt) stock

Preheat the oven to 180°C (350°F)/Gas 4.

Scrub the swede and peel it only if necessary. Grate 100g (4 oz) and dice the rest into 2cm (¾ in) pieces. Remove as much skin from the skirt as possible and lay it out flat, scoring it very slightly with a sharp knife to let it lie in an even square or oblong. Grate over a little nutmeg and sprinkle over half the cinnamon. Scatter over the grated swede and then the parsley. Roll up the meat and secure it with strong thread. Melt the butter in a flameproof casserole on a high heat. Put in the meat roll (or rolls) and brown it all over. Remove it and set it aside. Lower the heat and stir in the diced swede and onion. Cover, and let them sweat for seven minutes. Pour in the stock and add the remaining cinnamon and a little more nutmeg. Bring the stock to the boil and replace the meat. Cover, and put into the oven for 1¼ hours. Lift out the beef and remove the thread. Carve the beef into fairly thick slices — about six to each 450g (1 lb) roll. Arrange it on a warmed serving dish with the swede down each side. Pour any juices left in the casserole over the top.

Swede, like turnips, can be grated up into salads. This one makes a refreshing first course and it can be included on a table with a selection of salads. By halving the amount of yoghurt and keeping all the rest of the ingredients the same it will be suitable for serving as a side-salad.

Swede, Orange and Yoghurt Salad

350g (12 oz) swede
2 medium oranges (Spanish ones are the best)
4 cartons (20 fl oz) natural yoghurt

1 clove garlic crushed with a pinch of sea salt
freshly ground black pepper
juice of 1 lemon

Scrub and coarsely grate the swede. Cut the rind and pith from the oranges, slice them thinly and cut each slice into several pieces. Mix them into the swede. Mix the yoghurt, garlic, pepper and lemon juice and stir them into the swede and oranges.

Diced swede is often put into Scotch Broth which is an unblended soup. Try this hot, spicy one for a change.

Hot Swede and Carrot Soup

175g (6 oz) swede
175g (6 oz) carrots
25g (1 oz) butter
1 large onion, finely chopped
10ml (2 teaspoons) paprika

2.5ml (¼ teaspoon) cayenne
    pepper
10ml (2 teaspoons) tomato purée
10ml (2 teaspoons) flour
850ml (1½ pt) stock

Chop the swede and carrot into very small dice. Melt the butter in a saucepan on a low heat and stir in the swede, carrot, onion, paprika and cayenne. Cover and cook them gently for ten minutes. Stir in the flour and tomato purée and then the stock. Bring everything to the boil, stirring, and simmer, uncovered, for half an hour.

Carrots, old and new

Carrots are another vegetable with a long history. There are recipes in the Roman cookery book written by Apicius for fried carrots and for carrots cooked with parsnips, so like so many of our vegetables they were probably first cultivated in Britain in villa gardens.

After this they were mainly forgotten and left to grow wild and they were not adopted as a garden vegetable again until the fifteenth century. Like parsnips, carrots, if cooked in certain ways, can taste really sweet and they were valued most of all for this reason during Tudor and Stuart times, particularly by the poor. Even later in the eighteenth century when sugar was more readily available many recipes were written for sweet carrot puddings. Some were more like our Christmas puddings with dried fruits and spices and others were lighter in texture using the quarts of cream and dozens of eggs that so often went into the lavish sweets of the age.

I always use grated carrot for the Christmas pudding and in doing so never need any sugar, but simply rely on all the raisins, currants and sultanas to provide a natural sweetness with that of the carrots. Use grated carrot as well in fruit cakes and sweet tea breads to enable you to cut down on the sugar. They will be sweet, but not sugary sweet and much better for you.

Like turnips, when carrots were cooked in savoury ways they were roasted in hot ashes, and they have always been boiled and buttered or boiled and pureed with cream. Countless soups and broths have been made with carrots, and boiled beef and carrots has been popular for many years. A Frenchman, Henri Misson de Valbourg, writing of his travels in England during the 1690s says that the beef was salted for two or three days, boiled and then served up surrounded by 'five or six heaps of cabbage, carrots, turnips, or some other herbs or roots, well peppered and swimming in butter'.

The feathery leaves of new carrots were considered so attractive by the ladies of Charles I's court that they used to wear them for decoration. Add a few to a vase of flowers, and few people will ever be able to guess what they are!

Country wine can be made from carrots, similar to parsnip but not with quite so strong a flavour. A lovely golden-coloured brew can be made with carrots and wheat.

Carrots grow well on sandy soil, and when they were mainly a garden crop the area around Sandwich in Kent was famous for them. Suffolk became the main county for growing carrots as a field crop as early as the sixteenth century, and it has been so ever since.

If carrots are grown on a really large acreage, they can be dug up with a mechanical harvester that lifts them directly into large bins. Very often, though, they are lifted with a digger and picked up by hand and put into bags or nets in a similar way to parsnips. For the first part of the season their dark green, ferny tops are left on and the carrots are tied up in bunches out in the field. Later on they are snapped off and ploughed back in.

As the soil in which they mostly grow is so fine, carrots need little or no washing if they are to sent to market unwrapped as most of the dirt falls away from them as they are shaken over the belt of the digger. The bunches may be laid in plastic trays and sprayed with jets of water, but often they are left as they are. For packing into polythene bags, however, they are sometimes put through a rotating drum washer, like parsnips.

Even when you buy muddy carrots, very little preparation is involved before cooking. Unless they have a really dry outside (which they may towards the end of the season) there is no need at all to scrape or peel them, just scrub them well and grate, slice or chop them as you please to suit your particular method of cooking and serving. Carrots are an irreplaceable flavourer in stocks, sauces, pot-roasted dishes and stews, and they can also be a delicious vegetable in their own right, both cooked and in winter salads.

22

Taking a tip from roasting root vegetables in hot ashes, carrots can be baked. Choose ones about 10cm (4 in) long with the widest part about 3cm (1 in) in diameter, and leave them whole. They are best baked with a little butter, well-basted, in a moderate oven for 1¼ hours. They will brown on the outside and the sweetness of their flavour will be brought out. If you would like a softer outside that is still orange, and a milder flavour, wrap them in oiled foil and bake them for the same amount of time.

Here is another way of baking carrots that really brings out their sweetness and makes them rich and buttery.

Carrots Anna

450g (1 lb) large, thick carrots
25g (1 oz) butter plus a little more for greasing a piece of foil

freshly ground black pepper
freshly grated nutmeg

Preheat the oven to 180°C (350°F)/Gas 4.

Thickly butter a round 20cm (7 in) diameter cake tin or skillet. Slice the carrots into paper thin rounds. (Use a mandolin cutter if you have one). Put two layers of overlapping carrot rings in the base of the tin. Season with the pepper and nutmeg and dot with butter. Carry on layering until all the carrots are used. Season the top and cover with well-buttered foil weighed down with a fitting lid or heavy, oven-proof plate. Set the pan on a moderate heat on top of the stove for two minutes and then transfer it to the oven for 45 minutes. Turn out the carrots carefully so you have a round, flat orange cake, slightly browned on the top.

If you cook carrots on top of the stove, slice them and put them into a saucepan with 275ml (½ pt) of liquid and 15ml (1 oz) butter to the pound. You can use water or stock, wine or cider and flavour them with chopped herbs. Cook the carrots, covered, on a moderate heat for 20 minutes. They should be just tender and will have absorbed most of the liquid.

Here is an example of this method using wine and stock and using onions as well for flavour.

Carrots and Onions in White Wine

450g (1 lb) carrots
25g (1 oz) butter
2 medium onions, thinly sliced
60ml (4 tablespoons) chopped parsley

150ml (¼ pt) dry white wine
150ml (¼ pt) stock

Slice the carrots into 0.5cm (¼ in) rounds. Melt the butter in a saucepan on a low heat. Put in the onions and cook them until they are soft. Stir in the carrots and parsley and pour in the wine and stock. Raise the heat to moderate, cover and cook for 20 minutes.

Carrots can be grated, either alone or with other root vegetables, or chopped finely and mixed with celery or shredded cabbage, for all kinds of crunchy winter salads; and if you would rather have them hot, then there are hot salads to be made as well. Try this unusual one with leeks and currants.

Hot Carrot and Leek Salad

225g (8 oz) carrots
225g (8 oz) leeks
30ml (2 tablespoons) white wine
  vinegar
10ml (2 teaspoons) English

Vineyard or other granular
  mustard
60ml (4 tablespoons) olive oil
50g (2 oz) currants

Slice the carrots paper thin. Wash and thinly slice the leeks. Blend the vinegar and mustard together. Heat the oil in a heavy frying pan on a high heat. Put in the carrots, leeks and currants and move them around on the heat for two minutes. Stir in the vinegar and mustard, let them bubble, and serve immediately.

This simple raw salad of grated carrots has a light, almost sherbety taste which makes it ideal for serving as a refresher with curries. You could also serve it as a light first course or as an accompaniment to any cold meat.

Carrot and Apple Salad

For the dressing:

1 carton (5 fl oz) natural yoghurt
30ml (2 tablespoons) cider
  vinegar
1 clove garlic, crushed with a
  pinch of sea-salt
freshly ground black pepper

5ml (1 teaspoon) ground cumin
5ml (1 teaspoon) ground
  coriander

1 really large or 2 medium sized
  Bramley apples
2 large carrots

Mix all the ingredients for the dressing in a serving bowl. Quarter and core the apple, but do not peel it. Grate it immediately into the dressing, stirring it in as you go. Grate in the carrots and mix everything together well.

Grated carrots do not necessarily have to be made into salads. They can also be cooked in a number of ways. For example, put 450g (1 lb) of grated carrots into a vegetable steamer or colander covered with foil and steam them for 20 minutes, turning them over once. Then mix them on a gentle heat with 25g (1 oz) of melted butter and some chopped herbs and you will have a light and fluffy purée.

Here they are cooked gently in butter and then mixed with curd cheese for a refreshing first course.

Carrot and Orange Cheese

125g (4 oz) carrots
15g (½ oz) butter
50g (2 oz) finely chopped onion
100g (4 oz) curd cheese
grated rind and juice of 1 small
  orange

60ml (4 tablespoons) chopped
  watercress
1 small orange for garnish

Grate the carrots. Melt the butter in a frying pan on a low heat. Put in the onion and carrot and cook them until the onion is soft, stirring most of the time to prevent the carrot from overcooking. Put them into a bowl and work in the cheese and orange rind and juice. Put half the mixture into an earthenware bowl and smooth over the surface. Press on half the watercress and cover it with the rest of the cheese. Chill the cheese until it is firm. Scatter the remaining watercress over the top and garnish the edges of the bowl with thin slices cut from the remaining orange.

Grated carrots can also be braised in the oven like turnips and swede.

In this recipe, grated carrots are put with grated swede to make a stuffing for lamb.

Loin of Lamb with Swede and Carrots

1 piece loin of lamb weighing
  900-1.125kg (2-2½ lb), chined
15ml (1 tablespoon) plus 5ml
  (1 teaspoon) tomato purée
15ml (1 tablespoon) chopped
  thyme
350g (12 oz) swede

350g (12 oz) carrots
30ml (2 tablepoons) lamb fat or
  15g (½ oz) butter
150ml (¼ pt) dry white wine
150ml (¼ pt) stock
freshly ground black pepper
bouquet garni

Preheat the oven to 180°C (350°F)/Gas 4.

Remove the bones from the lamb and spread the cut surface with the 15ml (1 tablespoon) of tomato purée. Scatter over the thyme.

Grate a little of the carrots and swede to give you 30ml (2 tablespoons) of each. Mix them together and spread them over the purée and thyme. Season with freshly ground black pepper. Roll up the joint and secure it with strong thread or fine cotton string. Chop the remaining swede and carrots into 2cm (¾ in) dice. Heat the fat or butter in a flameproof casserole on a high heat. Put in the lamb and brown it all over. Remove it and set it aside. Lower the heat and cool the casserole a little. Stir in the prepared vegetables, cover them and let them sweat for five minutes. Pour in the wine and stock and stir in the 5ml (1 teaspoon) tomato purée. Bring them to the boil and replace the lamb. Tuck in the bouquet garni and season to taste. Cover the casserole and put it into the oven for 1¼ hours. Take out the lamb and carve it into fairly thick slices. Do this carefully and they will look extremely attractive with a thin stripe of red tomato purée round an orange filling.

Arrange the lamb down the centre of a serving dish with the vegetables down either side and any juices that are left in the casserole poured over the top. (N.B. there will only be a few tablespoons as most will have been absorbed by the vegetables.)

The following salt beef dish is really Boiled Beef and Carrots with a difference. I always salt a large piece of brisket at Christmas and have found this a good way of using it up. It is not too fatty as some salt beef dishes can be and the vinegar and the sweetness of the carrots counteract any over-saltiness.

Salt Beef and Carrots

675-900g (1½-2 lb) cooked salt
  brisket
2 medium onions, very thinly
  sliced
450g (1 lb) carrots, very thinly
  sliced

30ml (2 tablespoons) grated
  horseradish
60ml (4 tablespoons) red wine
  vinegar
30ml (2 tablespoons) chopped
  parsley

Trim any excess fat from the beef and chop it. Put it into a large heavy frying pan and set it on a low heat to render down to make enough fat for frying. Discard it when you have 60ml (4 tablespoons) liquid fat in the pan. Dice the lean meat. Raise the heat to moderate. Put in the onions and carrots and stir them around for three minutes. Mix in the beef, horseradish and vinegar and carry on cooking for ten minutes, stirring occasionally. Toss in the parsley and serve. Accompany it with potatoes baked in their jackets.

Carrots make delicious thick winter soups and I always think garlic is one of the essential ingredients. Here, tomatoes are used as well for freshness and a slight sharpness.

Carrot and Tomato Soup with Garlic

225g (½ lb) carrots
1 large onion
25g (1 oz) butter
225g (½ lb) ripe tomatoes (buy 'frying' ones)
850ml (1½ pt) stock

1 large or 2 small cloves garlic, crushed with a pinch of sea salt
30ml (2 tablespoons) grated raw carrot

Thinly slice the carrots and onion. Melt the butter in a saucepan on a low heat. Stir in the carrots and onion, cover and let them sweat for ten minutes. Scald and skin the tomatoes and cut them in half. Take the saucepan of carrots from the heat. Squeeze the tomato seeds into a sieve and rub the juice into the saucepan. Put in the tomato halves. Pour in the stock and bring it to the boil. Add the bouquet garni. Cover and simmer for 20 minutes. Cool the soup slightly and remove the bouquet garni. Add the crushed garlic and work the soup in a blender until it is smooth. Reheat it and serve it in individual bowls with the grated raw carrot floating on the top.

Carrots are so plentiful for most of the year that they are often taken for granted; but suddenly in May the big, firm tasty ones that we have been able to buy all through the winter and spring disappear and we realize what we have lost. For a couple of months we have to rely on the not-so-flavoursome foreign ones, until the new ones arrive, all tied up in bundles with the leaves attached. These not only make them look attractive, but help them to stay fresh in the warm summer weather.

As with old carrots, all you need to do to prepare these new carrots is trim off the long stringy root and give them a quick scrub.

Probably because there are so many other vegetables around in the summer that are eaten raw, new carrots are more often served hot or in cooked salads; but there is no real reason why you can't slice them thinly (they would be too fiddly to grate) and serve them raw. Be careful, though, which other ingredients you mix them with in respect of texture. They won't, for example, go with tomatoes because one is hard and the other too soft. Green peppers are ideal and so are cucumbers and the very firm hearts of lettuces.

At the very start of their season, green peas are tender enough to be served raw and in this salad the spices bring out the sweetness of the two new vegetables while the mayonnaise penetrates and softens them slightly.

27

Raw Pea and Carrot Salad

225g (8 oz) very young green
peas, weighed in their shells
225g (8 oz) new carrots
60ml (4 tablespoons)
mayonnaise
2.5ml (½ teaspoon) ground
coriander

2.5ml (½ teaspoon) ground
cardamon
2.5ml (½ teaspoon) curry
powder

Shell the peas and thinly slice the carrots and put them together in a bowl. Mix the mayonnaise into the spices and fold the resulting dressing into the salad. Let it stand for 15 minutes before serving.

When you put cooked new carrots into salads, mix them into the dressing while they are still warm so they soak up all the flavour. You can use a simple French dressing flavoured with different herbs to go with your main dish — tarragon for chicken; parsley and thyme for beef; savory for pork; or mint, Dijon mustard or capers for serving with lamb.

Here is a complete salad meal using cumin and coriander which are very refreshing spices in the summer especially with yoghurt. Serve it with a cold potato salad or some cold cooked brown rice mixed with a garlic-y French dressing.

Chicken and New Carrot Salad

One 1.5kg (3-3½ lb) roasting
chicken
2 sprigs mint
5ml (1 teaspoon) ground cumin
5ml (1 teaspoon) ground
coriander
5ml (1 teaspoon) curry powder

1 small onion
450g (1 lb) new carrots
1 carton (5 fl oz) natural yoghurt
30ml (2 tablespoons) olive oil
30ml (2 tablespoons) chopped
mint
1 small lettuce for serving

Put one sprig of mint inside the chicken. Truss the chicken. Mix the spices together and rub half of them into the skin of the chicken. Put it into a large saucepan or casserole with the remaining mint sprig, the onion (cut in half but not peeled) and two of the carrots, sliced. Cover it with water to just above the thighs. Bring it gently to the boil, cover and simmer for 50 minutes. Trim the remaining carrots and leave them whole. Add them to the pot for the final 20 minutes of cooking. Lift the chicken from the saucepan and let it cool completely. Strain the stock and discard the onion, mint sprig and chopped carrots. Cut the whole carrots into 1.5cm (½ in) pieces. Make the dressing by mixing the yoghurt, oil and remaining spices together and fold the carrots into it while they are still warm. Cool them completely and chill them slightly. Dice the chicken and combine it with the carrots in the dressing.

Serve the salad on a bed of lettuce leaves with the remaining mint scattered over the top.

Don't throw all the delicious stock from the poached chicken away. Use it to make a carrot soup. In this one the sweetness of the carrots and broad beans is brought out by the mint. You can serve it hot, but it is ideal for chilling as it is thick. Thin cold soups never seem very satisfying.

New Carrot and Broad Bean Soup

225g (½ lb) new carrots
450g (1 lb) broad beans (weighed
  in their shells)
25g (1 oz) butter
1 sprig mint

850ml (1½ pt) stock
15ml (1 tablespoon) chopped
  mint
30ml (2 tablespoons) chopped
  parsley

Thinly slice the carrots. Shell and chop the beans. Melt the butter in a saucepan on a low heat. Stir in the beans and carrots and tuck in the mint sprig. Cover, and let them sweat for ten minutes. Pour in the stock and bring it to the boil. Cover and simmer for 15 minutes. Cool the soup slightly and remove the mint sprig. Work the soup in a blender until it is smooth. Either, pour it back into the pan, stir in the herbs and reheat it; or, pour it into a bowl or tureen, stir in the herbs and chill.

When making cooked salads you need not always boil the vegetables first. You can simmer them gently in oil and mix in the vinegar when they are tender so no goodness and flavour has to be thrown away.

Cooked Carrot, Pea and Mint Salad

350g (12 oz) new carrots
350g (12 oz) green peas, weighed
  in their shells
2 sprigs mint
90ml (6 tablespoons) olive oil

45ml (3 tablespoons) white wine
  vinegar
45ml (3 tablespoons) chopped
  mint

Slice the carrots thinly. Shell the peas and reserve four of the best pods. Put the oil and mint sprigs into a heavy saucepan and warm on a low heat. Mix in the carrots, peas and pods. Cover, and simmer gently for 15 minutes, stirring once or twice. Take the pan from the heat, remove the pods and mint sprigs and stir in the vinegar and chopped mint. Turn the salad into a bowl to get quite cold.

If new carrots are small enough you can cook them whole. Use the summer herbs to flavour them. Here tarragon vinegar is used as well as the herb to give a slight sharpness which makes the carrots ideal for serving with pork. Use parsley alone if no tarragon is available.

Tarragon Flavoured Carrots

450g (1 lb) new carrots
275ml (½ pt) stock
25g (1 oz) butter
30ml (2 tablespoons) tarragon
  vinegar

15ml (1 tablespoon) chopped
  parsley
15ml (1 tablespoon) chopped
  tarragon

Scrub and trim the carrots and leave them whole. Put them into a saucepan with the stock and butter. Cover, and set them on a moderate heat for 20 minutes. Uncover the pan, raise the heat and cook until the liquid is almost all reduced and the carrots slightly glazed. Mix in the tarragon vinegar, parsley and tarragon and just heat them through.

And now for two hot meals, each with different flavourings to break away a little from the mint tradition. This first with nutmeg is a very attractive dish of dark browns and orange.

Lamb's Liver and New Carrots

900g (2 lb) lamb's liver
450g (1 lb) new carrots
25g (1 oz) butter
1 large onion, finely chopped
150ml (¼ pt) dry white wine
150ml (¼ pt) stock

freshly grated nutmeg (or 2.5ml
(¼ teaspoon) ground)
15ml (1 tablespoon) chopped
  marjoram
15ml (1 tablespoon) chopped
  parsley

Cut the liver into small thin slices. Trim and thinly slice the carrots. Melt the butter in a large frying pan or sauté pan on a high heat. Put in the liver in one layer and brown the pieces on both sides. (You will probably have to do this in two batches.) Remove all the liver and set it aside. Lower the heat, put in the onion and carrots and cook them until the onion is soft. Pour in the wine and stock and bring them to the boil. Add the nutmeg and herbs and replace the liver. Cover and simmer for 20 minutes.

Beef and carrots had to make an appearance somewhere. Instead of boiling beef with sliced large carrots, braise a joint of brisket with whole new ones and flavour them both with allspice.

30

Braised Brisket and Carrots

1 joint rolled brisket of beef
  weighing around 1.125kg
  (2½ lb)
450g (1 lb) new carrots
15g (½ oz) beef dripping
150ml (¼ pt) stock
150ml (¼ pt) sherry

1 small onion, peeled and stuck
  with 6 cloves
6 crushed allspice berries
15ml (1 tablespoon) chopped
  thyme
15ml (1 tablespoon) chopped
  parsley

Preheat the oven to 180°C (350°F)/Gas 4.

Scrub and trim the carrots and leave them whole. Melt the dripping in a large flameproof casserole on a high heat. Put in the beef and brown it all over. Pour in the stock and sherry and bring them to the boil. Add the onion with its cloves, allspice, thyme and parsley. Cover the casserole and put it into the oven for one hour. Put in the carrots, cover again, and continue cooking for a further 45 minutes. Remove the beef and carrots and keep them warm. Discard the onion. Skim any fat from the juices in the casserole. Let them simmer gently while you carve the beef and arrange it on a serving dish with the carrots. Pour over the sauce to serve.

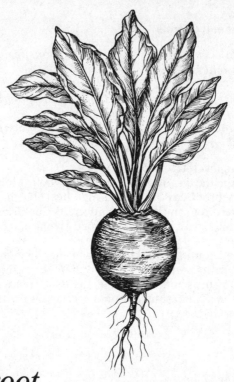

Beetroot

When we think of root vegetables, beetroot is very often left out, probably because ever since it was first introduced into this country in the fifteenth century it has been used mainly for salads and not for stews and soups like the other roots. The sweet soft, delicate flavour of boiled beetroot has been most often spiced up with vinegar; and it has been chopped or sliced and used as a tasty garnish for green salads, in earlier times with red barberries and nasturtium seeds and later with red cabbage or tomatoes.

The red colour of beetroot, so attractive in cold dishes, has probably had much to do with the fact that it was rarely, if ever, used in pottages and cooked meat dishes. One spiced beetroot and venison pottage was published in 1673, but this appears to be the first and only one. In the nineteenth century beetroot were boiled and buttered to be served as a hot vegetable dish, and they were also simmered in gravy with a dash of chilli vinegar.

The seeds of beetroot are drilled in the field fairly closely together so as they grow the rows of shiny purple and green leaves and purple stems get denser and denser. The first new beetroot are usually ready by the end of June. They can be dug up with a mechanical digger but they are very often pulled out of the ground by hand and tied up in bunches. I always enjoy buying the first bunch of the season and carrying them home with the long, brightly coloured leaves flapping over the top of my shopping basket. The bigger, later beetroot are all trimmed out in the field and the leaves are ploughed back in. They are all dug or pulled at the same time and stored in clamps to keep them cool and dry until they are needed.

Beetroot comes round or long and can vary from 3cm (1 in) to about 12cm (4 in). I always like to buy them raw so I can choose my cooking time, but to smell the pungence of a big, steamy red-stained bowl of freshly cooked beetroot in the greengrocers is one of the pleasures of winter shopping.

Whatever their size, beetroot should always be boiled unpeeled and still with the spindly root end and about 1.5cm (½ in) of the stalk attached. This will seal in all the colour, flavour and goodness. They need a fairly long cooking time, so to make sure they don't boil dry, keep the lid on the saucepan and just simmer them on a low to moderate heat. Large ones will take up to an hour and small ones 30 to 45 minutes depending on just how small they are. It's a great temptation to keep sticking a fork or sharp knife in to see if they are done, but try not to do this too often. Wait until near the end of cooking time before you try. When they are done, drain them and let them steam dry and peel them as soon as they are cool enough to handle. If they are going to be put into a salad, chop or slice the larger ones but leave the baby ones whole, and mix them with your vinegar or dressing while they are still warm.

During the winter and spring, when beetroot are large, they can be chopped and grated and mixed into cooked dishes and soups. All kinds of cheese can be served with beetroot and according to Eliza Acton it was fairly common in the later nineteenth century to serve cold, sliced beetroot with cheese as the last course of the meal.

These beetroot and cheese cakes make a good first course for a winter night. They are not really elegant, but extremely tasty, so I recommend they be served to a hungry family and not to dinner-party guests.

Beetroot and Cheese Cakes

225g (8 oz) beetroot
125g (4 oz) grated Farmhouse
  Cheddar cheese
2 eggs, beaten
15ml (1 tablespoon) chopped
  thyme

30ml (2 teaspoons) red wine
  vinegar
25g (1 oz) butter
1 medium onion, finely chopped

Boil the beetroot until they are tender. Peel and grate them. Mix them with the cheese, eggs, thyme and vinegar. Melt half the butter in a frying pan on a low heat. Put in the onion and let it brown. Mix it into the beetroot. Melt the remaining butter in the frying pan on a moderate heat and put in the mixture by the tablespoon (15ml spoon), flattening each blob to about 1.5cm (½ in) thick. You should have enough for eight small cakes. Cook them two at a time. After cooking for two minutes, turn them over carefully and cook the other side. They will go a very dark colour but this doesn't mean they are burnt. Lift them out and put them immediately onto individual serving plates. Serve piping hot.

If you have enough beef to serve it plain, then beetroot cooked with horseradish is a good accompaniment.

Hot Beetroot with Horseradish

450g (1 lb) beetroot
10ml (2 teaspoons) grated
  horseradish
6 crushed allspice berries

freshly ground black pepper
25g (1 oz) butter
275ml (½ pt) water

Peel the beetroot and slice them thinly — about 0.5cm (⅛-¼ in) thick. Put them into a saucepan with the rest of the ingredients. Set them on a high heat and bring them to the boil. Lower the heat, uncover, and simmer gently for 45 minutes, or until the beetroot are tender and slightly glazed.

And now let's break away from the more traditional ideas. In this beetroot and lamb dish the pickled onions counteract the sweetness of the beetroot without there being any evidence of sharp vinageryness. The mixture sounds extraordinary but the result is really good.

Lamb with Beetroot and Onions

675-900g (1½-2 lb) lean boneless
  lamb, cut from the shoulder
2 medium sized raw beetroot,
  weighing together 225-275g
  (8-10 oz)
125g (4 oz) chopped raw onions
8 pickled onions

60ml (4 tablespoons) lamb fat or
  olive oil
10ml (2 teaspoons) carraway
  seeds
275ml (½ pt) red wine (or 150ml
  (¼ pt) wine and 150ml (¼ pt)
  stock)

Cut the lamb into 2cm (¾ in) cubes and chop the beetroot into pieces the same size. Finely chop the raw onion and pickled onions separately. Heat the fat in a large frying pan or sauté pan on a high heat. Put in the

34

lamb and brown it. Remove it and set it aside. Lower the heat and cool the pan a little. Put in the raw onion, beetroot and carraway seeds and cook gently, moving everything around frequently until the onions are beginning to soften. Pour in the wine and bring it to the boil, stirring. Add the chopped pickled onions and replace the lamb. Cover the pan and set it on the lowest heat possible on top of the stove for one hour, stirring once or twice.

Serve it with wholemeal pasta which has been tossed with butter and grated Parmesan cheese, and a green salad.

Sour cream is often used in beetroot soups in Eastern European countries to add just a touch of freshness. Usually these soups are unblended, like, for example, Bortsch, but it works equally well in a blended soup.

Cream of Beetroot Soup

350g (12 oz) raw beetroot
25g (1 oz) butter
1 large onion, finely chopped
850ml (1½ pt) stock

60ml (4 tablespoons) red wine
* vinegar*
pinch ground allspice
30ml (2 tablespoons) sour cream

Chop 300g (10 oz) of the beetroot. Grate the remaining 50g (2 oz) and set them aside. Heat the butter in a saucepan on a low heat, stir in the beetroot and onion, cover and let them sweat for ten minutes. Pour in the stock and bring it to the boil. Add the vinegar and allspice. Cover and simmer for 15 minutes. Cool the soup slightly and work it in a blender until it is smooth. Return it to the pan, stir in the sour cream and reheat. Pour it into soup bowls and float the grated raw beetroot on the top for a contrast in colour, texture and flavour.

However many recipes there are for hot beetroot dishes, its most popular use is still in salads. Ring the changes a little by having it grated up raw instead of cooking it first. This salad is good with beef or egg dishes.

Raw Beetroot Salad

175-225g (6-8 oz) raw beetroot
15ml (1 tablespoon) grated
* horseradish*

5ml (1 teaspoon) mustard
* powder*
1 carton (5 fl oz) natural yoghurt

Peel and grate the beetroot and mix it with the horseradish. Mix the mustard and yoghurt together and stir them into the beetroot. Leave it standing for an hour before serving. You can even leave it overnight and you will still have a fresh-tasting salad.

If buying baby beets is a pleasure, then eating them is even more so. Very often the tail end of the old ones runs into the beginning of the new and at that time of the year the difference between the two kinds is tremendous. The old ones are dark and heavy, but the tiny ones are light and bright and almost translucent, and the flavour is so good that they are a treat to eat just plain and simply boiled with no garnish or dressing at all.

Take advantage of this in this simple salad with cottage cheese, which is a bright pink colour with the darker, whole beets on the top. Serve it for lunch or with a selection of salads on a cold table.

Baby Beet and Cottage Cheese Salad

12 very tiny (3cm (1 in) diameter) or 10 slightly larger (5cm (1½ in) diameter) new beetroot

450g (1 lb) cottage cheese
10ml (2 teaspoons) made English mustard

Boil the beets until they are tender. Drain them and let them steam dry. Peel them while they are still warm then let them get quite cold. If you are using the smallest beetroot, grate eight of them; if larger, grate six. Mix the grated ones and the mustard into the cheese. Pile the mixture into a dish and top with the four whole ones.

Mild Wensleydale cheese and new beetroot go well together in salads, particularly if the dressing is not too sharp. The white cheese and yoghurt here again pick up the jewel-like colour of the beets.

Beetroot and Wensleydale Salad

8 baby beets
175g (6 oz) Wensleydale cheese
6 large spring onions, chopped
60ml (4 tablespoons) natural yoghurt

30ml (2 tablespoons) olive oil
6 crushed allspice berries

Boil, drain and peel the beets as above. Let them cool completely and cut them into quarters. Dice the cheese. Put the beets and cheese into a bowl. Mix the yoghurt, oil and allspice and stir them into the salad. Serve it as a first course.

Yoghurt makes ideal dressings for beetroot as it is slightly tangy but not as sharp as vinegar. Use it again in this hot dish that is made pungent and spicy with juniper berries.

36

Baby Beets with Yoghurt and Juniper

8 baby beets
½ carton (2.5 fl oz) natural
  yoghurt

juice ½ lemon
10 crushed juniper berries

Boil the beets until they are tender. Drain and skin them while they are
still warm. Warm the yoghurt in the saucepan with the lemon juice and
juniper. Replace the beets and heat them through. In doing so you will
get a bright purply-pink sauce. Serve them all hot.

This cold salad of beets and eggs makes a light lunch or a first course.
For a main course salad, use ten baby beets — four to keep whole and
six to grate. Then double all the rest of the ingredients.

Ring of Baby Beets

6 baby beets
10g (½ oz) gelatine
juice 1 lemon
150ml (¼ pt) freshly made
  mayonnaise

½ carton (2.5 fl oz) sour cream
little oil for greasing 20cm (8 in)
  diameter ring mould

For the filling:

4 hard-boiled eggs
15ml (1 tablespoon) mayonnaise
15ml (1 tablespoon) sour cream

30ml (2 tablespoons) chopped
  chives

Boil the beets until they are tender. Drain them and peel them and let
them cool. Soak the gelatine in the lemon juice. Cut three of the beets
in half lengthways and grate the rest. (If some are larger than the
others use these for grating.) Arrange the halves, rounded side down
around the base of the lightly oiled mould. Mix the grated beets with
the mayonnaise and sour cream. Melt the gelatine in a small pan on a
low heat, without letting it bubble. Stir it quickly into the beetroot
mixture. Pour it evenly into the mould over the beetroot halves and
leave the ring in a cool place to set. N.B. It will only come half-way up
the mould. Chop the hard-boiled eggs and mix them with the remaining
mayonnaise, sour cream and chives. Turn out the ring by immersing
the base first in a bowl of hot water. Fill the middle with the egg salad.
It will be a Catherine wheel of bright colour, creamy in both texture
and flavour.

Baby beets can also be roasted in the oven, either plain or with onion.
The cheese is added here for extra flavour but you could easily omit it
for a plainer dish.

Baby Beets Roasted with Onion and Blue Cheese

25g (1 oz) butter
6 baby beets

1 large onion, thinly sliced
50g (2 oz) grated blue cheese

Preheat the oven to 200°C (400°F)/Gas 6.

Put the butter into a flat oven-proof dish and put it into the oven to melt. Trim and peel the beets and cut each one in half lengthways. Take the dish from the oven and roll the beets in the butter, setting them down rounded side uppermost. Scatter the onion rings over the top and put the dish back into the oven for 40 minutes. Scatter the cheese over the top and put the beets back until it has melted (about five mins).

Beetroot stay tiny from summer to autumn. We tend to fancy cold meals at the start of their season and hot ones towards the end. This beef recipe can fit the bill either way. Served hot, the beef has a small amount of spicy sauce, and cold it has a jellied red glaze. The beets pick up all the flavour of the beef and spices.

Pot-Roasted Brisket and Beetroot to serve either Hot or Cold

1 piece lean rolled brisket
* weighing 900-925g (2-2½ lb)*
6 allspice berries
6 juniper berries
8 baby beets

120ml (8 tablespoons) dry red
* wine*
60ml (4 tablespoons) red wine
* vinegar*

Preheat the oven to 160°C (325°F)/Gas 3.

Crush the spices together and rub them into the surface of the beef. Peel the beets and put them into a casserole with the beef. Pour over the wine and vinegar. Cover the casserole and put it into the oven for 1¾ hours.

To Serve Hot: Take the beef from the casserole and carve it. Arrange it on a warm serving dish with the beets. Skim any fat from the juices in the casserole and then spoon these over the beef.

To Serve Cold: Put the whole joint of beef into a dish and set the beets aside to cool. Skim the juices in the casserole and then brush them over the beef to give it a good, dark red spicy glaze. Let it cool and set and repeat several times using up all the glaze. After several goes, if there is still some left, just pour it all over the beef. Leave the beef in a cool place or in the fridge.

Serve it whole, with the beets surrounding it and carve it at the table. Accompany it with a green salad and a potato salad.

Celeriac

Try as I might, I have been able to find no historical reference to celeriac. It has never been widely grown in Britain either commercially or privately. This is a shame as it is perfect for winter salads. I always like to crunch the hard root-end of a head of celery and to have a great big root weighing about a pound with a similar flavour and texture is a real treat!

Celeriac is sown in boxes in January and kept under glass being heated gently from underneath. As soon as it begins to germinate the heat is turned off and the plants left to grow until late May or early June, when they are planted outside, either by hand or with a mechanical planter, depending on the size of the plot.

The leaves of celeriac look a little like celery leaves. In July they begin to get large and have to be picked off to let the root swell out as much as possible. This has to be done by hand, but in this case the grower is rewarded for his work. The large side-shoots can be used for stocks and soups and the more tender, lighter green ones for flavouring salads.

The roots should be ready for lifting by September. The easiest way of getting them up, or so I was told, is to dig them by hand as the actual bulb has a long root going deep into the ground. You get hold of the leaves, and pull and turn at the same time and up it all comes. The long roots and the leaves are chopped off, so by the time a celeriac root reaches the shops it will be clean and trimmed and have a stubble on top rather like a coconut. In colour and shape it resembles a slightly pointed white turnip, but it is much larger and each root weighs about 450g (1 lb). Celeriac is very sensitive to frosts, so all the roots have to be lifted by the end of October to be stored in clamps where it can last right round till April.

Celeriac is one of the few vegetables that I always peel as the outside is very tough and woody. Don't throw the peel away, though. Put it in a polythene bag and store it in the 'fridge for the stock-pot.

For salads, celeriac can be chopped or grated or cut into julienne sticks. It really is very crunchy, so you can soften it just a little by marinating it in a little vinegar or orange or lemon juice for about an hour before you prepare the final salad.

The most simple salad of all you can make with celeriac is to chop it finely and mix it with an equal amount of chopped celery. Just coat them with freshly made mayonnaise — nothing else is needed. Serve it with cold pork, or grilled sausages or pork pie.

This nutty salad can be served with cold lamb or egg dishes or on its own as a first course.

Celeriac and Hazelnut Salad

450g (1 lb) celeriac, or 1 big root	*1 clove garlic crushed with a*
75g (3 oz) hazelnuts	*pinch of sea salt*
juice 1 lemon	*freshly ground black pepper*
10ml (2 teaspoons) clear honey	*60ml (4 tablespoons) sour cream*

Peel the celeriac and chop it into dice the same size as the nuts. Put it into a bowl, mix in the lemon juice, and let it stand for one hour. Add the nuts. Mix the honey, garlic and pepper into the sour cream and mix this dressing into the bowl.

Cottage cheese and celeriac here make a healthy and cidery first course.

Hot Celeriac, Apple and Cheese Salad

350g (12 oz) celeriac	*30ml (2 tablespoons) cider*
2 medium sized cooking apples	*vinegar*
(Bramleys are best)	*100g (4 oz) cottage cheese*
60ml (4 tablespoons) olive oil	

Cut the celeriac into pieces about 2cm (¾ in) square and 0.5cm (⅛ in) thick. Quarter, core and slice the apples. Heat the oil in a large frying pan on a high heat. Put in the celeriac and apples and cook, moving them around, for two minutes. Pour in the vinegar and let it bubble. Take the pan from the heat and stir in the cottage cheese. Serve immediately.

You can fry celeriac in shallow fat. Butter preserves its delicate flavour best and bacon fat makes it nice and smoky in flavour. Cut the celeriac into small dice or sticks and fry them on a high heat until they are golden. They will be succulent and melt-in-the-mouth.

This next recipe carries the idea of frying celeriac a little further to make a hot first course. Recently, because of the subsidies on the plainer foreign cheeses, English cheese-makers have taken to making small quantities of really special cheeses like the one used here. If you are unable to find any or think it may be too expensive, use ordinary Farmhouse Double Gloucester and toss in 30ml (2 tablespoons) chopped chives or Welsh Onions with the cheese.

Celeriac and Double Gloucester with Chives

350g (12 oz) celeriac
125g (4 oz) Double Gloucester
   cheese with Chives
25g (1 oz) butter

120ml (6 tablespoons) stock
5ml (1 teaspoon) made English
   mustard

Dice the celeriac and cheese into 1.5cm (½ in) pieces. Heat the butter in a frying pan on a high heat. Put in the celeriac and stir it around until it browns. Pour in the stock and stir in the mustard. Bring them to the boil and let them almost reduce completely. Quickly mix in the cheese and let it heat through but not melt. Serve immediately.

Celeriac can be simmered on top of the stove with just enough stock to make it soft and tasty and slightly glazed. To 450g (1 lb) of celeriac you will need 150ml (¼ pt) stock and 15g (½ oz) butter or fat. Flavour it with parsley or sage and perhaps some chopped or sliced onion.

   The following recipe uses this basic method and has bacon for flavour.

Celeriac and Bacon

450g (1 lb) celeriac
125g (4 oz) lean bacon
15g (½ oz) bacon fat or butter
1 medium onion, thinly sliced

5ml (1 teaspoon) mustard
   powder
150ml (¼ pt) stock
10 chopped sage leaves

41

Peel the celeriac and cut it into cubes about 3cm (1 in) square. Dice the bacon. Melt the bacon fat in a heavy saucepan on a low heat, stir in the bacon and onion and cook them until the onion is soft. Mix in the celeriac. Add the mustard powder, stock and sage. Cover and keep the pan on a low heat for 30 minutes. The celeriac will be soft and tasty and the stock and mustard will make just enough thick sauce to coat it beautifully.

Celeriac, like most of the other root vegetables can also be braised in the oven. Here is a recipe using the basic method. You could add parsley or sage instead of the mustard; or use a granular or German mustard instead of Dijon.

Braised Celeriac and Mustard

450g (1 lb) celeriac   10ml (2 teaspoons) Dijon
25g (1 oz) butter   mustard
150ml (¼ pt) stock

Preheat the oven to 180°C (350°F)/Gas 4.
    Chop the celeriac into 2cm (¾ in) dice. Melt the butter in a flameproof casserole on a low heat. Stir in the celeriac, stock and mustard. Cover, and put into the centre of the oven for 30 minutes.

You can boil celeriac and serve it plainly, but it's a bit uninteresting. However if you boil it and mash it with an equal quantity of mashed potato you will have an accompaniment to any meat dish which is tastier and what's more lower in calories than the latter vegetable alone. Even better, make them into the following cakes.

Celeriac and Potato Cheese Cakes

350g (¾ lb) potatoes   Cheese, (or use Cheddar and
350g (¾ lb) celeriac   some chopped sage)
1 small onion   15g (½ oz) butter for greasing
25g (1 oz) butter   tray
75g (3 oz) grated Sage Derby   1 egg, beaten

Scrub the potatoes but leave the peel on. Cut them into convenient sized chunks for boiling. Scrub and peel the celeriac and chop it into pieces the same size. Thinly slice the onion. Boil the potatoes, celeriac and onion together for 20 minutes, or until the potatoes are tender enough for mashing. Drain them. Preheat the oven to 200°C (400°F)/Gas 6. Peel the potatoes and mash all the vegetables with the 25g (1 oz) butter and the cheese. Thickly butter a baking sheet and form the mixture into flat cakes about 8cm (2½ in) in diameter and

1.5cm (½ in) thick. Brush them with the beaten egg and bake them for three quarters of an hour or until they are golden brown and puffed up.

Nuts and celeriac always go well together in salads so I have put them together here for a winter beef stew.

Beef Stew with Celeriac and Walnuts

900g (2 lb) chuck steak or other   *150ml (¼ pt) red wine*
  good stewing beef   *150ml (¼ pt) stock*
450g (1 lb) celeriac   *bouquet garni*
25g (1 oz) beef dripping   *50g (2 oz) chopped walnuts*
1 large onion, thinly sliced   *30ml (2 tablespoons) chopped*
1 clove garlic, finely chopped   *parsley*

Preheat the oven to 180°C (350°F)/Gas 4.

    Dice both the beef and celeriac into 2cm (¾ in) pieces. Heat the dripping in a flameproof casserole on a high heat. Put in the cubes of beef and brown them all over. Do this in two batches if necessary. Remove the beef and set it aside. Lower the heat, put in the onion and garlic and cook them until they begin to turn golden. Pour in the wine and stock and bring them to the boil. Put in the celeriac and bring to the boil again. Replace the beef and tuck in the bouquet garni. Cover the casserole and put it into the oven for 1¼ hours. Remove the bouquet garni and mix in the walnuts and parsley. Return the casserole to the oven for five minutes.

Celeriac soups are thick and tasty and the tanginess of Cheshire cheese makes it an ideal garnish. There is no need to salt this soup — you can taste the natural salts in the vegetable itself.

Celeriac Soup

450g (1 lb) celeriac   *freshly ground black pepper*
25g (1 oz) butter   *bouquet garni*
1 large onion, thinly sliced   *75g (3 oz) grated Cheshire*
850ml (1½ pt) stock   *cheese*

Peel and quarter the celeriac and slice it thinly. Melt the butter in a saucepan on a low heat. Mix in the celeriac and onion, cover, and let them sweat for ten minutes. Pour in the stock and bring it to the boil. Season with the pepper and add the bouquet garni. Cover and simmer gently for 15 minutes. Remove the bouquet garni and cool the mixture slightly. Work it in a blender until it is smooth. Return it to the saucepan and reheat. Pour the soup into four heat-proof bowls and scatter over the cheese. Put the bowls under a hot grill for the cheese to melt.

Tubers

Tubers are the other family of vegetables whose edible parts lie deep in the earth. They are full of high energy starches and sugars and usually play the part of fillers in the meal — the plainer accompaniments to meat and other vegetable dishes.

Potatoes

Big or small, new or old, potatoes must be cooked by nearly every family in Britain at least once a day and many more are carried home hot and golden and smelling so tantalizing in their paper wrapping from fish and chip shops.

Despite their universal use now, potatoes were a late arrival to this country. The Spaniards found them first in Peru and by the 1570s were growing them fairly widely in their native country. A little of their crop was imported into England but scant notice was taken until Sir Francis Drake arrived with a boat load from Colombia in 1586. On the way home, he called in at Virginia, a stop which led to the idea that this was their country of origin; but they weren't grown there until the Pilgrim Fathers took them back on a return journey across the Atlantic.

Drake said of his discovery: 'These potatoes be the most delicate roots that may be eaten, and doe farre exceed our passeneps or carats . . . . . . the inside eateth like an apple but it is more delicious than any sweet apple, sugred.' That has probably been one of the most successful pieces of sales promotion.

Like all new-found luxuries, potatoes were relatively scarce at first, grown only as an exotic in the gardens of the rich. Sweet potatoes came with them and both were regarded not only as special foods but as aphrodisiacs fetching as much as £300 a pound at one time.

Whatever their effect, the most common way at first of cooking potatoes was to roast or boil them in their skins and then mash them with butter, salt, sack (which was like sherry), sugar, candied peel and spices. Sometimes they were baked in sweet pies and made into puddings. These sweet dishes were still common in the eighteenth century, but gradually the other qualities of potatoes were discovered and made use of.

Their plainness was appreciated as a contrast to richer dishes and they were served as a garnish for sauced meats and game; and their soft, creamy quality when they are mashed led them to be puréed and used as a basis for salad dressings.

With their increasing availability, potatoes were naturally made into more homely dishes, for the poor could not afford all the spices and elaborate trimmings. They wanted a cheap vegetable that could be boiled up in the pot and easily picked up the flavour of what little meat they had to make a wholesome and filling dish.

Potatoes were grown more widely in Ireland first, where they were boiled in their skins in a three-legged cauldron over the fire, and served with butter or bacon fat. Boxty was a favourite dish. This was grated raw potato boiled in hot milk until it was a fluffy purée and served with a well in the middle full of melted butter. Also in Ireland they were made into the knock-out brew called poteen.

From Ireland, potatoes came across to Lancashire and from then on they gradually became more and more important all over Britain. They were boiled with meat and broth to make the Lancashire dish called Lobscouse; baked with herrings in Wales; used to supplement flour in bread; put into sausages and stuffings; roasted in the dripping pan under the meat, and of course, in the eighteenth and nineteenth centuries, boiled and buttered.

Fish shops were common in the towns by the 1850s, set up to feed the industrial poor: men and women who had been working long hours in the factories and did not feel like cooking a meal at the end of the day. Fried cod or plaice were at first sold with a slice of bread or a baked potato, but when the idea of chips came from France around 1870, the English national dish had been born.

For a long time in England, Wales and Scotland, potatoes were grown mainly in gardens and on smallholdings, and it was not until the early nineteenth century that they were extensively grown as a field crop. They caught on sooner in Ireland as in that troubled country they could grow safely underground when cereals such as wheat or barley could be burnt. Lancashire and Norfolk led the way in England and in the eighteenth century the Norfolk Farmer, Arthur Young wrote that potatoes were 'one of the most profitable crops a farmer can cultivate'. He recommended planting them in March and that is still the best potato-planting month. Hand planting was the way in Young's time. A man went along the rows with a dibber that made three holes at a time and a boy followed along behind dropping in the seed potatoes.

Nowadays, potatoes are mostly planted by machine, although some farmers find planting by hand much faster and more efficient. The earth is laid aside first by a tractor — this is called drawing the baulks — the potatoes are laid equidistantly along the rows and then along comes the tractor again to split the baulks (cover over the potatoes with a ridge of earth).

By the end of April the first green leaves appear, neatly spaced along the baulks, and by the first week of June the early varieties from the warmest fields should be ready for the digger, being lifted either by machine or by hand.

If they are going to be stored they can be put first into small baskets or trugs which when they are full are tipped into wooden bins. These are in turn emptied into large, airy clamps which will keep the potatoes fresh and firm until the beginning of the next season, providing, that is, the stocks hold out that long.

Once the harvest has begun, potatoes should be plentiful. Usually they are the most plentiful vegetable of all and perhaps because of this and their regular appearance on every house-hold menu they are also the most unimaginatively cooked.

But how can anyone take those first new baby potatoes of the season for granted! Preserve all their flavour and their goodness as well by cooking them as often as possible in their skins. Wash them (but don't scrub hard), and toss them with butter and chopped herbs. Mint, chives and parsley are probably the most common, but you don't have to stick to these especially if your herb garden is a prolific one. Try thyme, savory or chervil instead. The best potatoes are the smallest — only about 2cm (¾ in) in diameter — but if you buy larger ones, boil them whole and slice them up, still with their skins on, and toss them with butter and chopped fennel.

New potatoes are far better for sautéeing than old ones as they are firm textured and don't break up in the pan or go floury. Boil them in their skins, peel them while they are still warm, slice them into halves or quarters if they are very tiny and dice them if they are larger, and fry them on a moderate heat in a mixture of butter and oil until they are golden. If you like, add some sliced onion or chopped salad onion to the pan as well and sprinkle in a little mustard powder or paprika while they are cooking.

The nearest taste I have ever found to that of potatoes roasted in the hot ashes of a bonfire is of par-boiled and then deep-fried baby potatoes as in the first recipe.

Deep-Fried Baby Potatoes

675g (1½ lb) new baby potatoes   deep fat for frying

Wash the potatoes and put them into a saucepan of lightly salted water. Set them on a high heat, bring them to the boil, and simmer for ten minutes. Drain them and let them steam dry. Heat a pan of deep fat on a high heat. Lower in the potatoes and cook them for five minutes in the bubbling fat. Drain them and serve them plain.

Alternative: Skin the potatoes after boiling and coat them with beaten egg and wholemeal flour before deep-frying.

You can also bake new potatoes in their jackets which is a good economical way of cooking if the oven is already on.

New Potatoes Baked in the Jackets

675g (1½ lb) new baby potatoes   25g (1 oz) butter

You can either have the oven at 160°C (325°F)/Gas 3, 180°C (350°F)/Gas 4 (this is the best), or 200°C (400°F)/Gas 6, depending on whatever else is cooking at the same time. Put the butter in an oven-proof dish and put it in the oven to melt. Wash and dry the potatoes. Roll them around in the melted butter to coat them, and bake them for one hour, 45 minutes or 30 minutes, again depending on your temperature.

Here is a way of baking new potatoes without their skins which makes them fluffy and crisp and golden brown.

Fluffy Baked New Potatoes and Onion

675g (1½ lb) small to medium   40g (1½ oz) butter
* new potatoes   1 medium onion, finely chopped*

Preheat the oven to 200°C (400°F)/Gas 6.

Boil the potatoes in their skins for ten minutes. Drain them and peel them as soon as they are cool enough to handle. Score them all over with a fork. Put the butter in an oven proof dish and put it into the oven to melt. Roll the potatoes around in the butter and scatter the onion over the top. Put them into the oven for 45 minutes, turning them and basting them half way through and keeping as many onions over them as possible.

Instead of boiling and slicing up new potatoes and tossing them with herbs, miss out the boiling altogether to bring out a really strong potato-y flavour. I have used fennel in this recipe to go with pork or fish, but you could use thyme, parsley, chervil or a very little of the pungent rosemary.

Sliced New Potatoes Simmered in Butter

675g (1½ lb) new potatoes
50g (2 oz) butter
30ml (2 tablespoons) chopped
  fennel

6 large or 12 small salad onions,
  finely chopped

Wash the potatoes and slice them into 0.5cm (¼ in) rounds. Melt the butter in a heavy saucepan on a low heat. Stir in the potatoes, herbs and onions. Cover tightly and keep on the low heat for 25 minutes, stirring around several times to make sure all the slices cook evenly.

Here is another way of cooking potatoes in butter on top of the stove.

Buttered New Potatoes with Paprika and Dill

675g (1½ lb) new baby potatoes
40g (1½ oz) butter

10ml (2 teaspoons) paprika
10ml (2 teaspoons) dill seeds

Scrape the potatoes. Melt the butter in a heavy saucepan on a low heat. Put in the potatoes and roll them around to get them well-coated. Scatter in the paprika and dill and roll the potatoes around again. Cover them with a butter paper and a lid (this steams them in their own moisture) and set them on the lowest heat possible for 30 minutes, shaking the pan occasionally.

New potato salads are always good with cold summer meals, and if the weather suddenly turns cooler then serve a hot salad with cold meat.

Hot in Two Ways Potato Salad

675g (1½ lb) new baby potatoes
45ml (3 tablespoons)
  mayonnaise
15ml (1 tablespoon) white wine
  vinegar

10ml (2 teaspoons) Tabasco
  sauce

Boil the potatoes in their skins. Drain them and skin them while they are still warm. Blend all the ingredients for the dressing together and put them in a saucepan. Gently turn the potatoes in the dressing taking care not to break them up. Cover the pan and set it on a low heat for one minute to heat the potatoes through. Serve the salad hot or let it cool completely and have it cold.

The best way with hot or cold potato salads is to mix them into the dressing while they are still warm so they absorb all the flavour. Then cool them all together.

Eggs and potatoes here make a lunch-time salad with a creamy dressing based on an eighteenth century Irish recipe.

Potato and Egg Salad

For the dressing:

1 egg
15g (½ oz) softened butter
pinch fine sea salt
5ml (1 teaspoon) mustard powder

15ml (1 tablespoon) flour
200ml (7 fl oz) milk
15ml (1 tablespoon) white wine vinegar

For the salad:

675g (1½ lb) new baby potatoes
6 hard-boiled eggs
30ml (2 tablespoons) chopped chives

30ml (2 tablespoons) chopped mint
parsley sprigs for garnish

First make the dressing. Soft-boil the eggs and remove the yolk while it is still hot. Work it with the butter, salt and mustard in a bowl. Blend the milk and flour in a saucepan. Set them on a low heat and bring them to the boil, stirring all the time with a wooden spoon. Take the pan from the heat. Gradually beat half the milk and flour mixture into the butter and the yolk, 5ml (1 teaspoon) at a time at first and increasing to 15ml (1 tablespoon). Return the resulting mixture to the saucepan. Set it on a low heat again and simmer, stirring, until the sauce is thick. Cover the dressing to prevent a skin forming on top, and leave it until it is cold. Stir in the vinegar. Boil the potatoes in their skins, drain and peel them while they are still warm. If they are very tiny cut them in half lengthways and if they are larger cut them into small dice. Mix the potatoes into the dressing while they are still warm and cool everything again. Chop four of the eggs and slice the other two. Mix the chopped eggs, chives and mint into the potatoes and put them into a bowl. Arrange the sliced eggs on top and garnish with the parsley sprigs.

In September and October, potatoes reach the in between stage. This way of cooking them is ideal. They have a fried taste but are moist and succulent as well.

Tortilla Potatoes

675g (1½ lb) small potatoes
60ml (4 tablespoons) olive oil
1 large onion, thinly sliced
1 large clove garlic (finely chopped)

275ml (½ pt) stock
30ml (2 tablespoons) chopped parsley

Heat the oil in a large heavy frying pan on a high heat. Put in the potatoes, onions and garlic and cook them until they are all brown, turning them frequently. Add the parsley. Pour in the stock and let it boil until it has almost completely reduced and the potatoes are slightly glazed.

Old potatoes are best cooked in their skins whenever possible. Peel them after cooking if you would rather serve them without.

Here are two ways of finishing off boiled potatoes.

Coddled Potatoes and Parsley

675g (1½ lb) fairly small old   *60ml (4 tablespoons) chopped*
  potatoes   *parsley*
50g (2 oz) butter

Boil the potatoes in their skins until they are just tender. Chop them, still with their skins, into 2cm (¾ in) dice. Melt the butter in the saucepan on a low heat. Stir in the potatoes and parsley. Cover and keep the pan on the heat for five minutes shaking it occasionally.

Very often yesterday's boiled potatoes are fried today perhaps with cabbage or Brussels sprouts to make bubble and squeak. Use freshly-cooked ones instead to make them into a brown-flecked hash. You could also try it with a mixture of potatoes and parsnips or potatoes and turnips.

Hashed Potatoes

675g (1½ lb) old potatoes   *freshly ground black pepper*
50g (2 oz) dripping

Boil the potatoes in their skins until they are just tender. Peel them as soon as you can pick them up and chop them. Melt the dripping in a frying pan on a low heat. Put in the potatoes and mash them down with a fork without turning them. Season the top with the pepper. Keep them on the heat until the underside browns well and turn them over in sections. Brown the underside again. Mix them all together and brown and turn twice more.

The best way to get really creamy-textured mashed potatoes is to melt the butter in a saucepan on a low heat first and then put in the potatoes and mash them into it. Do it quickly so they don't stick. Quickly mix in a little milk, or for a light, slightly tangy taste use a carton of natural yoghurt instead.

You can also try softening an onion in the butter before you put in the potatoes, or add some chives or parsley or any other herb you fancy.

This spicy dish of mashed potatoes goes well with winter salads.

Hot Mashed Potato Salad

675g (1½ lb) old potatoes
45ml (3 tablespoons) olive oil
15ml (1 tablespoon) white wine
  vinegar

5ml (1 teaspoon) Tabasco sauce
10ml (2 teaspoons) tomato purée

Boil the potatoes in their skins. Drain them and peel them as soon as they are cool enough to handle. Put them back into the saucepan and set it on the lowest heat possible. Quickly mash in the oil, vinegar, Tabasco sauce and tomato purée, being careful not to let anything stick. As soon as everything is well mixed and heated through take the pan from the stove and serve the potatoes really hot.

Roast potatoes are the traditional accompaniment to all our roast meats and in my own county dishes of them, steamy hot, crispy and golden brown are the accepted snack provided by pubs at darts matches. Sometimes, if you are lucky there will also be some on the counter at Sunday lunch time along with cubes of cheese.

This way of roasting potatoes is simple but it never fails to impress. The potatoes look so attractive and they probably taste better cooked this way than any other.

If you have an oven-to-table dish large enough, cook them in this and serve them still with all the butter and crumbs surrounding them.

Cut-Roasted Jacket Potatoes

12 small, even sized potatoes
50g (2 oz) butter

30ml (2 tablespoons) dried
  granary bread crumbs

Scrub the potatoes and make cuts in them 0.25cm (⅛ in) apart and at least three quarters of the way through on one of the flatter surfaces. Preheat the oven to 200°C (400°F)/Gas 6 and while it is heating put the butter inside in a flat oven-proof dish to melt. Roll the potatoes in the butter, set them cut-side-up and baste them. Put them into the oven for one hour, basting several times. Scatter over the crumbs and baste again. Put back into the oven for a further 15 minutes.

Cook sliced potatoes in stock on top of the stove with a little butter or dripping, and different herbs for flavour. Here is a basic recipe for this method of cooking. You could use beer instead of stock, or change to a different herb.

Glazed Lemon Potatoes

675g (1½ lb) old potatoes
25g (1 oz) butter
425ml (¾ pt) stock
grated rind and juice 1 lemon

30ml (2 tablespoons) chopped
   lemon thyme
pinch sea salt
freshly ground black pepper

Scrub the potatoes and cut them into rounds about 1cm (⅜ in) thick. Melt the butter in a heavy saucepan on a low heat. Put in the potatoes and mix them around so they get well-coated. Add the stock, lemon rind and juice, lemon thyme and seasoning. Bring them to the boil, cover and simmer for 20 minutes. Uncover, raise the heat and boil rapidly until most of the stock is absorbed and the potatoes are glazed.

Here is another tasty way of cooking potatoes in a liquid that also makes the sauce they are served in.

Potato Slices with Chives, Mace and Nutmeg

675g (1½ lb) fairly small old
   potatoes
little butter for greasing
30ml (2 tablespoons) chopped
   chives
30ml (2 tablespoons) chopped
   parsley

2.5ml (½ teaspoon) grated
   nutmeg
2.5ml (½ teaspoon) ground mace
fine sea salt and freshly ground
   black pepper to taste
up to 275ml (½ pt) milk
2 bayleaves

Preheat the oven to 200°C (400°F)/Gas 6.

Peel the potatoes and cut them into 0.5cm (¼ in) slices. Lightly butter an oven-proof dish. Put in the potatoes in layers, scattering the herbs, spices and seasoning in between. End with a layer of potatoes with just mace and nutmeg on top. Pour in enough milk to barely cover the last layer. Tear each bayleaf in half and tuck a piece into each quarter of the dish. Bake the potatoes for one hour and serve straight from the dish.

For a really special meal, make potatoes into a light and fluffy soufflé.

Potato Soufflé

675g (1½ lb) old potatoes
25g (1 oz) butter
75ml (3 fl oz) milk
freshly ground black pepper
6 chopped sage leaves

15ml (1 tablespoon) chopped
   parsley
2 eggs, separated
butter and crumbs for preparing
   a soufflé dish

Preheat the oven to 180°C (375°F)/Gas 5.

Boil the potatoes in their skins until they are tender. Drain them and peel them while they are still warm. Mash them well and beat in the butter, milk, pepper and herbs. Beat in the egg yolks. Stiffly beat the egg whites and fold them into the potato mixture. Pile them all into a prepared soufflé dish and bake for 45 minutes.

Jerusalem Artichokes

Jerusalem artichokes with their delicious, smoky flavour are still quite a rarity in provincial towns but they can be enjoyed as an equally filling but lower-caloried change from potatoes and a nutty addition to salads.

Artichokes are a well-travelled and confusingly named vegetable.

They were discovered in Massachusets in 1605 by the French explorer Champlain and taken back to France at the same time as natives of a primitive tribe called the Topinambour. Somehow then two new curiosities became muddled in people's minds and the vegetable ended up with the same name as the tribe. From France the vegetable Topinambour went to Holland where they were grown by a Dutch pastor called Ter Neusen. Someone then noticed that they had a similar flavour to the heart of the globe artichoke and so they were called Artischokappeln van Ter Neusen.

When they arrived in Britain soon after, they were called Canadian Potatoes, because they were a tuberous root like the potato that grew in that part of the world. But later the vegetable went to Italy and from thence came a new label — girasole articiocco; girasole because it was related to a species of sunflower of that name, called so because it followed the sun. It didn't take long for British tongues to slide into an easier word, so there we are — Jerusalem artichoke.

Once in Britain, the Jerusalem artichoke was cooked in a similar way to potatoes with at first all the same spices and sweeteners. It was baked or boiled and put into all manner of pies, both sweet and savoury. The smoky flavour was found to be very adaptable, and I have made one or two sweet pies by way of experiment.

The best way is to peel and thinly slice about 350g (12 oz), and mix them with 30ml (2 tablespoons) of clear honey, some ground cinnamon or nutmeg and a few raisins or sultanas. Put them in a shallow pie plate which you have lined with pastry, cover them with more pastry and bake the pie for 40 minutes in a hot oven (200°C (400°F)/Gas 6). The slices of artichoke will stay whole but will be soft and melty.

After the sweet-savoury time, Jerusalem artichokes were used purely for savoury dishes. In the eighteenth and nineteenth centuries they were boiled and mashed, boiled and buttered, or served au gratin with a Béchamel sauce.

Artichokes have a high starch content and so they have been fairly often made into country wine. This can be really excellent — strong, dry and full of flavour and usually a golden colour.

Mostly, artichokes have been a country garden vegetable and even now few growers have more than five acres of them, but I think this could soon increase as they are becoming more popular and easy to sell. They are set, usually with a machine, at around the same time of year as potatoes, and during the summer they grow higher and higher and really do seem to follow the sun. By the time harvest time comes around in late November most of this upper foliage has died down and what is left is usually burnt. If the season is a dry one artichokes are lifted by machine, again in the same way as potatoes, but they grow so deep that if it is wet and muddy they have to be dug out by hand.

Most of the things you do with potatoes you can do with artichokes, only usually the cooking time is much less. You can cook them in their skins and peel them afterwards, or you can peel them first. This is rather a sticky job and is best done in a big bowl of water with a little lemon juice or vinegar added to it. This stops both the vegetable and your fingers from going a dirty, reddish brown colour.

Boiled artichokes can be tossed with herbs or lemon juice, or mixed with mayonnaise or French dressing while they are still warm to make them into a salad. If you boil them whole and in their skins make sure when you are testing them to stick your skewer or fork into the fat part. The long, pointed end is tough and fibrous and if you wait until that part is tender you may end up with an unworkable mush at the other end. If the pointed part obstinately stays hard then cut it off and throw it away.

54

Like potatoes, artichokes can be baked in their jackets, and they can be roasted whole or in slices in butter or dripping, or round a joint.

Cut them into rings without peeling them and fry them until they are golden in a mixture of olive oil and butter. Like turnips they will have a soft, melty middle and crispy outside.

For an even crisper coating, dip the artichokes in batter and make them into fritters, and serve them instead of potatoes.

Wholemeal Artichoke Fritters

900g (2 lb) Jerusalem artichokes

For the batter:

100g (4 oz) wholemeal flour
10ml (2 teaspoons) curry powder
5ml (1 teaspoon) paprika
pinch fine sea salt

1 egg, separated
150ml (¼ pt) milk
150ml (¼ pt) water
deep fat for frying

Peel the artichokes and discard the long, pointed ends. Cut the rest into 0.5cm (¼ in) slices. Put the flour, spices and salt into a bowl and make a well in the centre. Put in the egg yolk and gradually beat in the water and milk. Stiffly beat the white and fold it into the batter last of all to make it light and fluffy. Dip the artichoke slices in the batter and deep fry them in hot oil until they are golden. The crisp tasty batter will enclose a soft melty slice of artichoke.

Potatoes in soups can be a little floury, but artichoke soups are always creamy and have a slightly smoky flavour.

If you haven't Sage Derby cheese for this one, use a Farmhouse Cheddar, and garnish the top with chopped sage instead of bacon.

Artichoke and Sage Derby Soup

450g (1 lb) Jerusalem artichokes
25g (1 oz) butter
1 large onion, thinly sliced
850ml (1½ pt) stock

seasoning to taste
100g (4 oz) Sage Derby cheese
50g (2 oz) lean bacon

Peel and thinly slice the artichokes, discarding any really tough parts of the pointed ends. Melt the butter in a saucepan on a low heat. Stir in the artichokes and onion, cover, and let them cook gently for ten minutes. Pour in the stock, season, and simmer uncovered for a further ten minutes. Meanwhile, grill the bacon until it is crisp and either crumble or finely chop it. Cool the soup slightly and work it in a blender until it is smooth. Put 150ml (¼ pt) back into the saucepan, set it on a low heat, bring it just to simmering point and beat in the cheese. When it has all melted, pour in the rest of the soup. Reheat without boiling. Serve it in individual soup bowls with the bacon sprinkled over the top.

The bacon in the recipe above goes well with the artichokes as both their flavours are smoky. In the same way artichokes and kippers are a good combination. Make a salad with cooked artichokes and cooked flaked kippers, or make them into a substantial soufflé.

Artichoke and Kipper Soufflé

450g (1 lb) Jerusalem artichokes
1 large onion, thinly sliced
25g (1 oz) butter
150ml (¼ pt) milk
10 chopped sage leaves
freshly ground black pepper
4 eggs, separated

225g (8 oz) kipper fillets
15ml (1 tablespoon) grated
  Parmesan cheese
butter, crumbs and greaseproof
  paper for preparing an 18cm
  (7 in) diameter soufflé dish

Peel the artichokes and cut them into 1cm (½ in) dice. Melt the butter in a saucepan on a low heat, put in the onion and cook it until it is soft. Stir in the artichokes, milk, sage and pepper. Bring them just to the boil and simmer, uncovered for 20 minutes, beating frequently with a wooden spoon so the artichokes cook down to a thick pulp. Cook the kippers while the artichokes are simmering. Put them into a shallow pan and cover them with water. Cover, bring them to the boil and simmer for two minutes. Lift them out, drain and flake them, discarding the skin and bones. Preheat the oven to 190°C (375°F)/Gas 5. Beat the fish, egg yolks and half the Parmesan cheese into the artichokes. Stiffly whip the whites and quickly fold them into the mixture with a metal spoon. Pile the mixture into the prepared soufflé dish and bake for 30 minutes.

Raw Jerusalem artichokes have a nutty flavour, rather like almonds, which makes them a good ingredient in winter salads. Only use the thick ends as the thin parts are much too tough and you will be chewing for ages! Either slice the rounded ends paper thin or grate them straight into the dressing to prevent them turning brown.

    Artichokes and Seville oranges are usually in the greengrocer's at the same time, so put them together into a salad.

Artichoke and Orange Salad

350g (¾ lb) Jerusalem artichokes
2 Spanish oranges
½ bunch watercress
grated rind and juice 1 Seville
  orange

60ml (4 tablespoons) olive oil
1 clove garlic crushed with a
  pinch of sea-salt
freshly ground black pepper
125g (4 oz) curd cheese

Scrub and very thinly slice the round ends of the artichokes without peeling. Cut the rind from the oranges, slice them and cut each slice into quarters. Chop the watercress. Put the artichokes, sliced orange and watercress together and divide them between four small bowls. Mix together the grated Seville orange rind and juice, oil, garlic and pepper and mix equal portions of this dressing into the bowls. Top each one with a blob of curd cheese. Serve as a first course.

The Onion Family

All kinds of onions were known in Anglo-Saxon times, but their names were different then. The ordinary onion was called 'ynioleac', leeks were 'porleac', garlic 'garleac', and the chive-types 'cropleac'. Two others were listed as 'hol-leac' and 'brade-leac'.

Large Onions

The goodness and flavour of onions has been highly valued for thousands of years and bread, onions and beer have always been served together. They were the basic diet of peasants in ancient Egypt, and with a hunk of cheese as well have been the English countryman's favourite lunch since Medieval times.

Onions were used in classical Greece, where they were served with wine as a kind of appetizer; and by the Romans who used them fresh and dried, in sauces and as a vegetable.

It was probably the Romans who first brought the cultivated onions to Britain, but there were wild ones growing here before then which were no doubt eaten raw and also roasted in their skins in hot ashes. Later, onions were a common addition to the pottage pot, particularly with cabbage, and as early as 1393 they were listed along with parsley, sage, garlic and other herbs as one of the essential ingredients in a salad.

In the fifteenth century it was the practice to boil up the umbels (or offal) of an animal, particularly venison, with onions, to counteract their strong flavour, and this led to our dish of liver and onions.

At this time, onions were a common vegetable in gardens all over the country, but even so, supply couldn't keep up with demand and both onions and onion seed were imported from Spain and Holland.

Elizabethan recipes were full of onions. They were in pottages and pies and were included, both raw and cooked, in salads. Often they were boiled in their skins, peeled and mixed with a simple oil and vinegar dressing.

58

The idea of sticking cloves into an onion to flavour braised and pot-roasted meat came from France in the seventeenth century and was quickly adopted. Since then they have been used as flavourers in all kinds of ways.

A field of growing onions is not a spectacular sight; in fact if you drove past one you would probably never notice there was anything quietly growing under the ground at all. The tops are green and straggly and fairly widely spaced. Sometimes, before onions are dug up, a roller is towed over the field behind a tractor to bend over these tops and make them wither and eventually drop off. This cuts down the time when they are lifted. If it were not done they would all have to be broken off separately later.

Onions are either dug up with the same kind of machine that is used for potatoes, or lifted by hand. A freshly dug onion is fairly moist and white on the outside, and to cure their skins they are left on top of the earth for several days for the sun and wind to dry them and make them golden brown.

All the onion crop is lifted in the autumn, and for the winter they are stored in clamps. Kept in these airy conditions, they will last until April or May, or until the stocks run out and we have to rely on imported ones again.

Onions are so widely used that instructions as to how to prepare them are not really necessary. Whenever I slice or chop them, unless I want rings for garnish, I always cut them in half lengthways first so they don't roll around on the chopping board. If they are really large, then it is often best to cut them into quarters.

For golden brown stocks and broths, where the onions are included for flavour and discarded before the final dish is made, keep the skins on and just cut the onion in half.

Medium sized to large onions can be baked whole in their skins in a moderate oven for 1½ hours. Then each person can cut open their own steamy bundle of leaves and quickly push in a knob of butter so it sinks all through the layers.

Those onions that are just a little larger than the button or pickling onions are ideal peeled and baked in an oven proof dish for 1¼ hours in stock or milk.

Cooked in the following way with cheese, they can be a first course or an accompanying vegetable.

Onions Covered with Cheese

12 small onions	*Edam cheese*
1 large bayleaf	*15ml (1 tablespoon) browned*
150ml (¼ pt) stock	*crumbs*
12 wafer-thin triangular slices	*little butter for greasing dish*

59

Preheat the oven to 190°C (375°F)/Gas 5.

Peel the onions and cut a small slice from the bottom of each so they stand upright. Stand them in a lightly greased oven-proof dish so they aren't touching. Tear the bayleaf in half and tuck it between the onions. Pour in the stock. Put the onions into the oven for an hour and 10 minutes, basting them occasionally. Take the dish from the oven and lay a slice of cheese over each onion. Scatter the crumbs on top. Put the dish back into the oven for a further ten minutes, or until the cheese has softened and folded itself over the onions but not run into the stock.

Serve them whole either straight from the dish or in another serving dish having taken care when lifting them out not to disturb the cheese.

Another way of cooking onions in the oven is to stuff them. This recipe, on first looking at the ingredients appears as though it will taste sharp and spicy, but in actual fact, all the sharpness is taken away in the cooking, leaving only a pleasant, savoury flavour. The meat mixture will be creamy-textured as the chopped turnip will have melted into it.

Stuffed Turnips and Onions

4 small white turnips (each weighing around 125g (4 oz)
4 medium onions (each weighing around 125g (4 oz)
25g (1 oz) butter
900g (2 lb) best quality minced beef
60ml (4 tablespoons) malt vinegar
30ml (2 tablespoons) Worcestershire sauce
pinch ground mace
15ml (1 tablespoon) chopped savory
30ml (2 tablespoons) chopped parsley
4 pickled walnuts, finely chopped

Preheat the oven to 180°C (350°F)/Gas 4.

Cut the bottom off the turnips so they stand upright. Hollow them out so you have four shells 0.25-0.5cm (⅛-¼ in) thick. Chop the tops and scooped out pieces. Peel the onions carefully, leaving the outer white layer intact. Cut off the tops and scoop out the middle as with the turnips. Chop the tops and scooped out pieces. Melt the butter in a large, flameproof casserole on a low heat. Put in the chopped onion and turnip and cook them, stirring occasionally until the onion is soft. Raise the heat, put in the beef and brown it, stirring it around all the time to break it up well. Put in the vinegar, sauce, mace, herbs and chopped pickles. Bring everything to the boil and take the casserole from the heat. Stuff as much mixture as possible into the hollowed-out onions and turnips. Stand these amongst the rest of the beef mixture in the casserole. Cover, and put the casserole into the oven for 1¼ hours.

Serve the stuffed onions and turnips on top of all the rest of the beef in a serving dish.

This recipe for pork and onions is hot and spicy and very quick to make, provided you have the sauce handy.

Hot Pork Slices and Onions

675g (1½ lb) thin slices of pork
* cut from the lean end of the*
* belly*
10ml (2 teaspoons) paprika
2.5ml (½ teaspoon) cayenne
* pepper*
2 cloves garlic
pinch sea salt

15ml (1 tablespoon) olive oil
1 large onion, thinly sliced
275ml (½ pt) brown sauce (made
* from root vegetable trimmings*
* — see under Parsnips — A*
* Good Brown Gravy)*
15ml (1 tablespoon) tomato
* purée*

Pound the paprika, cayenne pepper, garlic and salt together with a pestle and mortar. Work in the olive oil. Spread this mixture over both sides of the pork slices. Preheat the grill to high. Lay the pork on the hot rack and scatter over the onion rings. Grill them close to the heat for about five minutes on each side, moving the onions to the edge of the pan if they keep the heat from the pork too much. Put the pork and onions into the bottom of the grill pan. Pour in the sauce and stir in the tomato purée. Put the pan back under the hot grill for five minutes.

These simple onion kebabs can be served hot on a bed of brown rice, or cold with salads. They are also ideal to take on a picnic. If you are going to carry them around, stick corks on the ends of the skewers to prevent them from damaging anything in transit.

Chicken and Onion Kebabs

1 roasting chicken weighing
* 1.5kg (3-3½ lb)*
1 really large or 2 medium
* onions*
50g (2 oz) butter

1 large clove garlic, crushed
* with a pinch of sea salt*
10ml (2 teaspoons) curry powder
10ml (2 teaspoons) ground
* cumin*

Joint the chicken, cut the meat from the bone and cut it into 3cm (1 in) cubes. Cut the onion into 3cm (1 in) squares by cutting it lengthways into about six pieces and then in half crossways. Alternate pieces of onion and chicken onto four skewers, starting and ending with onion. Melt the butter in a small saucepan on a low heat. Add the curry powder, cumin and garlic and let them simmer gently for two minutes. Brush this mixture over the kebabs. Preheat the grill to high. Put under the kebabs and cook them until they are golden brown all over, taking care not to overcook the chicken. They should only need about five minutes all together.

This next dish sounds a little peculiar, but it is absolutely delicious. It is based on a fourteenth century Italian recipe which originally used cream cheese and saffron.

Scrambled Beef and Onions

350g (12 oz) lean stewing beef
450g (1 lb) onions, thinly sliced
45ml (3 tablespoons) olive oil
little freshly grated nutmeg
2.5ml (½ teaspoon) ground
  cinnamon

2.5ml (½ teaspoon) freshly
  ground black pepper
125g (4 oz) curd cheese
2 eggs, beaten

Cut the beef into small, thin slivers. Wash the onions in a colander under the hot tap. Heat the oil in a heavy frying pan on a high heat. Put in the meat and brown it well, stirring it around all the time. Lower the heat right down and stir in the onions and spices. Cook them slowly until the onions are beginning to brown. Stir in the cheese. When it is well mixed in, stir in the eggs. Continue to stir until the eggs are cooked like scrambled eggs. Like scrambled eggs, it is best served as soon as possible.
  Potatoes baked in their jackets and a green salad are the best accompaniments.

Onion soup is traditionally made in France with champagne, to be served as a pick-you-up in the small hours of the morning at a party.
  This one is made with a plain white wine and is spiced with mustard.

Onion Soup with Mustard, Watercress and White Wine

25g (1 oz) butter
225g (8 oz) onions, thinly sliced
15ml (1 tablespoon) wholemeal
  flour
10ml (2 teaspoons) mustard
  powder

575ml (1 pt) stock
1 bayleaf
275ml (½ pt) dry white wine
½ bunch watercress, finely
  chopped
1 egg, beaten

Melt the butter in a saucepan on a low heat. Put in the onions and cook them until they are golden. Stir in the flour and mustard and let them bubble. Take the pan from the heat and stir in the stock. Bring it to the boil, stirring. Put in the bayleaf and simmer for ten minutes, uncovered. Pour in the wine and bring the soup to the boil. Remove the bayleaf.

Add the watercress and quickly whisk in the egg with a fork. Keep whisking until it scrambles into strands.

Serve the soup with brown toast.

Button Onions

Button onions are essentially an autumn treat. Their season usually lasts from September to December, but I have found that if they are stored in a cool, dark, dry place it is possible to keep them for about two months longer without their going soft or sprouting green shoots.

Often they are called 'pickling onions', but this is by no means their only use. You can make stews, casseroles and braised dishes attractive as well as tasty if you use the buttons instead of large onions. They can be served alone as a vegetable dish, or they can be boiled, or simmered in olive oil, and made into salads.

This first recipe for a salad is based on the Elizabethan idea of cooking them in their skins first. It really does keep in all their flavour. Cheshire cheese is ideal for this salad and soaks up a little of the dressing so all the flavours blend. There is no difference in taste between the white and red Cheshire cheeses, but the white one looks the more attractive against the red dressing and light-coloured onions. Serve the salad as a first course.

Cheese and Onion Salad

16 button onions
15ml (1 tablespoon) tomato
  purée
15ml (1 tablespoon)
  Worcestershire sauce
60ml (4 tablespoons) olive oil

30ml (2 tablespoons) white wine
  vinegar
175g (6 oz) white Cheshire
  cheese
1 box mustard and cress

Bring a pan of lightly salted water to the boil. Put in the onions, still in their skins and simmer them, covered for 20 minutes. Make the dressing while they are cooking. Put the tomato purée and Worcester sauce into a bowl and work in first the oil and then the vinegar. Drain the onions and peel them while they are still warm. Put them immediately into the dressing. Let them get quite cool. Cut the cheese into 0.75cm (½ in) dice. Mix it into the salad with the cress. Let the salad stand for a further 15 minutes for the cheese to soak up a little dressing.

Serve it in small earthenware bowls with brown bread and butter.

Here is an attractive beef and onion stew, flavoured with orange. Be careful when you are serving it not to put all the onions on the same plate!

Beef Stew with Orange and Button Onions

900g (2 lb) lean stewing beef
2 small oranges (if it's November onwards use Spanish ones)
bouquet garni
24 button onions
3 large sticks celery
30ml (2 tablespoons) beef dripping

15ml (1 tablespoon) wholemeal flour
150ml (¼ pt) dry red wine
275ml (½ pt) stock
1 clove garlic, finely chopped
1 small leek (optional)

Preheat the oven to 180°C (350°F)/Gas 4.

Cut the beef into 3cm (1 in) cubes. Thinly pare four strips of rind from one of the oranges and tie them into the bouquet garni. Peel the onions and slice the celery. Melt the dripping in a flameproof casserole, put in the beef, in two batches, and brown it well. Remove it and set it aside. Lower the heat and cool the casserole a little. Put in the onions and celery and cook them until the onions are beginning to look translucent. Stir in the flour and then the wine and stock. Bring them to the boil and replace the beef. Add the bouquet garni and the garlic. Cover the casserole and put it into the oven for 1½ hours. Pare all the rind from the other orange and cut it into 0.25cm (⅛ in) slivers. Thinly slice the leek. Bring a small pan of water to the boil when the casserole is nearly ready. Put in the orange peel and leek and cook them for two minutes. Drain them and keep them warm. Squeeze the juice from one of the oranges. Cut any remaining rind and pith from the other and slice it thinly. Cut each slice into quarters. When the beef is done, remove the bouquet garni and stir in the orange juice and pieces of orange. Heat it through again and put it into a warm serving dish. Scatter the orange rind and the leek over the top.

Served as a vegetable alone, button onions are best slightly glazed with a little butter and stock. Soy sauce here makes them nice and sticky, but you could instead use 5ml (1 teaspoon) of soft brown sugar or honey.

Saute of Button Onions with Soy Sauce

350g (12 oz) button onions
15ml (½ oz) butter
2.5ml (¼ teaspoon) ground ginger

15ml (1 tablespoon) soy sauce
60ml (4 tablespoons) stock

Peel the onions. Melt the butter in a sauté pan or heavy frying pan on a low heat. Put in the onions and cook them until they are lightly browned, turning them frequently. Sprinkle over the ginger and add the soy sauce and stock. Cover the pan and cook gently for ten minutes, by which time the onions should be brown and tender and just coated in a syrupy sauce.

This lamb dish is cooked in a similar way to give just a little rich sauce. Serve it with spinach noodles or wholemeal pasta, and a plain green salad, or a salad of watercress and orange.

Lamb with Button Onions and Button Mushrooms

675-900g (1½-2 lb) lean boneless lamb, cut from the shoulder
225g (½ lb) button onions
12 black olives
6 flat anchovy fillets
60ml (4 tablespoons) lamb fat or 25g (1 oz) butter

225g (½ lb) button mushrooms
150ml (¼ pt) dry red wine
15ml (1 tablespoon) chopped thyme
15ml (1 tablespoon) chopped parsley

Cut the lamb into 2cm (¾ in) dice. Peel the onions. Stone and quarter the olives. Chop the anchovies. Heat the fat or butter in a large frying pan or sauté pan on a high heat. Put in the lamb and brown it well, moving it around to drive away any moisture that may collect. Remove it and set it aside. Lower the heat, cool the pan slightly and put in the onions and mushrooms. Cook them until the onions are beginning to look translucent. Pour in the wine and bring it to the boil. Stir in the olives, anchovies and herbs and replace the lamb. Cover the pan tightly and set it on a low heat for 45 minutes.

However much I may cook with button onions, I always pickle some every year as well. Pack all the pickling spices into the jars to make them hot and flavoursome.

Pickled Onions

900g (2 lb) button onions
30ml (2 tablespoons) sea salt
625ml (1¼ pt) malt vinegar
15ml (1 tablespoon) black peppercorns

15ml (1 tablespoon) cloves
6 dried red chillies

Peel the onions and layer them in a large bowl with the salt. Cover them and leave them to stand overnight. Wash them in a colander, drain them well and pack them into jars. Put the vinegar, peppercorns, cloves and chillies into a saucepan. Bring them to the boil and simmer them, covered, for 15 minutes. Let the vinegar get quite cold and pour it over the onions. Let some of the spices and chillies find their way into the jars too to make the onions hot and spicy.

Fattier cuts of meat such as breast of lamb often benefit from the sharpness of pickles. Here the onions are rolled up in the lamb for the final stages of cooking so you get meat and pickles all in one.

Breast of Lamb with Pickled Onions

2 pieces breast of lamb

For boiling:

1 small onion
1 small carrot
1 stick celery plus a few leaves
10 black peppercorns
10 cloves

1 blade mace
piece cinnamon stick about
*   10cm (3 in) long*
bouquet garni including
*   rosemary and thyme*

For roasting:

8 flat anchovy fillets
15ml (1 tablespoon) capers

8 pickled onions, finely chopped

Put the boiling ingredients into a large pan with just enough water to cover the lamb. Bring them to the boil and simmer for ten minutes. Put in the lamb and simmer gently for 1½ hours. Cool the lamb in the liquid until it is lukewarm. Lift each piece out separately and remove all the bones and skin and as much fat as possible. Press each piece overnight under a heavy weight. When you are ready for the final cooking, preheat the oven to 180°C (350°F)/Gas 4. Pound the anchovies and capers together with a pestle and mortar. Spread them over the underside of the pieces of lamb and scatter the chopped pickled onions evenly over the top. Roll up the two pieces separately and tie them round and lengthways with fine cotton string. Put them in a roasting tin and put them into the oven for 45 minutes so they go brown and crisp on the outside. This is excellent hot or cold.

Salad Onions

Despite all our sophisticated methods of planting and storing we have
never been able to adequately fill
the gap between the end of one onion
season and the beginning of another.
Imported ones first came from
Holland, and later in the nineteenth
century, from Brittany. Now we get
them from Spain, Cyprus and even
California to help us through the
difficult time in the late spring and
early summer.

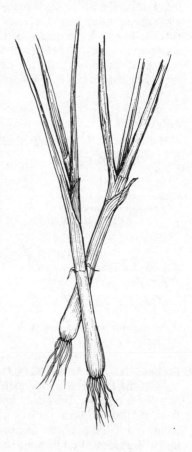

We are not left entirely without
home-produce, however, as we have
salad onions available nearly all the
year round, not just in the spring as
was once the case.

They are what is called 'continuity
grown'. Some are sown in the
autumn so they can over-winter and
be ready very early in the year, and
some are sown in the spring to
provide a crop for the summer.
Salad onions are one of the most
labour-intensive crops. They are so
tiny and grow so close together and
have to be bunched in such small
amounts that it takes a long time to
clear even half an acre. First of all, the onions are combed with a swift,
upward movement of the hands to untangle the tops and remove the
worst of the dead leaves. Then they are pulled up, separated out and
bunched with an elastic band. The way and the extent to which the
muddy, slimy salad onions are washed and trimmed depends on the
size and facilities of the farm and their eventual market.

A small market-gardener supplying local shops, for example, may
wash them by rubbing the mud off in a large tank of water, pull the
dead leaves off by hand and trim off only the tips of the long green
parts. On the larger farms, supplying big supermarket depots, the
process can be far more involved using all kinds of equipment and
water sprays.

67

With all this work in mind, it is really worth making the most of salad onions in all kinds of recipes, as well as putting them into salads and serving them with cold meats and cheese. Whatever you do with them, always use the green parts as well — they are just as good as the white and make dishes attractive as well.

Eggs always seem to be the perfect spring-time ingredient and they often benefit from a mild onion flavour.

This soufflé is light and fluffy and should rise really high so prepare the dish with buttered and crumbed greaseproof paper first. Use Gruyere cheese if you can, but, failing this, a good strong Cheddar.

Salad Onion Soufflé

4 eggs separated
25g (1 oz) butter
15ml (1 tablespoon) wholemeal
  flour
275ml (½ pt) milk infused with
  1 bayleaf, 1 blade mace,
  bouquet garni, 6 black
  peppercorns, small piece
  onion
8 large salad onions, finely
  chopped

15ml (1 tablespoon) chopped
  parsley
12 chopped sage leaves
75g (3 oz) grated Gruyere
  cheese
15ml (1 tablespoon) browned
  crumbs
butter and crumbs for preparing
  greaseproof paper and 20cm
  (7 in) diameter soufflé dish

Preheat the oven to 200°C (400°F)/Gas 6.

Melt the butter in a saucepan on a moderate heat. Stir in the flour and let it bubble. Take the pan from the heat and stir in the milk. Return it to the heat and stir until you have a thick, bubbly sauce. Remove it from the heat again and beat in the chopped onions, herbs and all but 15ml (1 tablespoon) of the cheese. Beat in the egg yolks, one at a time. Mix the remaining cheese with the crumbs. Stiffly whip the whites and fold them into the rest with a metal spoon. Pile the mixture into the prepared soufflé dish and scatter the crumb and cheese mixture over the top. Put the soufflé into the centre of the oven and as soon as you have closed the door turn the heat down to 190°C (375°F)/Gas 5. Bake for 30 minutes.

Angels-on-Horseback is the name usually given to oysters rolled up in bacon, but the poor man's way is bacon and cheese. You can serve these as a first course either straight from the dish or laid on pieces of fried brown bread. Use Cheddar cheese if there is no Sage Derby.

Angels and Onions on Horseback

4 large collar rashers bacon
175g (6 oz) Sage Derby cheese

8 salad onions (with fairly
straight white ends, not big
bulbous ones)

Cut each bacon rasher in half. Cut the cheese into even-sized wedges about 1.5cm (½ in) square and 3-4cm (1-1½ in) long. Cut the onions into lengths the same size as the width of the bacon rashers. Lay a wedge of cheese and one onion on each bacon piece and roll them up. Lay them on a heatproof dish or plate. Preheat the grill to high and grill the rolls on all sides until the bacon is cooked and the cheese just beginning to melt.

This chicken dish is again quick to prepare and is really attractive and tasty. Larger, stronger onions could mask the flavour of the chicken, but salad onions here are ideal.

Grilled Chicken and Salad Onions

One 1.5kg (3-3½ lb) roasting
  chicken
30ml (2 tablespoons) olive oil
freshly ground black pepper
60ml (4 tablespoons) grated
  Parmesan cheese

60ml (4 tablespoons) double
  cream
10ml (2 teaspoons) Dijon
  mustard
12 medium salad onions, finely
  chopped

Joint the chicken. Brush the joints with the oil and grind over some black pepper. Mix the cheese, cream, mustard and onions together. Preheat the grill to high, and grill the chicken pieces, skin-side down first and as close to the heat as possible, until they are cooked through and the juices run clear when they are pricked. (About 15 minutes.) Turn all the chicken pieces skin-side up and spread over the cheese and onion mixture. Put them back under the grill until they are golden brown.

This meat loaf will make a main meal for two to three people, but it is best cut in slices and taken on a spring picnic.

Spring Beef Loaf

450g (1 lb) best quality minced
  beef
6 large or 10 small salad onions
30ml (2 tablespoons) chopped
  parsley
15ml (1 tablespoon) chopped
  capers

10ml (2 teaspoons) Dijon
  mustard
5ml (1 teaspoon) Dill seeds
30ml (2 tablespoons) dry white
  wine

Preheat the oven to 160°C (325°F)/Gas 3.

Put the beef into a large bowl. Chop the salad onions, green parts as well. Put the onions and all the rest of the ingredients into the bowl with the beef and beat them all together well. Press the mixture into a 450g (1 lb) loaf tin and put it into the oven for one hour. Leave the loaf to get quite cold before turning it out.

N.B. For a main meal for four, use half as many ingredients again, use a 900g (2 lb) loaf tin, and add 15 minutes to the cooking time.

Most cream of onion soups are creamy white, but this one, if you use the green parts of the salad onions, will be a soft green.

Cream of Salad Onion Soup

Two 125g (4 oz) bunches of salad onions (or four 50g (2 oz))
25g (1 oz) butter
15ml (1 tablespoon) wholemeal flour

850ml (1½ pt) stock
bouquet garni
seasoning to taste
60ml (4 tablespoons) sour cream

Chop the salad onions finely and set aside 30ml (2 tablespoons) of the green ends for garnish. Melt the butter in a saucepan on a low heat. Stir in the onions, cover them, and let them sweat for ten minutes. Stir in the flour and the stock and bring them to the boil, stirring. Add the bouquet garni and salt and freshly ground black pepper to taste and simmer, uncovered, for five minutes. Cool the soup slightly and remove the bouquet garni. Work the soup in a blender until it is smooth. Return it to the pan, stir in the sour cream, and reheat. Serve the soup in small bowls with the chopped green parts floating on the top.

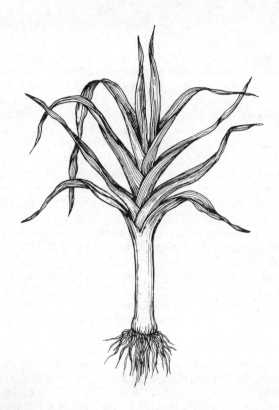

Leeks

Leeks are increasing in popularity in Britain at the moment and their season seems to be getting longer and longer. There are about fifty different types grown in the country varying considerably in size and shape and time of availability. There are the almost miniature ones for cooking whole, the long slender ones with only a small amount of green that are best for cooking in short lengths, the really big fat ones for slicing up for frying or for salads and garnishes, and all the others in between.

Leeks were brought to Britain by the Romans, but they were most widely grown from Anglo-Saxon times until the sixteenth century, when they were even more popular than onions. A book of laws drawn up in Wales before the Norman conquest only mentions two vegetables — leeks and cabbages. It stipulated that they had to be well fenced-in against straying cattle. The two Anglo-Saxon names for 'garden' were 'leac-tun' and 'wyrt-tun', 'tun' meaning enclosure, and 'leacs' and 'wyrts' being leeks and cabbages.

Leeks were the vegetable that was most often used for the thick, boiled, Medieval broth called pottage, and during Lent when no meat was allowed to be eaten they were often, in poor houses at least, its main ingredient and flavourer. The poor stewed them up with cabbage and sometimes a little salt fish, but the rich could afford many more elaborate ways of getting round the strict religious laws. They made an expensive substitute milk from ground almonds and the leeks were boiled with this and a little ground rice, spices and honey to be served as an accompaniment to eels. On non-fasting days the leeks were boiled in ham or meat stock with bacon or poultry. Another popular dish of the time was to simmer the leeks with wine and spices and serve them on well-toasted bread.

Pottages were still common in the fifteenth century and leeks were stewed with the 'umbels' of pork in the same way as onions were with those of venison. They remained the standard Lenten dish until Elizabethan times after which they gradually began to disappear from the recipe books due to the relaxation of the laws and the availability of many more different kinds of vegetables.

Eighteenth century cooks rarely used leeks, but they remained ever-popular in Wales, and one or two regional dishes were kept in other parts. The Scots have their cock-a-leekie, a real descendant of the pottage days. There must be many different recipes for it but basically it consists of a cock or chicken stuffed with prunes and simmered with leeks until it is tender, to make a good thick broth. In the West Country there is Licky Pie, usually a flat pie with a filling of leeks, bacon and a savoury custard.

Lines and lines of leeks with long wavy green tops standing up straight like soldiers on parade are a spectacular sight when seen growing on a large scale. There are all sorts of machines to be used for leek-digging. The grower I went to see was using an elevator-digger that is normally used for potatoes, towed along behind a tractor. Then comes the tiring and dirty part of gathering up, trimming and washing. On market gardens this is done by hand while on large farms that supply supermarkets they are laid on a conveyor belt, sprayed, then topped and tailed and their outer sheath stripped off. They go through another washing system, again based on a conveyor-belt, with strong jets of water being sprayed at them from all directions. This still isn't enough, however and at the end they are each hand-sprayed individually. As they go through the process they get more and more shining white and the departments through which they travel get cleaner and cleaner. Then at the opposite end of the shed to which they came in they are laid in pure white containers and wrapped up in polythene.

If you are buying ready-washed leeks all you need to do to clean them is to hold the ends under a running tap, gently easing all the layers apart so the water runs through. Those that you buy unpacked may sometimes need to have their outer layer removed, but if it is white and sound you can leave it. Making slits right through the ends of the leeks to wash them may make them come apart during cooking especially if you want to cook them in short lengths, so if you can see obstinate dirt lurking under the surface, make short slits at regular intervals with a sharp knife and run the water through these.

One of the best ways to cook leeks is to cut them into 5cm (2 in) lengths and cook them on top of the stove with a little butter and a small amount of liquid. Add some chopped herbs, a little spicy mustard or some lemon juice to vary the flavour. In fact, leeks and lemon go very well together. Here is a more unusual way of combining them.

Julienne of Leeks and Lemon

450g (1 lb) leeks
25g (1 oz) butter
150ml (¼ pt) stock

juice ½ lemon
30ml (2 tablespoons) chopped
  parsley

Cut the leeks in half lengthways and then into pieces 3cm (1 in) long and 0.5cm (¼ in) wide. Heat the butter in a heavy frying pan on a high heat. Put in the leeks, stir them around and lower the heat to moderate. Let the leeks brown, stirring frequently. Raise the heat again and add the stock, lemon juice and parsley. Let the liquid boil until it has almost reduced completely and serve immediately.

Leeks can be braised in the oven and the very tiny, almost miniature leeks can be very attractive if they are baked whole. They can, however, be quite difficult to wash. Make an incision with a sharp knife from about 5cm (2 in) from the top to about 1cm (½ in) from the bottom and wash them under running water, gently pulling the layers apart. When all the dirt is gone, push them together to reshape them.

Use an oven-to-table serving dish to bake them in and arrange them with the white parts and the fan-like green ends facing in different directions.

Leeks Baked with Cheese

8 tiny leeks
15g (½ oz) butter
60ml (4 tablespoons) stock

15ml (1 tablespoon) grated
  Parmesan cheese

Preheat the oven to 200°C (400°F)/Gas 6.

Trim and wash the leeks as described above. Grease a large flat oven proof dish with half the butter and use the other half to grease a piece of foil. Lay the leeks in the dish, pour in the stock and scatter the cheese over the top. Cover with the foil and bake for 45 minutes. For a change of flavour, omit the cheese and use 150ml (¼ pt) dry cider instead of the stock.

Chicken always goes well with leeks. The spices used in this recipe give it a very mellow flavour which blends well with the lemon, making nothing too strong or pronounced.

Spiced Chicken and Leeks

one 1.5kg (3-3½ lb) roasting
    chicken
450g (1 lb) leeks, about 3cm
    (1 in) in diameter if possible

½ lemon, sliced
5ml (1 teaspoon) ground cumin
5ml (1 teaspoon) ground
    coriander

For the sauce:

25g (1 oz) butter
5ml (1 teaspoon) ground cumin
5ml (1 teaspoon) ground
    coriander
15ml (1 tablespoon) flour

275ml (½ pt) poaching liquid
juice ½ lemon
30ml (2 tablespoons) chopped
    parsley

Cut the leeks into 4cm (1½ in) lengths. Put the sliced lemon inside the chicken and rub the spices into the skin. Put the chicken into a large casserole or saucepan and surround it with the leeks. Pour in water to just cover the legs and cover. Bring to the boil and simmer for 50 minutes. Lift out the chicken and let it cool. Lift out all the leeks with a perforated spoon and reserve them. Strain off 275ml (½ pt) stock for the sauce. Melt the butter in a saucepan on a low·heat and cook the spices gently in it for five minutes. Stir in the flour and let it bubble and blend in the stock. Bring it to the boil, stirring. Add the lemon juice and parsley and simmer for two minutes. Dice the chicken into pieces about 3cm (1 in) square and add these and the leeks to the sauce. Reheat gently without letting the chicken over-cook and serve with brown rice, made like a risotto with the remaining chicken stock.

The Romans liked to put olives into leek salads. Use them together here to flavour a quiche which you can have either hot or cold.

Leek and Chicken Quiche

For pastry to line a 20cm (8 in) diameter flan ring:

175g (6 oz) 85% wholemeal flour
100g (3 oz) butter

pinch sea salt
water to mix

For the filling:

350g (12 oz) leeks, both white
and green parts
225g (8 oz) cold cooked chicken
3 eggs
30ml (2 tablespoons) chopped
parsley

15ml (1 tablespoon) chopped
thyme
6 flat anchovy fillets
8 black olives (or more if you
wish)

Preheat the oven to 200°C (400°F)/Gas 6.

Make the pastry and line the flan-ring. Thinly slice the leeks and cook them in lightly salted boiling water for ten minutes. Drain, refresh and drain again. Dice the chicken into 1cm (½ in) pieces. Beat the eggs with the herbs and mix in the chicken and cooked leeks. (N.B. There will be a lot more filling than egg. The eggs form a binder to hold everything together.)

Put the mixture into the lined flan-ring. Cut the anchovies in half lengthways and arrange them in a lattice-work over the top. Stone and halve the olives and decorate the top with them. Bake in the centre of the oven for half an hour.

Pork, ham and bacon have probably been cooked with leeks more than any other meat. This next recipe uses the spices that were put into the pottage pot.

Old Spiced Pork Chops and Leeks

4 pork chops
2.5ml (½ teaspoon) ground
cloves
2.5ml (½ teaspoon) ground
cinnamon
2.5ml (½ teaspoon) ground
nutmeg

30ml (2 tablespoons) pork fat or
15g (½ oz) butter
275ml (½ pt) dry cider
450g (1 lb) 3cm (1 in) diameter
leeks, sliced

Mix the spices together and rub them into both sides of the chops. Heat the fat in a large sauté pan or shallow casserole on a moderate heat, put in the chops and brown them on both sides. Remove them and set aside. Pour in the cider and bring it to the boil. Replace the chops and put in the leeks. Cover and cook on a low heat for 30 minutes. Serve the chops surrounded by the leeks and with any remaining juices spooned over the top.

Use ham that you have cooked yourself for this next recipe or bought ham cut from the bone in thick slices. The thinly sliced pressed ham doesn't work half as well.

Lamb, Ham, Leeks and Mushrooms

450g (1 lb) lean boneless lamb,
  cut from the shoulder
225g (8 oz) ham
225g (8 oz) leeks
125g (4 oz) flat mushrooms
30ml (2 tablespoons) lamb fat or
  25g (1 oz) butter

275ml (½ pt) dry cider
15ml (1 tablespoon) chopped
  marjoram
15ml (1 tablespoon) chopped
  thyme

Dice the ham and lamb into 2cm (¾ in) pieces. Thinly slice the leeks and chop the mushrooms. Heat the fat in a heavy sauté pan or shallow casserole on a high heat. Put in the lamb and brown it. Remove and set it aside. Lower the heat and put in the leeks. Cook them gently until they soften. Raise the heat to moderate, put in the mushrooms, and stir them around for one minute. Pour in the cider and bring it to the boil. Replace the lamb together with the ham and herbs. Cover, and set on a low heat for 40 minutes.
    Serve it with brown rice or wholemeal spaghetti.

For a complete change, put leeks with fish. Greenland Halibut is a good, meaty, fairly cheap white fish.

Halibut and Leeks

4 Greenland halibut steaks
60ml (4 tablespoons) seasoned
  wholemeal flour
350g (12 oz) leeks

25g (1 oz) butter
150ml (¼ pt) white wine
2.5ml (½ teaspoon) ground mace

Skin the fish steaks and coat them in the flour. Thinly slice the leeks. Melt the butter in a heavy frying pan on a moderate heat, put in the fish steaks and brown them on both sides. Remove them and set aside. Lower the heat, stir in the leeks and cook them gently for two minutes. Pour in the wine and bring it to the boil. Add the mace, cover and simmer for five minutes. Set the fish on top, cover again and continue cooking for a further five minutes so the fish picks up all the flavour of the leeks and mace.

76

Leeks often benefit from the spiciness of a granular mustard, and there are some new English ones on the market now made with white wine. Use one of these to flavour the following soup.

Leek and Mustard Soup

350g (12 oz) leeks
25g (1 oz) butter
15ml (1 tablespoon) flour
850ml (1½ pt) stock

10ml (2 teaspoons) English
  granular mustard
30ml (2 tablespoons) chopped
  parsley

Finely chop the leeks. Melt the butter in a saucepan on a low heat, stir in the leeks, cover, and let them sweat for ten minutes. Stir in the flour, stock and mustard. Bring them gently to the boil, stirring, and add the parsley. Simmer gently, uncovered, for 15 minutes. To make the soup really special, use only 725ml (1¼ pt) stock at first and when the leeks have simmered pour in 150ml (¼ pt) dry white wine and reheat.

Cabbages, Leaves and Sprouts

The cabbage family of vegetables is a very large one indeed and so is the variety of tastes, textures and colours that they supply.

During the winter there are the green kinds that are best for simmering on top of the stove or braising in the oven, there are the crinkly leaved Savoys for stuffing; hard, solid white cabbages for salads; and shiny red ones, again for braising. Late April and May bring the firm, pointed, fresh green spring cabbage; and in summer there are the round, delicate green Primos.

Brussels sprouts are also related to the cabbage and so are spring greens and curly kale.

In history, it is quite difficult to distinguish which types of cabbages were used when and for what purpose. Most of our present-day kinds are all descended from the wild cabbage of which both the leaves and seeds were put into pottages as early as Neolithic times.

The Romans brought an open-headed cabbage to Britain and this remained the commonest type throughout the Anglo-Saxon and Medieval periods, known as cole-plant, cole-worts, worts, or wyrts. It was put into pottage with salt pork, spiced with cinnamon and saffron, or stewed with marrow-bone and hare or goose in a dish called 'long worts de char'. It was also simmered in a large quantity of butter, or boiled and chopped and served over small squares of toast.

By the sixteenth century, the headed types of cabbage had arrived from Holland and it was from these that the actual name of cabbage was derived. They were called at first by the French word for head, 'caboche' which is still sometimes used in the Channel Islands. From this came cabochis, caboges and later cabbages.

In Elizabethan times, cabbages were usually boiled and buttered or sometimes shredded and put into salads. Boiling and buttering seems to have been the most popular way of cooking cabbage from then until the present day, but since Medieval times, cooks have realized that this way is not necessarily the best. A fourteenth century recipe says 'take a large quantity of the worts — and shred them, and put butter thereto and seethe them and serve forth — and let nothing else come nigh them'. Hannah Glasse, 400 years later, gives only one recipe for cabbage and this is very similar. 'Most people,' she says, 'spoil garden things by over-boiling them. All things that are green should have a little crispness, for if they are over-boiled, they neither have any sweetness or beauty.' Cabbage is 'best chopped and put into a saucepan with a piece of butter, stirring it for about five or six minutes, till the butter is all melted, and then send it to table.' These two very simple methods still make a good deal of sense.

All types of cabbages can either be set in the fields as seeds or as plants, and usually they grow about 28cm (12 in) apart. The plants can either be raised in boxes under glass or they can be drilled in a propagation field first, very close together, and planted out when they are about 10cm (4 in) high, sometimes taking out every plant from the original field and sometimes just replanting all those between the twelve inches and leaving the evenly spaced ones.

Green Cabbages for Autumn and Winter

There are two basic types of green cabbages, those which are cut in September and October, and those which last from November to April, providing fresh, light-textured leaves to contrast well with the heavier roots and warming dishes of winter.

The seeds of the Autumn cabbage (usually Autumn Supreme and Autumn Victory) are drilled in March, and those of the winter ones (Christmas Drumhead, January King or a newer one called Celtic) in April and May.

Attractive as they may look when ready for cutting, gathering them is sometimes not a particularly attractive occupation as it has to be done in all weathers, rain and wind and sometimes even snow. They are cut still with their outer leaves attached, with long sharp knives, and put into wooden crates or large nylon nets. They are taken just as they are to markets and sometimes direct to local greengrocers. For supermarkets, they may be trimmed and wrapped in polythene. No washing is necessary as the inner heart is kept clean and guarded from frost by the large protecting leaves.

Once in the kitchen, these outer leaves are not so useful for they are very tough and if they are cooked with the rest of the cabbage, even if they are shredded up small, they will remain quite chewy when all the rest is ready to eat. Use some of them in the stock-pot and perhaps a few chopped very small in vegetable soups, but I'm afraid you may have to throw the rest away, or if you have a vegetable garden, put them on the compost heap.

The flattish round heads of all kinds of green cabbage, although firm, are quite loosely packed and their texture makes them far better for cooking than for salads. Cut them in half, quarter them and cut away the tougher part of the stalk. If there is any dirt lurking amongst the layers hold them under running water. Then shred them finely.

Cooked on top of the stove, one average-sized cabbage needs no more than 150ml (¼ pt) of liquid, and you can vary the flavour by using water, stock, wine or cider; by adding different herbs to the saucepan, or a spoonful of tomato purée or spicy mustard. Add a knob of butter or 30ml (2 tablespoons) of olive oil for extra richness, cover tightly, and set on a moderate heat for 20 minutes, stirring occasionally.

Cabbage and apples are always a good combination and here there is celery as well to provide an additional savoury flavour. Serve it with lamb, chicken or pork.

Cabbage, Celery and Apple in Cider

1 medium green autumn or winter cabbage
4 large sticks celery
1 medium sized Bramley (or other cooking apple)

25g (1 oz) butter
1 clove garlic, finely chopped
150ml (¼ pt) dry cider
15ml (1 tablespoon) chopped savory

Remove the outer leaves from the cabbage and shred it. Slice the celery thinly. Peel, core and slice the apple. Put the butter into the bottom of a large saucepan and put in the cabbage, celery, apple and garlic. Pour in the cider and mix in the savory. Cover and set on a moderate heat for 20 minutes, stirring around several times. By the end of cooking time the vegetables will still be firm and all the liquid will have evaporated to a cidery glaze.

Cabbage can also be braised in the oven to make a richer dish. This cabbage recipe has a very dry and unusual flavour.

Cabbage and Green Peppers with Soy and Ginger

½ medium sized green autumn
    or winter cabbage
2 large green peppers
25g (1 oz) butter
1 large onion, thinly sliced

1 clove garlic, finely chopped
15ml (1 tablespoon) soy sauce
5ml (1 teaspoon) ground ginger
150ml (¼ pt) stock

Preheat the oven to 180°C (350°F)/Gas 4.
Shred the cabbage. Core and slice the peppers. Melt the butter in a flameproof casserole on a low heat. Put in the onion and garlic and cook them until the onion is soft. Stir in the cabbage, peppers, soy sauce and ginger. Cover, and put into the oven for 45 minutes.

Green cabbage is not as suitable for salads as some of the other varieties, but its texture and colour when shredded are very similar to those of chicory. In this salad, the grapefruit provides a subtle contrast in colour and the whole is refreshing and attractive in its creamy white dressing.

Chicory, Cabbage and Grapefruit Salad

225g (½ lb) chicory (this will
    either be 2 small or 1 large
    bulb)
2 grapefruit
½ medium sized green autumn
    or winter cabbage

1 carton (5 fl oz) natural yoghurt
30ml (2 tablespoons) white wine
    vinegar
1 clove garlic crushed with a
    pinch of fine sea salt
freshly ground black pepper

Chop the chicory. Shred the cabbage finely. Put them together in a bowl. Combine the yoghurt, vinegar, garlic and pepper and mix them into the salad. Let them stand for half an hour. Peel, quarter and slice the grapefruit and mix them into the salad just before serving.

When green winter cabbages are at their most plentiful, Spanish oranges and satsumas are in the shops. Put them together for just another version of Boef a l'Orange.

Beef Braised with Orange and Cabbage and served with Satsumas

piece of rolled Sirloin weighing
    about 1.15kg (2½ lb)
1 medium sized green winter
    cabbage
25g (1 oz) butter
1 large onion, thinly sliced
2.5ml (½ teaspoon) ground
    allspice

little freshly grated nutmeg
grated rind and juice 1 small
    Spanish orange
2 satsumas
10ml (2 teaspoons) grated
    horseradish

Preheat the oven to 160°C (325°F)/Gas 3.

Discard the outer leaves of the cabbage and shred it. Melt the butter in a flameproof casserole on a high heat. Put in the beef and brown it all over. Remove it and set it aside. Lower the heat, stir in the onion, and cook it until it is soft. Stir in the cabbage, spices and grated orange rind and juice and bring the juice to simmering point. Replace the beef and surround it with the cabbage. Cover the casserole and put it into the oven for 1½ hours. Peel the satsumas, pull them into quarters and thinly slice them. Remove the beef from the casserole. Mix the satsumas and horseradish into the cabbage and heat them through while you carve the beef. Arrange the beef down the centre of a serving dish with the cabbage down either side.

Cabbage is a relatively cheap vegetable so sometimes for a special meal it is worth combining it with a few more expensive ingredients, such as an unusual cheese or a small quantity of another vegetable which is out of season, like the green pepper in the following recipe.

Casserole of Chicken and Cabbage

One 1.5kg (3½ lb) roasting
  chicken
30ml (2 tablespoons) chicken fat
  or 15g (½ oz) butter
1 large onion, thinly sliced
1 medium sized green autumn or
  winter cabbage, shredded

1 large green pepper, deseeded
  and sliced
30ml (2 tablespoons) chopped
  parsley
50g (2 oz) Sage Derby cheese,
  grated
150ml (¼ pt) stock

Preheat the oven to 180°C (350°F)/Gas 4.

Joint the chicken. Heat the fat or butter in a large casserole on a moderate heat. Put in the chicken pieces, skin side down first and cook them until they are golden brown, turning them once. Remove them and set them aside. Lower the heat, put in the onion and cook it until it is soft. Stir in the cabbage, green pepper and parsley and when they are all well mixed together, take out half the mixture. Lay the chicken pieces on top of the cabbage still in the casserole and scatter the cheese over this. Cover with the reserved cabbage and pour in the stock. Cover and put into the oven for 45 minutes.

Serve the chicken arranged on a bed of cabbage. The cheese will just melt and provide just a hint of cheese and sage flavours mingled together.

In this next recipe the cumin and coriander give a light and refreshing flavour and the almonds and currants turn the simple cabbage into a dish fit for an Eastern Prince.

Eastern Lamb and Cabbage

675g (1½ lb) lean boneless lamb
   cut from the shoulder
60ml (4 tablespoons) lamb fat
   made from the trimmings or
   25g (1 oz) butter
1 large onion, thinly sliced
5ml (1 teaspoon) ground cumin
5ml (1 teaspoon) ground
   coriander
1 medium sized green autumn or
   winter cabbage.

50g (2 oz) almonds, blanched
   and slivered
50g (2 oz) currants
15ml (1 tablespoon) tomato
   purée
225g (½ lb) tomatoes, scalded,
   skinned and roughly chopped
150ml (¼ pt) dry white wine

Cut the lamb into small dice about 2cm (¾ in) square. Heat the fat or
butter in a large casserole on a high heat. Put in the lamb and brown it
well, moving it around and keeping the heat high to drive away any
moisture. Remove it and set it aside. Lower the heat and stir in the
onion, cumin and coriander. Cook them until the onion is soft. Stir in
the cabbage, almonds, currants, tomato purée and tomatoes and pour
in the wine. Bring them to the boil, replace the lamb, cover and cook
them on a low heat for 30 minutes.

One Medieval recipe that I found was for cabbage cooked in beef
broth. The final instructions were 'Thick it with grated bread, but for a
lord it shal be thicked with the yolks of eggs, beaten.' This soup is not
for a lord as I've used breadcrumbs which make it substantial and
tasty. Serve it before a light meal or at lunchtime before bread and
cheese. Use home-cooked ham or ham cut from the bone.

Cabbage, Ham and Cider Soup

1 small green autumn or winter
   cabbage
25g (1 oz) butter
1 medium onion, finely chopped
100g (4 oz) lean ham, very finely
   diced

575ml (1 pt) stock
50g (2 oz) granary or wholemeal
   breadcrumbs
275ml (½ pt) dry cider

Remove the outer leaves from the cabbage. Do not shred it, but chop it
very finely. Melt the butter in a saucepan on a low heat, mix in the
cabbage, onion and ham. Cover and cook gently for ten minutes. Pour
in the stock and bring it to the boil. Cover again and simmer for ten
minutes. Meanwhile, soak the breadcrumbs in the cider. Pour the
cider and crumbs into the soup and simmer for five minutes more.

White and Red Cabbages

The hard, solid red and white cabbages came to England from Holland in the fifteenth century, and during Elizabethan times they were both shredded up raw and put into salads, usually dressed with oil and vinegar. One cookery book of the time suggests that you 'take a good, hard cabbage, and with a sharp knife shave it so thin you may not discern what it is'.

By the seventeenth century, white cabbages were usually boiled and buttered but the red were still used in salads in the eighteenth century, both for the crunchy texture and the bright red colour which garnished the plate beside beetroot, barberries and nasturtium flowers.

The red cabbage had always stirred more culinary imagination than the white, probably because when it is just plain boiled it becomes rather tasteless and unless an acid is added in the form of vinegar or lemon juice the colour is a rather horrid blue. In the nineteenth century it was often simmered, tightly covered, for a considerable time with butter and lemon juice or chilli vinegar, and sometimes it was stewed in brown gravy and served with sausages.

Its main use in later years has been in pickles to serve with cold meats, but gradually it is being accepted as an interesting and different vegetable and more and more are being grown.

Likewise, the white cabbage is also enjoying a new popularity as more and more people are serving a salad with the main meal to replace at least one of our 'two veg'.

In order to obtain the solid, round, tightly-packed heads of white and red cabbages they have to be allowed to grow slowly for a good long time. Most of the seeds used in this country still come from

84

Holland and they are drilled in early March to be ready usually by the end of August. The crop lasts until the end of April and on many farms they are left growing in the fields until they are needed. This is a cheaper way of keeping them than cutting them first and storing them in specially built clamps.

Both white and red cabbages have more stalk than the green kinds and the hearts are protected by bushy outer leaves, those of the mature white cabbage being a deep green and the red a dull, dark purple.

Towards the end of the season the stalk grows upwards and the leaves spread out making the plants look more like miniature exotic pine-trees than cabbages. When they are cut, the outer leaves are pushed down and the glossy-sheened reddy-purple or soft green centres are cut out with a sharp butcher's knife. On farms that specialize in vegetables, the outer leaves and stems are ploughed back in, but on mixed farms sheep are sometimes let out into the stubble to feed and to manure the field as they go.

How the cabbages are actually taken from the fields depends on the density of the crop. If it is fairly thick, each cutter has her own sack (a purple one for red cabbages and a green one for the white) and is responsible for a certain block of the field; but if it is towards the end of the season and the cabbages are fewer on the ground all the women follow a tractor, cutting as they go and tossing the cabbages into a container which is towed behind.

When the cabbages are cut they are either taken to the packing shed or to the corner of the field to be put into sacks. No other washing or trimming is needed, but if they are to be sent to supermarkets they are stretch-wrapped in polythene and sometimes if they are large they are cut in half.

In the kitchen, both kinds of cabbage need little preparation. The ends of the stalk should be cut away, and in the case of red cabbages where it can be very tough some of the inside of the stalk as well. Then, depending on the recipe, they can either be chopped into small square pieces or shredded or 'shaved thin' exactly as recommended in Elizabethan times.

White cabbages are the best kind of winter cabbage for salads as they are crisp and yet not at all tough.

This salad is a real English flavoured one. It is perfect for serving with cold beef, steak and kidney pudding, and beef pies.

Cabbage and Horseradish Salad

1 small white cabbage
90ml (6 tablespoons) olive oil
45ml (3 tablespoons) malt
  vinegar

5ml (1 teaspoon) made English
  mustard
15ml (1 tablespoon) grated
  horseradish

Shred the cabbage and put it in a bowl. Beat the oil, vinegar and mustard together and mix in the horseradish. Stir the dressing into the cabbage.

Hot salads are always a good idea during the winter. This spicy one goes well with pork or chicken.

Hot Cabbage, Apple and Cinnamon Salad

1 small white cabbage
1 really large or 2 medium sized
  Bramley apples
60ml (4 tablespoons) olive oil
1 large clove garlic, finely
  chopped

5ml (1 teaspoon) ground
  cinnamon
30ml (2 tablespoons) cider
  vinegar

Shred the cabbage. Quarter, core and slice the apples. Heat the oil in a large skillet or frying pan on a moderate heat. Put in the cabbage, apple, garlic and cinnamon and stir them around on the heat for two minutes. Pour in the vinegar, let it bubble and serve immediately.

This hot salad is a meal in itself. Serve it for lunch or supper.

Egg, Bacon and Hot Cabbage Salad

1 small white cabbage
60ml (4 tablespoons) olive oil
1 large onion, thinly sliced
175g (6 oz) lean bacon, diced
30ml (2 tablespoons) white wine
  vinegar

5ml (1 teaspoon) made English
  mustard
8 eggs
12 chopped sage leaves

Shred the cabbage. Heat the oil in a large skillet or frying pan on a moderate heat. Put in the onion and bacon and cook them until the onion is soft. Meanwhile, blend the vinegar and mustard together. Soft-poach the eggs in lightly simmering salted water, drain them and keep them warm. When the onion is ready, put in the cabbage and sage and stir them around for one and a half minutes. Raise the heat and pour in the vinegar and mustard. Blend them in well and let the resulting dressing bubble. Put the salad onto a warmed serving dish and put the eggs on the top. If you like, scatter a little chopped parsley over them for garnish.

Plain cooked white cabbage is very bland and needs some additional flavouring added to the pot such as Worcester sauce or bacon if it is going to be served as a cooked hot vegetable.

White Cabbage and Orange

1 small white cabbage
1 clove garlic

15ml (1 tablespoon) Worcester
sauce
1 large orange

Chop the cabbage and garlic and put them into a saucepan with about 1.5cm (½ in) water. Add the sauce. Cover the pan and set it on a moderate heat for 15 minutes, stirring occasionally. Cut the rind from the orange, slice it and cut each slice into quarters. When the cabbage is tender and slightly glazed brown mix in the orange and just heat it through.

White Cabbage Wedges with Bacon and Onion

1 small white cabbage
50g (2 oz) lean bacon
7.5ml (½ tablespoon) pork
  dripping
1 small onion, thinly sliced

150ml (¼ pt) stock
1 bayleaf
freshly ground pepper
15ml (1 tablespoon) chopped
  parsley

Cut the cabbage in half and cut each half into four wedges, lengthways. Dice the bacon. Melt the dripping in a heavy frying pan on a low heat. Put in the bacon and onion and cook them until the onion is soft. Add the cabbage, stock and bayleaf and season with the pepper. Bring the stock to the boil and add the parsley. Cover, and simmer for 20 minutes. Most of the stock will have evaporated and the cabbage will be moist and tasty. Discard the bayleaf and serve the wedges with the bacon and onion and any stock that is left spooned over the top.

Red cabbage is not now as popular a salad ingredient as white as it can sometimes be a little tough, but if you let it stand for a while in the dressing before serving you can overcome this problem. Hot salads are ideal for red cabbage, too, as the small amount of cooking also helps to soften it.

In the spring there should be plenty of dandelion leaves around to make the following hot salad, and at the same time small blood oranges arrive from Spain. As substitutes during the middle of winter use ordinary Spanish oranges and parsley.

Hot Red Cabbage and Orange Salad

1 small red cabbage
2 blood oranges
45ml (3 tablespoons) olive oil
1 large clove garlic, finely
  chopped

30ml (2 tablespoons) red wine
  vinegar
10 chopped dandelion leaves

87

Shred the cabbage. Cut the rind from the oranges and slice them. Cut each slice into quarters. Heat the oil in a large frying pan or skillet on a high heat. Put in the garlic and cook it until it begins to brown. (This will make it taste really nutty.) Put in the cabbage and stir it around for three minutes. Mix in the orange and pour in the vinegar. Bring the dressing to the boil and mix in the dandelions. Serve the salad immediately.

Use a top-quality braising steak for this complete salad meal then the short cooking time won't matter at all.

Hot Beef and Red Cabbage Salad

900g (2 lb) lean braising steak
½ small red cabbage
15ml (1 tablespoon) clear honey
45ml (3 tablespoons) red wine
  vinegar

15ml (1 tablespoon) grated
  horseradish
60ml (4 tablespoons) olive oil
1 large onion, thinly sliced
1 clove garlic, finely chopped

Cut the beef into small thin slivers about 3cm by 0.5cm (1 in x ¼ in). Shred the cabbage. Blend the honey, vinegar and horseradish together. Heat the oil in a large frying pan or skillet on a high heat. Put in the beef and brown it well, moving it around to drive away any moisture that may collect. Lower the heat and put in the cabbage, onion and garlic. Continue cooking until the onion is soft. Raise the heat again and stir in the honey mixture. Bring the dressing to the boil and serve the salad immediately.

The best way of cooking red cabbage is to braise it in the oven. Try it with apples and red wine and serve it with casseroles and stews or with game.
    Braise red cabbage and meat or fish together to make the most of all their flavours and textures.
    Prunes and anchovies have often been used to stuff a joint or a fillet of pork. Here they flavour the cabbage as well.

Pork with Prunes and Red Cabbage

1 joint shoulder or spare rib of
  pork weighing about 1-1.25kg
  (2½ lb)
8 prunes
150ml (¼ pt) red wine

2 medium sized cooking apples
1 small red cabbage
4 flat anchovy fillets
15g (½ oz) lard or pork dripping

Soak the prunes in the wine for three hours.

Preheat the oven to 180°C (350°F)/Gas 4.

Cut the prunes in half and remove the stones. Peel, quarter, core and slice the apples. Shred the cabbage and chop the anchovies. Heat the lard in a flameproof casserole on a high heat. Put in the pork and brown it all over, remove it and set it aside. Lower the heat and cool the pan a little. Put in the onion and garlic and cook them until the onion is soft. Stir in the apples, cabbage, anchovies and prunes. Pour in the wine and bring it to the boil. Replace the pork and surround it with the cabbage. Cover the casserole and put it in the centre of the oven for 1½ hours. Remove the pork, carve it and arrange it down the centre of a warm serving dish. Put the cabbage mixture on either side and spoon any juices left in the casserole over the pork.

The herrings in this recipe are pickled first to add just a slight touch of sharpness. As they cook they become really meaty and the cabbage maintains a slight crispness.

Pickled Herrings and Red Cabbage

4 large herrings
150ml (¼ pt) red wine vinegar
5ml (1 teaspoon) black
  peppercorns
1 bayleaf
5ml (1 teaspoon) mustard seed

1 small onion, thinly sliced
1 small red cabbage
1 large onion, thinly sliced
1 large cooking apple (or 2 small
  ones)
25g (1 oz) butter

Fillet the herrings and lay the fillets in a flat dish overlapping as little as possible. Put the vinegar, peppercorns, bayleaf, mustard seed and small onion into a saucepan. Bring them gently to the boil and simmer for five minutes. Let them get quite cold and strain the vinegar over the herrings. Leave them for four hours at room temperature, cut-side down. Preheat the oven to 180°C (350°F)/Gas 4. Shred the cabbage. Peel, quarter, core and slice the apples. Lift the herrings from the vinegar and reserve both. Melt the butter in a large wide-based casserole on a low heat. Stir in the large onion and the apple and cook them until the onion is soft. Stir in the cabbage and pour in the reserved vinegar. Bring it to the boil and bury the herrings in the cabbage. Cover the casserole and put it into the oven for 45 minutes. Serve the cabbage with the herrings on top.

And now for a real luxury meal for a special dinner party. You could even serve it for Christmas dinner if you were only entertaining a few people and wanted a change. It is also ideal for New Year or Twelfth Night. These amounts will serve six people.

Braised Duck with Red Cabbage and Apples

one 2kg (4½ lb) duck, (a fresh
  one if possible)
12 black peppercorns
12 juniper berries
1 medium sized red cabbage
1 large onion, thinly sliced
1 large or 2 medium sized
  cooking apples

5ml (1 teaspoon) carraway seeds
150ml (¼ pt) dry red wine
30ml (2 tablespoons) red wine
  vinegar
10ml (2 teaspoons) clear honey
15ml (1 tablespoon) flour

Preheat the oven to 180°C (350°F)/Gas 4.

Joint the duck and remove as much of the excess fat as you can. Put this fat in a large casserole and set it on a low heat to render down for cooking. You will probably get enormous amounts but will only need 15ml (1 tablespoon) for the actual recipe. Crush the peppercorns and juniper berries together and rub them into the cut surface and skin of the duck pieces. Pour off any excess fat from the casserole and set your 15ml (1 tablespoon) on a moderate heat. Put in the duck, skin-side down first, and brown it, turning once. Remove it and then set it aside. By this time more fat will have collected so again pour off all but 15ml (1 tablespoon). Lower the heat, stir in the onion, apple and carraway seeds and cook them until the onion is soft. Stir in the cabbage, pour in the wine and vinegar and mix in the honey. Bring them to the boil and bury the pieces of duck in the cabbage. Cover the casserole and put it into the oven for one hour. Lift out the pieces of duck and keep them warm. Take out the cabbage with a perforated spoon and put it in a flat serving dish. Keep it warm. Skim all the fat from the juices in the casserole and blend 15ml (1 tablespoon) of this fat with 15ml (1 tablespoon) flour. Whisk this into the casserole and let the resulting sauce simmer for one minute. Mix all but 60ml (4 tablespoons) of the sauce into the cabbage. Set the duck on top and spoon over the rest of the sauce.

Savoy Cabbages

Savoys are the most attractive cabbages of all with their masses of velvety textured, crinkly, dark green outer leaves. They, too are a winter vegetable and you can usually buy them from November to March. A native of Italy, they were taken first to France in 1533 by Catherine de Medici when she married Henry IV and arrived in Britain shortly after.

Their texture is not really suited to salads and like other green vegetables they have been mostly boiled and served with butter. Few recipes actually specify Savoy cabbage over any other type.

The outer protecting leaves are very tough and so are fit only for the stock-pot, but those just inside are perfect for stuffing as they become tender during cooking but just stay firm enough to hold their shape. Shredded and simmered or braised Savoys are really succulent and can be a vegetable dish alone or can incorporate meat to make a complete meal.

This first recipe is plain, simple and refreshing and can be served with any meat, fish or egg dish.

Savoy with Tomatoes

*1 medium sized Savoy cabbage,
    outer leaves removed
1 medium onion, thinly sliced
1 clove garlic, finely chopped*

*30ml (2 tablespoons) olive oil
150ml (¼ pt) water
8 firm tomatoes*

91

Shred the cabbage. Put it with the onion, garlic, oil and water in a saucepan. Cover, and set them on a moderate heat for 20 minutes, stirring occasionally. Scald and skin the tomatoes and slice them into rounds. Mix them into the cabbage at the last minute and let them just heat through.

Usually, Savoy leaves are stuffed with a meat or meat and rice mixture. Stuff them instead with the rest of the cabbage and serve them as an unusual accompanying vegetable.

Packets of Savoy

1 medium to large Savoy   *2.5ml (¼ teaspoon) ground*
  cabbage   *allspice*
25g (1 oz) butter   *30ml (2 tablespoons) sour cream*
1 medium onion, finely chopped   *150ml (¼ pt) stock*

Preheat the oven to 200°C (400°F)/Gas 6.

Remove and discard all the really tough outer leaves of the Savoy. Take off and wash the next 12. Blanch them by putting them into lightly salted simmering water for two minutes and drain them well. Finely chop the rest of the cabbage. Melt the butter in a large frying pan on a low heat. Put in the onion and cook it until it is soft. Put in the cabbage and stir it around on the heat for one minute. Add the allspice and sour cream. Divide this mixture between the 12 blanched leaves. Roll them up, stem end first, then the sides and then the top. Lay the packets in a flat oven-proof dish, not overlapping if possible. Pour in the stock and put uncovered into the oven for 40 minutes.

For this recipe, pack the Savoys tightly in the casserole so they will hold their shape.

Serve either as a first course or as an accompanying vegetable.

Savoy Stuffed with Stilton

1 medium sized Savoy   *100g (4 oz) Stilton cheese*
25g (1 oz) butter   *30ml (2 tablespoons) chopped*
1 medium onion, thinly sliced   *parsley*

Preheat the oven to 180°C (350°F)/Gas 4. Cut the Savoy in half and wash it well. Hollow out the centre of each half leaving an outer shell of about 3cm (1 in) thick. Blanch each shell in lightly salted simmering water for two minutes. Drain them well. Chop the middles. Melt the butter in a casserole large enough to take the two halves packed together. Put in the onion and let it soften. Take the casserole from the heat and stir in the chopped cabbage, Stilton and parsley. Fill the two halves with this mixture and put them into the casserole. Cover and put it into the centre of the oven for 45 minutes.

Casseroles of pork and cabbage are usually fairly heavy, but this one is light in both texture and flavour. Serve it with a vegetable that contrasts well in substance and colour. Carrots are perfect.

Pork with Savoy and Celery

900g (2 lb) lean end of belly of
  pork
1 small Savoy cabbage
6 sticks celery
1 large onion

1 clove garlic, finely chopped
2.5ml (½ teaspoon) ground mace
150ml (¼ pt) dry white wine
150ml (¼ pt) stock

Preheat the oven to 200°C (400°F)/Gas 6.
  Dice the pork. Shred the cabbage and thinly slice the celery and onion. Heat a flameproof casserole on a high heat with no fat. Put in the cubes of pork and move them around on the heat until they are brown and any excess moisture that collects in the pan is driven away. Remove the pork and set it aside. Lower the heat and cool the pan a little. Put in the onion and cook it until it is soft. Stir in the cabbage, celery, garlic and mace. Pour in the wine and stock and bring them to the boil. Replace the pork. Cover and put into the oven for one hour.

Pigeons make a fairly cheap meal but can be made to look and taste really expensive. The final appearance of this dish is absolutely beautiful. You have the bright orange carrots and bright green Savoy, just slightly glazed by the sauce.

Pigeons with Bacon and Savoy

4 pigeons
3 collar rashers bacon
15g (½ oz) fat or pork dripping
1 large onion, thinly sliced
225g (8 oz) carrots cut in
  julienne sticks

30ml (2 tablespoons) stock
1 medium sized Savoy cabbage,
  shredded

For the sauce:
2 collar rashers bacon
15g (½ oz) bacon fat or dripping
1 small onion, finely chopped
1 small carrot, finely chopped
1 small stick celery, finely
  chopped
15ml (1 tablespoon) wholemeal
  flour

15ml (1 tablespoon) tomato
  purée
425ml (¾ pt) stock
1 chopped mushroom
bouquet of sage
30ml (2 tablespoons) dry white
  wine

First, make the sauce. Dice the bacon, rinds as well. Heat the dripping in a small heavy saucepan on a low heat. Put in the bacon, onion, carrot and celery and let them brown. Stir in the flour and brown it. Stir in the tomato purée. Take the pan from the heat and stir in the stock. Set it back on the heat and bring the stock to the boil. Skim, add the mushroom and sage, cover and set on the lowest heat possible for ¾ hour. Strain through a conical strainer or a sieve pressing down hard. Mix in the wine. Preheat the oven to 180°C (350°F)/Gas 4. Put two sage leaves inside each pigeon and tie the legs of each one together. Dice the bacon and put it into a large flameproof casserole with the fat. Set it on a low heat and brown it. Take it out and reserve it. Raise the heat to high, put in the pigeons and brown them all over. Remove them and lower the heat. Stir in the onion and carrots, cover them with a butter paper and a lid and let them sweat for five minutes. Set the pigeons on top and spoon in the stock. Cover with the paper and lid again and put them into the oven for one hour. Lift out the pigeons and vegetables and stir any juices that are in the pan into the sauce. Replace the vegetables and mix in the Savoy and the reserved bacon pieces. Mix in all but 60ml (4 tablespoons) of the sauce. Put the pigeons on top and spoon the remaining sauce over each one. Cover with the lid only this time and put back into the oven for 45 minutes. Serve the pigeons on the bed of cabbage.

Spring Cabbages

Spring cabbages are the pale, conical types that are usually only in the shops during late April and all through May. Occasionally they last into the beginning of June. Spring cabbages vary in appearance.

Sometimes their pointed hearts are hard and solid and sometimes they are darker in colour with many more outer leaves. This is because they are actually spring greens that have either been allowed to heart or that have been grown in a specific way to enable them to do so. When they are grown specially, they are raised first in a seed bed and are then all planted at the same time so that they will all heart together. All drilled spring greens will eventually do this but not together and this makes picking fairly difficult and lengthy. The field will have to be gone over several times and the cutters must inspect every cabbage and decide whether it is ready or not.

Spring cabbages have a light, refreshing texture and flavour, quite unlike that of spring greens. You can cook them or shred them up into salads, so they are ideal to bridge the gap between the winter cabbages and the summer Primos and salad vegetables.

One of their most distinctive features is their shape, so make the most of it by cooking them whole.

Whole Spring Cabbage in Stock

1 medium sized spring cabbage   150ml (¼ pt) stock

Break the outer leaves from the cabbage and save them to cook separately or with spring greens. Trim the stalk at the base, leaving a flat surface. Put the stock into a saucepan large enough to hold the cabbage lying on its side and bring it to the boil. Put in the whole cabbage. Lower the heat, cover, and simmer for 25 minutes, turning the cabbage about three times so it cooks evenly. By the end of cooking time most of the stock will have evaporated. Serve the cabbage standing on its flat base.

To make whole spring cabbage just that bit tastier, make a deep cross cut in the top and pour in some melted butter and scatter over some chopped herbs or grated Parmesan cheese. You could also fill the cut with grated Farmhouse Cheddar or Sage Derby cheese.

Here is another way of serving spring cabbage whole.

Whole Spring Cabbage with Mushrooms and Lemon

1 medium sized spring cabbage   juice 1 lemon
150ml (¼ pt) stock   30ml (2 tablespoons) chopped
25g (1 oz) butter   parsley
100g (4 oz) flat mushrooms,
  finely chopped

Cook the whole cabbage according to the method above and while it is cooking prepare the following filling.

Melt the butter in a frying pan on a moderate heat. Put in the mushrooms and cook them for two minutes, stirring once or twice. Pour in the lemon juice and add the parsley. Lower the heat, cover and simmer for two minutes.

Set the cooked cabbage upright in a serving dish and make a deep cross-cut in the top. Spoon in all the mushroom sauce so it fills the gap and falls over the edges.

Another way of making use of the shape of spring cabbage is to stuff the bottom halves. They stay a light fresh green colour and look as attractive as stuffed globe artichokes. In a way they are better as they are far easier to eat, more substantial and cheaper.

Stuffed Spring Cabbage

2 medium sized spring cabbages
175g (6 oz) collar rashers of
    bacon
675g (1½ lb) best quality minced
    beef
1 clove garlic, finely chopped

12 large salad onions, finely
    chopped
15ml (1 tablespoon) tomato
    purée
10 chopped sage leaves
150ml (¼ pt) dry white wine

Remove the outer leaves from the cabbages and trim the bases so they stand upright. Cut off the tops, leaving a base about 12cm (4 in) high. Chop and reserve the tops. Hollow out the bottom parts with a sharp knife leaving a shell about 2cm (¾ in) thick. Chop the hollowed out pieces and put them with the tops. Chop the bacon and put it in a large heavy saucepan or flameproof casserole and set it on a low heat. When the fat begins to run, raise the heat, add the beef and garlic and stir everything around until the beef is broken up and browned. Mix in the onions, tomato purée and sage and pour in the stock. Bring everything to the boil and lower the heat. Put the cabbage shells on a dish (this will catch any drips) and quickly stuff as much as possible of the meat mixture into them. Mix the chopped cabbage into the casserole. Set the stuffed cabbages in the mixture and pour in any juices that have collected in the dish. Bring everything to the boil again, cover and simmer gently for 40 minutes.

Serve with the stuffed bases sitting on top of the beef and cabbage mixture. You will need no other vegetable, and instead of potatoes have wholemeal spaghetti.

You can shred spring cabbages and use them like any of the winter types. It is a matter of choice whether you cook the outer leaves. They cook down as well as the lighter parts and you will have a dish of light and dark green.

Both these following recipes have light, spring-like flavours.

Spring Cabbage with White Wine and Dill

*1 spring cabbage, both inner
  heart and outer leaves
25g (1 oz) butter*

*1 large onion, thinly sliced
10ml (2 teaspoons) dill seeds
150ml (¼ pt) white wine*

Shred the cabbage. Melt the butter in a saucepan on a low heat. Stir in
the onion and dill and cook them until the onion is soft. Mix in the
cabbage and pour in the wine. Cover, and keep on the low heat for 20
minutes.

Spring Cabbage with Fennel and Salad Onions

*1 spring cabbage, both inner
  heart and outer leaves
25g (1 oz) butter
150ml (¼ pt) stock*

*8 salad onions, chopped
30ml (2 tablespoons) chopped
  fennel*

Shred the cabbage. Put the butter and stock in a saucepan and set
them on a low heat until the butter has melted. Stir in the cabbage,
onions and fennel. Cover, and set on a moderate heat for 20 minutes,
stirring occasionally.

English cucumbers start to get much cheaper in May, so put them with
spring cabbage to make a hot salad.

Hot Spring Cabbage and Cucumber Salad

*inner heart of 1 small spring
  cabbage
1 medium sized cucumber
60ml (4 tablespoons) olive oil
10ml (2 teaspoons) soft brown
  sugar*

*30ml (2 tablespoons) white wine
  vinegar
5ml (1 teaspoon) mustard
  powder
30ml (2 tablespoons) chopped
  chives*

Shred the cabbage. Wipe and slice the cucumber. Heat the oil in a
large frying pan on a moderate heat. Put in the cabbage and cucumber
and cook them until the cabbage is just beginning to wilt. Blend the
wine, vinegar, sugar and mustard together. Raise the heat under the
pan and stir in the chives and the vinegar mixture. Let the dressing
bubble and serve the salad immediately.

Use the first of the season's radishes with spring cabbage to make a raw
salad. Serve it with cold meats, grills and sausages, patés, terrines or
quiches.

Spring Cabbage, Radish and Cheese Salad

inner heart of 1 small spring
  cabbage
1 bunch radishes
100g (4 oz) grated Farmhouse
  Cheddar cheese

150ml (¼ pt) freshly made
  mayonnaise

Shred the cabbage and slice the radishes. Mix the cheese and mayonnaise together in a salad bowl. Thoroughly mix in the cabbage and radishes and let the salad stand for half an hour before serving so all the flavours can blend.

In this recipe with pork, it seems when you first put the cabbage in the pot that you are going to have enormous amounts, but it cooks down considerably when you braise it. The brighter green outer leaves make the final dish really attractive.

Sweet and Sour Pork with Spring Cabbage

1 joint lean end of the belly of
  pork weighing about 1.125kg
  (2½ lb)
6 large salad onions
10ml (2 teaspoons) chopped
  rosemary
150ml (¼ pt) stock
15ml (1 tablespoon) tomato
  purée

15ml (1 tablespoon) soy sauce
1 medium sized spring cabbage,
  both inner heart and outer
  leaves
30ml (2 tablespoons) pork fat or
  olive oil
1 clove garlic, crushed with a
  pinch of fine sea salt
15ml (1 tablespoon) clear honey

Preheat the oven to 180°C (350°F)/Gas 4.

Remove the bones, rind, and any excess fat from the pork. Finely chop two of the onions and scatter these and 5ml (1 teaspoon) of the rosemary over the cut surface. Roll the joint (or simply fold it in half if it is easier) and tie it with strong thread or fine cotton string. Blend the stock, purée and soy sauce together. Shred the cabbage and chop the remaining four onions. Heat the oil or fat in a large flameproof casserole on a moderate heat. Put in the pork and brown it all over. Remove it and set it aside. Lower the heat and pour off all but a thin film of fat from the pan. Keep the pan off the heat and pour in the stock mixture and stir in the honey and garlic. The pan should still be sufficiently warm to allow the honey to dissolve easily. Set the pan back on the heat, bring the liquid just to simmering point and replace the pork. Baste it. Put the cabbage, onions and remaining rosemary all round the pork. Cover the casserole and put it in the oven for 1¼ hours.

Serve the carved pork on a bed of cabbage.

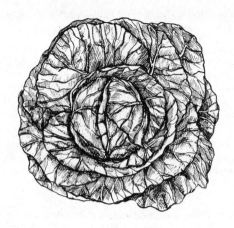

Summer Cabbages

The most universally grown variety of summer cabbage that we have is the Primo. The early ones can be raised under glass and planted at the beginning of March and the ones for cutting later in the summer are usually drilled. During the first few months of growing the deep green leaves become large and fairly spread out, and when the weather begins to get warm at the end of May the inner ones start to turn in and form the solid round heart that is more densely packed than those of winter cabbages but not as firm as the hard Dutch kinds. The heart finally ends up a bright shiny green and is surrounded by velvety outer leaves.

Primos can be cut like red and white cabbages, taking only the heart and leaving the outer leaves, or they can be cut at the base. If this is the case, the leaves serve as a protection during travelling and they can also be chopped up with the cabbage and put into the pot, or cooked separately like spring greens. Apart from trimming and shredding, Primos need little preparation. The stalk is fairly tender and cooks down, so you need only trim away the very end.

Like winter cabbages, they are best cooked. You can simmer them and braise them or par-boil them and make them into cooked salads. You can cook them with meat or poultry or serve them with fish. Whatever your cooking method, the leaves maintain a slight, crisp freshness and are an attractive, almost translucent green — just right for all kinds of summer meals.

On hot summer days, if you are not serving a salad with the meal, vegetables are often better for being simply cooked. Simmering cabbage in just a little water keeps it as light as possible. Add a little garlic and black pepper for additional flavour.

Simple Cabbage and Garlic

firm heart of 1 Primo cabbage
1 large or 2 small cloves garlic
liberal amount of freshly ground
  black pepper

small pinch fine sea salt
3cm (1 in) water in the bottom
  of a saucepan

Shred the cabbage and finely chop the garlic. Put them into the saucepan with the pepper, salt and water. Cover, and set on a moderate heat for 15 minutes. All the water steams away and the cabbage stays just slightly crisp.

Although Primo cabbage can be cooked in many of the same ways as winter ones, it is always good to vary your methods with the seasons. These following dishes cooked with oil and vinegar are rather like cooked salads in which the crisp texture of the cabbage is maintained and in appearance it is bright green and slightly glazed. The vinegar just gives flavour but no striking sharpness. The salads are superb hot, but not suitable for serving cold as the flavour becomes too cabbagey when they cool. Always take advantage of the herbs and fruits of summer when you are cooking Primos and then you will be certain that cabbage can be a different and interesting vegetable the whole year round.

This first salad goes well with chicken or pork.

Primo Cabbage and Peaches

inner heart of 1 medium sized
  Primo cabbage
1 small onion, thinly sliced
45ml (3 tablespoons) olive oil
30ml (2 tablespoons) tarragon
  vinegar

1 large peach (or 2 small ones)
10ml (2 teaspoons) chopped
  tarragon

Shred the cabbage and put it into a saucepan with the onion. Put in the oil and tarragon vinegar. Cover the saucepan and set it on a very low heat for 20 minutes, stirring occasionally. Stone and slice the peaches and mix these and the tarragon into the cabbage. Just heat them through and serve the salad as soon as possible so they stay firm.

In this recipe the new carrots add a touch of sweetness and the poppy seeds a slightly nutty flavour.

Cooked Salad of Primo Cabbage and Carrots

inner heart of 1 medium sized
   Primo cabbage
225g (½ lb) new carrots
60ml (4 tablespoons) olive oil

30ml (2 tablespoons) white wine
   vinegar
15ml (1 tablespoon) poppy seeds

Shred the cabbage and cut the carrots into julienne sticks. Put them into a saucepan with the oil, vinegar and poppy seeds. Cover and set on a very low heat for 20 minutes, stirring occasionally.

This recipe takes the basic cooked salad idea a little further and brings in meat as well. It is a good way of cooking beef in the summer as it is far lighter than a stew or a braised dish.

Cooked Salad of Primo Cabbage and Beef

inner heart 1 large Primo
   cabbage
900g (2 lb) lean stewing steak
90ml (6 tablespoons) olive oil
1 clove garlic, finely chopped
6 flat anchovy fillets, finely
   chopped

2.5ml (½ teaspoon) ground mace
45ml (3 tablespoons) white wine
   vinegar
15ml (1 tablespoon) chopped
   thyme

Shred the cabbage. Cut the beef into small, thin slivers. Heat the oil in a large flameproof casserole on a high heat. Put in the beef and cook it until it browns. Move it around all the time and keep the heat high to drive away all the moisture that will collect at first. Keep cooking until the beef is a good brown and the moisture all gone. Turn down the heat and keep moving the beef around until the pan cools a little. Mix in the cabbage, garlic, anchovies, mace, vinegar and thyme. Cover and cook on a very low heat for 30 minutes.

Primo cabbage can also be made into the quickly cooked hot salads in the same way as winter ones. Again, use the summer herbs to make them individual. In the following one, the lamb provides the fat for cooking both the chops and the cabbage which brings the flavours together. It does necessitate, however, that you really do serve it hot.

Hot Primo Cabbage and Lamb Chop Salad

8 small lamb chops
2 cloves garlic
inner heart of 1 medium Primo
   cabbage
60ml (4 tablespoons) lamb fat
   made from the chop trimmings

30ml (2 tablespoons) chopped
   tarragon
60ml (4 tablespoons) tarragon
   vinegar

Trim all the excess fat from the chops and render it down in a large frying pan on a low heat for cooking. Make insertions in the chops with a sharp knife and insert small, thin slivers from one of the cloves of garlic. Shred the cabbage and finely chop the remaining garlic. Heat the fat on a moderate heat, put in the chops and fry them for 15 minutes, turning frequently. Half way through, scatter over half the tarragon. Remove the chops and keep them warm. Put the cabbage and remaining garlic and tarragon into the pan and stir them around for two minutes. Pour in the vinegar, mix it in and let it bubble.

Turn the salad into a warm serving dish and set the chops on top. They will be golden brown against the bright green cabbage.

Primo cabbages usually last right round to August when the first of the season's cooking apples are picked. Put them together for a harvest meal with pigeons. It has a light texture, colour and flavour that is quite different to the pigeons cooked with Savoy cabbage.

Primo Cabbage and Pigeons in White Wine

4 pigeons
25g (1 oz) pork dripping
1 large onion, thinly sliced
inner heart 1 medium sized
   Primo cabbage, shredded

2 new cooking apples, peeled,
   quartered, cored and sliced
200ml (7 fl oz) dry white wine
25g (1 oz) kneaded butter

Preheat the oven to 180°C (350°F)/Gas 4.

Melt the dripping in a large, flameproof casserole on a high heat. Put in the pigeons and brown them all over. Remove them and set them aside. Lower the heat, put in the onions and apples and cook them until the onion is soft. Stir in the cabbage, replace the pigeons, and pour in the wine. Bring it to the boil, cover the casserole and put it into the oven for 1½ hours. Remove the pigeons and keep them warm. Set the casserole on top of the stove on a moderate heat and stir in the kneaded butter. Keep it on the heat for one minute. Put the cabbage into a warmed serving dish and set the pigeons on top.

Spring Greens

Spring greens, or collards, are a particularly British vegetable and they are the nearest we have to the Medieval cole-plant. They were the most popular kind of cabbage until the sixteenth century and they were sown all through the year to provide a good supply. Round cabbages need warm weather during their growing periods to produce the firm heads, but greens can grow in the cold and take a shorter time to mature and so they can easily be drilled in the autumn to be ready for cutting early in the following year. Not long ago, they were only sown once a year to be ready for cutting in April and May, but now they are what is known as an all-year cash crop available from October to May, and on some farms all through the summer as well.

As with all cabbages, they are cut by hand with long, sharp knives. They grow close together and so each cutter has her own green net or wooden box, which as soon as they are full, are lifted onto a trailer. To get the spring greens into their polythene bags the packers sometimes use a large funnel, putting the narrow end into the bag and pushing the greens through. In another method, the bag is put inside out on a circular wire frame, the greens are pushed through the middle, and the bag turns right way out all round them.

At different times of the year, the size and the tenderness of the leaves of greens can vary quite considerably. In the autumn they are fairly soft but small and tightly packed, and in the winter months they are larger but fleshier and the stalks are tough and have to be removed. Both these kinds are good for simmering on top of the stove and for braising in the oven. Use 150ml (¼ pt) of liquid to 450g (1 lb) of greens and flavour them with herbs, spices, sauces and spicy sausages, or mix in some grated Parmesan cheese just before serving.

The cooking liquid can also be changed (use stock, wine or water); and you can add some leeks or sliced onion and in the spring a bunch of chopped salad onions.

Serve this one with pork or lamb.

Spring Greens and Leeks in Red Wine

175g (6 oz) leeks	*15g (½ oz) butter*
225g (8 oz) spring greens	*150ml (¼ pt) dry red wine*

Cut the leeks in half lengthways and slice them thinly. Remove the stems from the greens and chop the leaves. Put the butter into the bottom of a heavy saucepan. Mix the leeks and greens together and put them on top of the butter. Pour in the wine. Cover the pan and set it on a moderate heat for 20 minutes, stirring occasionally.

Braising greens in the oven makes a really succulent dish. Cook them with herbs or wine (or both), or more simply with stock and onions. This one goes with all roast meats, and it can be quite economical too, cooking everything in the oven.

Spring Greens Braised with Onions

225g (½ lb) spring greens	*25g (1 oz) butter*
225g (½ lb) onions	*150ml (¼ pt) stock*

Preheat the oven to 180°C (350°F)/Gas 4.

Remove the stalks from the greens. Wash and chop the leaves. Thinly slice the onions. Melt the butter in a flameproof casserole on a low heat. Put in the onions and cook them until they are soft. Stir in the greens and pour in the stock. Cover and put into the oven for one hour, stirring everything around once about three quarters of the way through.

Here spring greens and lamb make another warming casserole.

Lamb and Spring Green Casserole

675-900g (1½-2 lb) lean boneless lamb cut from the shoulder
60ml (4 tablespoons) lamb fat or olive oil
2 medium onions, thinly sliced
1 large or two small cloves garlic, finely chopped

450g (1 lb) spring greens
350g (12 oz) ripe tomatoes
12 black olives
15ml (1 tablespoon) chopped marjoram
150ml (¼ pt) dry white wine

Cut the lamb into 2cm (¾ in) cubes. Wash and chop the greens. Scald skin and roughly chop the tomatoes. Stone and slice the olives. Preheat the oven to 180°C (350°F)/Gas 4. Heat the fat in a flameproof casserole on a high heat. Put in the lamb and brown it, moving it around to drive away any moisture that collects. Remove it and set it aside. Lower the heat and cool the casserole a little. Put in the onions and garlic and cook them until the onions are soft. Pour in the wine and bring it to the boil. Stir in the greens, tomatoes, olives and marjoram. Bring everything to the boil again and replace the lamb. Cover the casserole and put it into the oven for 1¼ hours.

In March and April the leaves of spring greens get large and soft and the stalks less stringy. Use them like vine leaves and stuff them, or line a loaf tin or pudding basin with them.

This curry-flavoured dish is absolutely delicious. The nuts are juicy and just slightly crunchy and the sultanas make a fruity contrast in flavour. Although the stuffed leaves look light, they are very filling and combine all kinds of goodness together.

Curried Stuffed Greens

675g (1½ lb) large leaved spring greens

For cooking:

25g (1 oz) butter
1 large onion, finely chopped

5ml (1 teaspoon) hot Madras curry powder
150ml (¼ pt) stock

For the filling:

350g (12 oz) raw chicken off the
  bone (use 2 large chicken legs
  or boneless breast)
15g (½ oz) butter
1 small onion, finely chopped

2 hard boiled eggs
75g (3 oz) peanuts
50g (2 oz) sultanas
5ml (1 teaspoon) hot Madras
  curry powder

Preheat the oven to 190°C (375°F)/Gas 5.

Make the filling first. Mince the chicken finely. Melt the butter in a frying pan on a low heat. Put in the onion and cook it until it is soft. Mix the onion and butter into the chicken. Finely chop the eggs and mix these in with the peanuts, sultanas and curry powder. Take 12 of the outer leaves of the greens and cut away the toughest part at the very end of the stalk. Put a portion of stuffing onto each of the leaves and roll them up, stem first, then the sides and lastly folding over the top. Finely chop the remaining leaves. Melt the butter in a flameproof casserole on a low heat. Stir in the onion and curry powder and cook them until the onion is soft. Stir in the chopped greens and put the stuffed leaves on top. Pour in the stock. Cover the casserole and put it into the centre of the oven for 45 minutes.

Serve on a warm dish with the stuffed leaves on top of the braised greens.

A traditional Buckinghamshire dish called Bucks Badger consists of equal parts of chopped bacon and onion with sage and sometimes a little potato all steamed together in a suet pudding. You could call this next recipe a Slimming Badger for it uses greens instead of suet! It is light so serve it for lunch or supper.

Green Bacon Pudding

450g (1 lb) large leaved spring
  greens
175g (6 oz) streaky bacon
6 large or 8 small salad onions
10ml (2 teaspoons) chopped
  rosemary

little pork dripping or bacon fat
for greasing a large pudding
  basin

For finishing:

6 eggs
either 100g (4 oz) grated
  Farmhouse Cheddar cheese

or 275ml (½ pt) thick cheese
sauce

Wash the greens and set aside enough of the largest leaves to line the pudding basin, and to cover the top. Finely chop the rest. Dice the bacon, chop the onions and mix with the chopped greens and rosemary for the filling. Line the greased pudding basin with leaves, put in the filling, and cover the top with leaves. Cover the pudding with lightly greased greaseproof paper and foil. Bring some water to boil in a large saucepan. Put in the pudding and steam it for 1½ hours. Towards the end of cooking time, hard boil the eggs so they will be ready at the same time as the pudding. Make the sauce if you are using it. Turn the pudding out onto a plate. Cut the eggs in half lengthways and arrange them round it. Either, scatter over the grated cheese or pour the cheese sauce over the pudding and the eggs.

Here's a green loaf which is best served hot. Be careful turning it out as it is very juicy.

Green Loaf

40g (1½ oz) butter
350g (¾ lb) spring greens
1 large onion, finely chopped
675g (1½ lb) best quality minced beef
6 flat anchovy fillets, finely chopped
15ml (1 tablespoon) mixed chopped thyme and savory

30ml (2 tablespoons) chopped parsley
little freshly grated nutmeg
freshly ground black pepper
45ml (3 tablespoons) dry white wine

Preheat the oven to 180°C (350°F)/Gas 4.
Use a little of the butter to grease a 900g (2 lb) loaf tin. Remove any tough parts of stem from the greens. Line the tin with some of the larger leaves and finely chop the rest. Melt the remaining butter in a frying pan on a low heat. Put in the onion and cook it until it is soft. Stir in the chopped greens and keep moving them around on the heat for two minutes. Put the onions, greens and meat in a large mixing bowl. Beat in the anchovies, herbs, nutmeg, pepper and wine. Pile the mixture into the lined tin. Cover it tightly with foil. Bake au bain marie for 1½ hours. Turn it out and serve it hot.

Use eggs and spring greens instead of batter for a light toad-in-the-hole. Use good, herby butcher's sausages — not the pink bready mass-produced ones.

Green Toad-in-the-Hole

225g (½ lb) spring greens

15g (½ oz) butter

*10ml (2 teaspoons) chopped
  rosemary
8 sausages (about 450g (1 lb))
4 eggs, separated
15ml (1 tablespoon) Parmesan
  cheese
30ml (2 tablespoons) chopped
  parsley*

*1 medium onion, thinly sliced
4 small, firm tomatoes, cut in
  half
little butter for greasing 25cm
  (9 in) diameter pie plate or
  flat oven proof dish*

Wash and chop the greens. Put them into a saucepan with the rosemary and 3cm (1 in) water. Cover and cook them on a moderate heat for 20 minutes, stirring occasionally. Preheat the grill to high and half-cook the sausages evenly all round. Beat the egg yolks with the Parmesan cheese and parsley. Melt the butter on a low heat, put in the onion and cook it until it is golden. Mix it into the egg yolks and then mix in the cooked greens. Stiffly beat the whites and fold them into the mixture with a metal spoon. Pile everything into the greased pie plate and arrange the tomato halves and sausages on top in a pattern. Bake in the centre of the oven for half an hour, or until the egg mixture rises golden brown round the sausages.

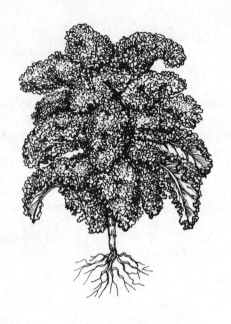

Curly Kale

Curly Kale is one of the hardiest vegetables there is — it absolutely
thrives in the cold. Because of this it, or one of its varieties, was the
most popular vegetable in Scotland from Medieval times until the
eighteenth century, and one of their words for a cottage garden was
'kailyard'. It was cooked in broths sometimes with barley and
sometimes in an oatmeal pottage called 'brochan'. 'Muslin Kale' was a
lowland dish, which was a pottage thickened with oats and barley and
containing kale and onions.

Kale hasn't been grown so much in England, but it has been known
here since Anglo-Saxon times, called 'winter greens' and sometimes
'borecole' from the Dutch 'boerenkool' or 'peasant's cabbage'. Just
lately there seems to have been an increasing demand for kale. Try it
during its short season in January and February.

Once in the kitchen, kale needs to be washed well as dirt gets inside the crinkles of the leaves and if you leave it you will have Crunchy Kale Special! Break off all the stalk below the leaf and if it is very thick tear it out of the leaf completely. For most dishes the leaves are best torn into pieces about 3cm (1 in) square as it is one of the few vegetables that does not diminish in the pot too much.

In Medieval and Tudor times, when kale was in season the only meat around was bacon or salt pork. The flavours still go well together and here they make an accompanying vegetable dish.

Kale and Bacon

450g (1 lb) kale
125g (4 oz) lean bacon
25g (1 oz) butter

1 large onion, thinly sliced
1.5cm (½ in) water in the bottom
of a saucepan

Wash the kale and tear it into small pieces. Dice the bacon. Melt the butter in a saucepan on a low heat. Put in the onion and bacon and cook them until the onion is soft. Stir in the kale and add the water. Cover, and cook on a moderate heat for 15 minutes, stirring occasionally and checking that the pan doesn't become dry.

Make a savoury dish with another traditional flavouring — mustard — and serve it with chicken or beef.

Kale and Mustard

450g (1 lb) kale
25g (1 oz) butter
1 large onion, thinly sliced

10ml (2 teaspoons) made English
mustard
300ml (½ pt) stock

Wash the kale and tear it into small pieces. Melt the butter in a heavy saucepan on a low heat. Stir in the onion and cook it gently for one minute. Mix in the kale. Mix the mustard and stock together and add them to the pan. Cover, and keep on the low heat for 20 minutes, stirring occasionally.

One of the best ways with Kale is to stir-braise it. Use as large a pan as possible as there is quite an amount to fit in.

This makes an extremely tasty dish for serving with pork, chicken or egg dishes.

Stir-Braised Kale with Chorizo Sausage

450g (1 lb) curly kale
75g (3 oz) Chorizo sausage

1 small onion, thinly sliced
150ml (¼ pt) stock

Wash the kale and tear it into small pieces. Cut the Chorizo in half lengthways and slice it thinly. Put the pieces into a large frying pan. Set

109

it on a low heat and when the red fat begins to run, put in the onion. Cook it until it is soft. Raise the heat to moderate and put in the kale. Stir it around for one minute and pour in the stock. Bring it to the boil, cover and lower the heat again. Cook gently for seven minutes.

For a complete change, use anchovies and mace to give a very eighteenth century flavour.

Stir-Braised Kale with Anchovies

450g (1 lb) curly kale   25g (1 oz) butter
4 flat anchovy fillets   pinch ground mace
150ml (¼ pt) stock

Wash the kale and tear it into small pieces. Pound the anchovy fillets to a paste and mix them with the stock. Melt the butter in a large frying pan on a high heat. Put in the kale and stir it around for one minute. Pour in the stock and anchovy mixture and bring it to the boil. Sprinkle in the mace. Cover and set on a very low heat for seven minutes.

Put kale into an egg custard for a lunch or supper dish for four or a main meal for two people.

Savoury Kale Custard

225g (½ lb) kale   100g (4 oz) grated Farmhouse
25g (1 oz) butter   Cheddar Cheese
1 large onion, thinly sliced   butter for greasing 25cm (8 in)
150ml (¼ pt) milk   diameter pie plate or
4 eggs   ovenproof dish
10ml (2 teaspoons) made English
    mustard

Preheat the oven to 200°C (400°F)/Gas 6.
    Wash the kale and tear it into small pieces. Melt the butter in a saucepan on a low heat. Put in the onion and cook it until it is soft. Mix in the kale and pour in the milk. Cover and keep on a low heat for 20 minutes. Take the pan from the heat and let the kale cool slightly. Beat the eggs with the mustard and stir these and the cheese into the kale. Put the resulting mixture into the buttered pie plate. Bake it in the centre of the oven for 30 minutes when it should be golden brown and slightly risen.

Cook salt pork with kale in true peasant fashion for a winter meal.

Salt Pork, Kale and Potatoes

piece salt belly of pork weighing
around 1.125kg (2½ lb)

For boiling:

1 small carrot
1 small onion, cut in half
1 stick celery, broken into 3
* pieces*
6 black peppercorns
bouquet garni

1 large onion, thinly sliced
450g (1 lb) curly kale
4 medium sized potatoes
275ml (½ pt) milk
10ml (2 teaspoons) made English
* mustard*

For finishing:

10ml (2 teaspoons) mustard
* powder*
15ml (1 tablespoon) dry cider

or
10ml (2 teaspoons) made English
* mustard*

Put the pork and boiling ingredients into a saucepan and cover them with water. Bring them gently to the boil, skim, and simmer for one hour. Cut the rind and any thick fat from the pork while it is still warm and pull out the bones. Reserve the rind and fat. Preheat the oven to 190°C (375°F)/Gas 5. Cut the pork into 1cm (¼-½ in) slices. Peel and dice the potatoes. Wash the kale and tear it into small pieces. Mix the milk and mustard together. Chop the reserved fat and put it into a large flameproof casserole. Set it on a low heat until you have about 15ml (1 tablespoon) of fat in which to cook the onion. Remove the pieces of fat. Put in the onion and soften it. Stir in the kale and potatoes and pour in the milk and mustard. Put the pork slices on top. Put the casserole into the oven for 45 minutes. Lift out the pork slices and set them aside. Mash the kale and potatoes together, with a potato masher if you have one to get the mixture smooth. If there is too much liquid in the pan, set it on a low heat as you mash and it will soon dry sufficiently. Put the kale and potato mixture into a heatproof serving dish and set the pork on top. Make a thin mustard with the mustard powder and cider and spread it over the pork. (Or use the extra made mustard.) Put the dish under a hot grill for the pork to brown.

Brussels Sprouts

The Romans grew several types of cabbage for the tiny sprouts which hid under the leaves, but these weren't crops that they left behind in Britain.

Sprouts as we know them today were first grown around the city of Brussels in the thirteenth century but cultivation here only began in the late seventeenth century. They came too late for pottages and no-one seemed to think of putting them into salads and so mostly they have been boiled, usually for a short time to keep them just firm. After boiling they have been tossed with butter or mixed with gravy or lemon juice.

Brussels sprouts are best when they are small and nutty, when they have been firmed by the first frosts but are not overblown. They are a real winter crop and this, combined with their size makes them one of the most fiddly and unpleasant of vegetables to pick, the worst hazard being cold fingers. Several days before picking all the leaves are stripped from the stalks, which makes the small stems die and the sprouts easier to break off. A Brussels sprout field is usually picked twice. The bottom half of the stems are picked first and the top sprouts carry on growing and filling out ready for the second time around. Sometimes, in the weeks just after Christmas, when other vegetables may be scarce, you can buy Brussel tops, which are like slightly Brussels sprout flavoured spring greens suitable for cooking in many of the same ways. They are not as common as I would like them to be, however, as if the tops are picked no more sprouts will grow, the field can only be covered once and the yield per acre will be cut. The ideal way really of buying sprouts and tops would be to have a whole stem and use it as you please, but no-one at the moment that I know of is marketing them in this way.

Sprouts are usually past their best in early spring and out in the country in March you can often come across sprout fields full of munching sheep, finishing off the last of the leaves and stubble.

The taste and texture of Brussels sprouts can vary considerably according to how they are cooked.

This is a simple recipe. The butter just glazes the sprouts slightly but they remain light in flavour and are still only just tender.

Buttered Sprouts

450g (1 lb) Brussels sprouts *30ml (2 tablespoons) chopped*
pinch sea salt   *parsley*
25g (1 oz) butter

Trim the sprouts and leave them whole. Put barely enough water in a saucepan to cover them, add the salt and bring it to the boil. Put in the sprouts and butter and cook on a moderate heat, covered, for ten minutes. Mix in the parsley just before serving.

Steamed sprouts maintain all their freshness and goodness. Nutmeg is the best flavourer you can use for them.

Steamed Sprouts and Nutmeg

450g (1 lb) Brussels sprouts   *25g (1 oz) butter*
freshly grated nutmeg to taste

Slice the sprouts crossways and put them into a double boiler or into a pudding basin with the nutmeg. Put the butter on top. If you are using a basin put it on a stand in a saucepan of boiling water. Cover the sprouts and steam them for 45 minutes, stirring them around occasionally so they cook evenly.

Use nutmeg again for a completely different way of cooking sprouts to make them rich and creamy-textured. Serve them with lamb, beef and poultry.

Braised Brussels Sprouts with Onions, Nutmeg and Mace

450g (1 lb) Brussels sprouts   *pinch ground mace*
25g (1 oz) butter   *little grated nutmeg*
1 large onion, thinly sliced   *150ml (¼ pt) stock*

Preheat the oven to 190°C (375°F)/Gas 5.
    Trim the sprouts and leave them whole. Melt the butter in a flameproof casserole on a low heat. Put in the onion and cook it until it is soft. Stir in the sprouts, mace and nutmeg and pour in the stock. Bring it to the boil. Cover the casserole and put it into the oven for 45 minutes.

This is the thickest and richest way of cooking Brussels sprouts that I know. Serve them for supper or for lunch on a cold day with crispy grilled bacon.

Brussels Sprouts in Their Own Brown Gravy

450g (1 lb) Brussels sprouts,   *10ml (2 teaspoons) wholemeal*
  trimmed and left whole   *flour*
25g (1 oz) butter   *150ml (¼ pt) stock*
1 small onion, finely chopped

Preheat the oven to 180°C (350°F)/Gas 4.
    Melt the butter in a small flameproof casserole on a high heat. Put in the Brussels sprouts and onion and just let them brown. Dust in the flour and let it cook for one minute. Stir in the stock and bring it to the boil. Cover and put into the oven for 30 minutes.

Raw, Brussels sprouts have a nutty flavour, and by one of those delicious coincidences all kinds of nuts are in the shops when they are at their best.

Try them in a creamy salad with almonds.

Brussels Sprout and Almond Salad

450g (1 lb) Brussels sprouts
100g (4 oz) almonds, shelled
10ml (2 teaspoons) tarragon (or Dijon) mustard

150ml (¼ pt) freshly made mayonnaise

Trim the sprouts and cut them crossways into thin slices. Blanch and shred the almonds. Put them together in a bowl. Mix the mustard into the mayonnaise and stir them into the salad. Let them all stand for at least 15 minutes before serving.

If you only have a little meat left over from the day before which won't make a complete meal, supplement it by making a cream that turns out a beautiful fresh green colour and is full of goodness.

Brussels Sprout Cream

450g (1 lb) Brussels sprouts, trimmed
little butter for greasing
275ml (½ pt) milk
1ml (¼ teaspoon) ground mace
freshly ground black pepper
25g (1 oz) butter
1 large onion, thinly sliced

1 clove garlic, finely chopped
15ml (1 tablespoon) wholemeal flour
2 eggs, beaten
15ml (1 tablespoon) mixed chopped marjoram and parsley
25cm (8 in) diameter ring mould

Lightly grease a saucepan with butter. Put in the milk and bring it to the boil. Add the Brussels sprouts, mace and pepper and simmer for 15 minutes. Drain, reserve the milk and mash the sprouts. Melt the 25g (1 oz) butter in a saucepan on a low heat. Put in the onion and garlic and cook them until the onion is golden. Stir in the flour and the reserved milk. Bring the sauce to the boil and stir until it is thick and bubbly. Stir in the mashed sprouts, the eggs and the chopped marjoram and parsley. Put this into the lightly greased ring mould and cover with foil. Set it over a saucepan of boiling water and steam for 35 minutes. Turn it out and serve it hot.

If you like you can fill the centre with some plainly cooked Brussels sprouts such as the Simple Sprouts and Garlic.

This dish is quick to prepare and very cheap.

114

Minced Beef and Brussels Sprouts

450g (1 lb) Brussels sprouts
900g (2 lb) best quality minced
*   beef*
1 large clove garlic, finely
*   chopped*
45ml (3 tablespoons) chopped
*   parsley*

150ml (¼ pt) dry white wine
150ml (¼ pt) stock
15ml (1 tablespoon) Dijon
*   mustard*
15ml (1 tablespoon) chopped
*   capers*

Trim the sprouts and slice them into 0.5cm (¼ in) rounds. Heat a large sauté pan or frying pan on a high heat with no fat. Put in the minced beef and garlic and cook them, moving them around all the time until the beef is browned. Lower the heat. Mix in the parsley and the sprouts and cook everything for two minutes, stirring occasionally. Pour in the wine and stock and bring them to the boil. Stir in the mustard and capers. Cover the pan and simmer for 20 minutes. Serve it with brown buttered rice.

Brussels sprout soups are usually creamy, blended ones, but here they are chopped finely to make a thick, nutty-flavoured pottage kind of soup with orange.

Brussels Sprout and Orange Soup

225g (½ lb) Brussels sprouts
25g (1 oz) butter
1 large onion, finely chopped
2.5ml (½ teaspoon) ground mace
15ml (1 tablespoon) wholemeal
*   flour*

850ml (1½ pt) stock
grated rind and juice 1 large
*   orange (Spanish are best)*
15ml (1 tablespoon) chopped
*   thyme*
freshly ground black pepper

Finely chop the sprouts. Melt the butter in a saucepan on a low heat. Stir in the onion and cook it until it is soft. Add the mace, and stir in the flour and stock. Bring the stock to the boil, stirring, and add the orange rind, chopped sprouts, thyme and pepper. Simmer for 20 minutes, uncovered. Stir in the orange rind and reheat to serve.

If you ever buy brussel tops, the dark green, leafy crown on the sprout stem, cook them like spring greens. They have a flavour that is a cross between the two vegetables.

Flowers

Cauliflowers and purple sprouting broccoli are both members of the cabbage family that have been grown for their flowers instead of their leaves, and because of this they will have here a section of their own.

They are the cook's flowers of spring that can always be relied on for most of April and the first weeks of May which, according to the eighteenth century farmer Arthur Young are the 'most pinching six weeks in the whole year'. They are both versatile vegetables which is good when others may be short. Both can make meals in themselves, accompanying vegetables, first courses and cooked salads; and cauliflowers can be blended into soups or chopped up raw.

Cauliflower

Cauliflowers arrived in Britain from Cyprus at the very beginning of the seventeenth century and our name for them comes from 'cole-flower' or cabbage-flower.

For a short time they were chopped up, leaves as well, and put into pottage but more often they were boiled alone until they were barely tender and then plainly buttered or used for cooked salads. The dressings for these were made of oil and vinegar or butter and vinegar, and they were flavoured with herbs or with spices and sugar.

In the eighteenth century cauliflowers were boiled and buttered and sometimes simmered in milk or a rich brown gravy. Cheese always seems to have been the favourite flavouring. Cheshire cheese was used first, strewn thickly over the top and browned with a salamander that was put into a really hot fire and then held over the cheese. In the nineteenth century Parmesan cheese and Béchamel sauce became the most popular coverings.

I have found one seventeenth century recipe for a sweet dish in which the cauliflower was simmered in milk and then coated in a rich creamy custard flavoured with nutmeg, sugar, mace, cinnamon, sack (which was like sherry) and orange-flower water. Then it was baked and served with a sweet, rich wine sauce. I haven't actually tried this one and am still wondering how you would mask that definite cabbagey flavour that, however delicate, is always there with cooked cauliflower.

Cauliflowers are usually available now for most of the year, but their best season is from March to June when you get the spring varieties. In the farming world they are actually called 'broccoli'.

At the farm I visited the cauliflowers were cut by hand, the women followed behind the tractor cutting the well-grown cauliflowers, slashing the mass of green leaves across the front or (more technically) the face, and slinging them high into the air into the bodge.

When the bodge was full it was taken off to the end of the field where just one lady was responsible for all the grading and packing. The cauliflowers were left with most of their leaves on to protect them and keep them from rolling around in the wooden crates.

You need not throw away the tougher, outer leaves of cauliflowers. They are extremely useful in the stock-pot, especially when root vegetables begin to disappear. The inner ones can be broken into small pieces and cooked with the cauliflower itself or put into vegetable soups.

When you prepare a cauliflower for cooking, keep the fleurettes whole by breaking them away from the main stem. Use the stalk as well and either cut a section of it with a sharp knife before you pull off the fleurette, or chop it separately.

The best way to cook cauliflower is with as little water as possible — about 150ml (¼ pt) in the bottom of a saucepan for one medium sized head. Put in a bayleaf or a bouquet garni for flavouring or a thinly pared piece of orange or lemon peel. Add a little butter if the cauliflower is to be served plain, but not if you are going to add some kind of sauce later. Cover the saucepan and set it on a moderate heat for 15 minutes, turning the cauliflower once or twice to make sure it cooks evenly. Using this basic method, you can produce a different flavour to accompany any kind of main dish.

This mustardy one is perfect for serving with pork.

Cauliflower and Mustard

1 medium sized cauliflower
10ml (2 teaspoons) English
Vineyard or other English
granular mustard
150ml (¼ pt) stock

Break the cauliflower into small fleurettes and break some of the more tender inner leaves into small pieces. Mix the mustard into the stock, put them into a saucepan, set them on a moderate heat and bring them to the boil. Mix in the cauliflower and cook for 20 minutes. All the stock should be absorbed and the cauliflower covered in tiny granules of mustard.

You can also add a small amount of another vegetable, such as a diced green pepper to the pan, and you can vary the cooking liquid by using white wine instead of stock.

Plainly cooked cauliflower can be made into a cauliflower cheese or into a seventeenth century cooked salad, which is best served with cold meats.

Cauliflower, Anchovy and Lemon Salad

1 medium sized cauliflower
bouquet garni
2 thinly pared strips lemon rind
4 flat anchovy fillets

60ml (4 tablespoons) olive oil
juice 1 lemon
30ml (2 tablespoons) chopped
  parsley

Break the cauliflower into small fleurettes and keep a few of the inner leaves. Put them into a saucepan with the bouquet garni and lemon rind and about 1.5cm (½ in) water. Cover them and set on a low heat for 15 minutes, when the cauliflower should be just tender and all the water steamed away. Let the cauliflower cool completely. Pound the anchovies to a paste and work in the oil and lemon juice. Put the cauliflower into a bowl and mix in the dressing and parsley.

Another very effective way of serving cauliflower is to cook it whole, sprinkle it with grated cheese and brown it under the grill. Put the trimmed cauliflower into a saucepan with about an inch of water to immerse the stalk but not the flower. Simmer it, covered, for 20 minutes. Add flavourings such as bouquet garni, bayleaf or a strip of lemon rind.

In the following recipes, part-cooked cauliflower is incorporated into the main dish for the final stages of cooking. The first is for whiting which is both very cheap and low in calories so as a special treat I've added almonds.

Whiting with Cauliflower and Almonds

4 medium-sized whiting
60ml (4 tablespoons) seasoned
  wholemeal flour
50g (2 oz) shelled almonds
1 medium sized cauliflower
1 bayleaf

75g (3 oz) butter
30ml (2 tablespoons) chopped
  mixed herbs
6 flat anchovy fillets, finely
  chopped
juice 1½ lemons

118

Remove the heads and fins from the whiting and clean them, keeping in the backbone. Coat them in the seasoned flour. Blanch the almonds and split them in two. Divide the cauliflower into fleurettes and put them into a saucepan with the bayleaf and 3cm (1 in) water. Set them on a moderate heat for ten minutes. Drain the cauliflower if necessary and keep it warm. Discard the bayleaf. Melt 15g (¾ oz) of the butter in a large frying pan on a moderate heat. Put in the whiting and fry them until they are golden brown on both sides. (You will probably have to do this in two batches.) Arrange the fish on a warmed serving dish. Add a further 10g (½ oz) butter to the pan and when it has melted put in the cauliflower and brown it fairly quickly. Arrange it round the whiting. Put all the remaining butter into the pan and raise the heat. Put in the almonds and brown them quickly, moving them around constantly. Stir in the herbs and anchovies and pour in the lemon juice. Take the pan from the heat immediately and pour the sauce and almonds over the whiting and cauliflower.

The delicate flavours of calves liver and cauliflower complement each other in this dish which is quick to prepare and easy to serve.

Calves Liver and Cauliflower with Lemon

675g (1½ lb) calves liver
1 large cauliflower
1 bay leaf
1 strip thinly pared lemon rind
150ml (¼ pt) water

25g (1 oz) butter
juice ½ lemon
150ml (¼ pt) dry white wine
30ml (2 tablespoons) chopped parsley

Cut the calves liver into small, thin pieces. Break the cauliflower into small fleurettes and some of the inner leaves into 3cm (1 in) pieces. Put it into a saucepan with the bayleaf, lemon rind and water. Set it on a moderate heat for seven minutes. Drain if necessary, and discard the bay leaf and lemon rind. Heat the butter in a large frying pan or sauté pan on a high heat. Put in the liver and stir it around until it browns (in two batches if necessary). Stir the cauliflower quickly into the pan. Pour in the lemon juice and wine and bring them to the boil. Scatter the parsley over the top. Cover the pan and keep it on a very low heat for five minutes.

The substantial cauliflower makes good vegetarian meals. Here is an egg curry, which fills four people very well. For the sauce, use the brown gravy made from the trimmings of root vegetables (see under parsnips). If you can, use a live yoghurt bought from a whole food shop. One made from goat's milk is perfect but not essential.

119

Curried Eggs and Cauliflower

8 eggs
1 large cauliflower
25g (1 oz) butter
1 large onion, thinly sliced
15ml (1 tablespoon) hot Madras
  curry powder
5ml (1 teaspoon) ground
  turmeric

5ml (1 teaspoon) ground
  coriander
150ml (¼ pt) stock
1 bayleaf
275ml (½ pt) brown sauce
1 carton (5 fl oz) natural yoghurt

Hard boil and peel the eggs. Break the cauliflower into small fleurettes and the inner leaves into small pieces. Heat the butter in a heavy saucepan or large flameproof casserole on a low heat. Stir in the onion, curry powder, turmeric and coriander. Cook them until the onion is soft and mix in the cauliflower. Pour in the stock and tuck in the bayleaf. Cover and set on a low heat for 20 minutes, stirring occasionally. Remove the bayleaf and mix in the brown sauce. Put in the eggs. Cover again and cook for a further ten minutes. Turn off the heat and when the sauce has stopped bubbling, stir in the yoghurt. Cover, and let the flavours blend for two minutes before serving.

Brown rice is the best accompaniment.

Cauliflower isn't often used as a raw ingredient in salads, but I think it makes a very good one. It crumbles under your tongue and is very easy to eat, not at all chewy like some raw vegetables. Mix it with a plain French dressing or with mayonnaise for side salads, or make it into a main-course salad with cheese such as the following. Serve it for lunch with brown bread and butter.

Spicy Cauliflower and Cheese Salad

1 small cauliflower
1 medium sized green pepper
225g (8 oz) strong Farmhouse
  Cheddar cheese
50g (2 oz) Polish Cabanos
  sausage or salami

6 pickled onions
45ml (3 tablespoons) chopped
  chives
60ml (4 tablespoons)
  mayonnaise
5ml (1 teaspoon) Tabasco sauce

Chop the cauliflower into small pieces. Dice the pepper and the cheese. Slice the sausage thinly. If you are using salami, chop it into small dice if it is one piece, or if it is in slices, cut each one into quarters. Chop the pickled onions. Put them all into a bowl with the chives. Mix the mayonnaise and the Tabasco sauce together and stir them into the salad.

Another thing you can do with the versatile cauliflower is make into a soup that is creamy in both texture and colour.

Almonds are used again here as the flavours do go together so well.

Cauliflower and Almond Soup

1 small cauliflower	*850ml (1½ pt) stock*
50g (2 oz) plus 8 shelled almonds	*freshly ground black pepper*
1 medium onion, thinly sliced	*pinch sea salt*
1 bayleaf	*pinch ground mace*

Break the cauliflower into small pieces. Blanch all the almonds. Split the extra eight and break each sliver in half. Set these aside. Put the cauliflower, whole almonds, onion and bayleaf into a saucepan with the stock. Season, bring them to the boil, cover and simmer for 20 minutes. Remove the bayleaf and add the mace. Work everything in a blender until you have a smooth, creamy soup. Return it to the saucepan. For the garnish, toast the split almonds under a high grill until they are brown. Reheat the soup and pour it into four small bowls. Float the toasted almonds on the top.

Purple Sprouting Broccoli

There is purple sprouting broccoli and white sprouting broccoli, but the purple is the type that is the most popular and is the most readily available. It is usually only picked during late March and April and sometimes into early May, but I have known some unusual years when it was in the shops at Christmas.

The name broccoli comes from the Italian 'brocco' meaning a shoot, and it has been a favourite vegetable in that country since Roman times.

Sprouting broccoli was another of the vegetables taken to France by Catherine de Medici, bride of Henry IV, in 1533, but it probably reached Britain a little before this.

Most commonly it was boiled and buttered, and in the seventeenth and eighteenth centuries it was treated in a similar way to asparagus, tied in bundles, boiled, and served on toast with a butter sauce.

Lately, though, it hasn't received as much respect and although it is becoming more popular, it can still cause some confusion when people fail to recognize it. The situation is slowly being remedied. Some supermarkets actually give sample cooking instructions that are tried and tested.

Purple sprouting broccoli grows in fairly bushy clumps, and as the actual flowers hide under the leaves, a field full of it is a deep green. The stalks are usually picked by hand and packed straight into sacks or crates. These are then taken either direct to small shops and markets or, if the sprouting is destined for the supermarket, it is weighed and packed in a similar way to spring greens.

To prepare purple sprouting, break off all the small heads and leaves from the main stem and use only these. The stem itself can be tough and a bit stringy, so it is best put into the stock pot or onto the compost heap. This in fact may have been the culprit in putting people off the vegetable.

Once you have the small, tender parts, wash them in cold water and put them into a saucepan. Add 150ml (¼ pt) of water, stock or even white wine to the pound (450g). Cover them and set them on a moderate heat for 20 minutes, turning them over several times. Add a little butter to the pan as well if you like, and some chopped herbs or a bouquet garni. By the end of cooking time all the liquid should have evaporated and the purple sprouting will be just tender. If you are cooking in this way for the first time, check, when you turn the vegetable, that the liquid is not disappearing too quickly. Lower the heat slightly if it is, and add more water by the tablespoon (15ml).

The market gardener's word for purple sprouting broccoli (which is really rather a mouthful) was 'purples' (far easier), so I have used it most often in the recipes.

Purples and Parmesan Cheese

Parmesan cheese is the perfect flavourer for purples. Strew it thickly over the top just before serving. In this way, especially if you have put butter into the saucepan as well as water, the vegetable could easily make a course in itself, either before the main dish or after as a vegetable and cheese course. Don't be sparing with the cheese. Use about 45ml (3 tablespoons) to 450g (1 lb) of purples.

The anchovies and olives together in this recipe make the purple sprouting rich and succulent without your having to use butter or oil. By the end of cooking time they will have given a subtle flavour to the vegetable and the stock will have evaporated to a slight glaze.

Purples, Anchovies and Olives

450g (1 lb) purple sprouting   4 green olives
4 flat anchovy fillets   150ml (¼ pt) stock

Break the purple sprouting into small heads and leaves. Chop the anchovies and olives and pound them together with a pestle and mortar to a smooth paste. Mix them with the stock. Put the purple sprouting into a saucepan with the stock mixture. Cover, and set on a moderate heat for 20 minutes, stirring around once or twice.

Bacon is a good flavourer for many vegetables. In most recipes it is chopped up, but keeping it in pieces more or less the same length as the purple sprouting makes it look attractive and also ensures that everyone gets their fair share. This makes a good vegetable dish with eggs, soufflés and quiches.

Purples and Bacon

25g (1 oz) butter   1 large onion, thinly sliced
4 rashers green streaky bacon,   450g (1 lb) purple sprouting
  cut in half crossways

Melt the butter in a large saucepan on a low heat. Put in the bacon and onions and cook them gently until the onion is soft. Break the purple sprouting into small leaves and heads and put them on top of the bacon. Add 2cm (½ in) of water to the pan. Cover, and keep on a low heat for 20 minutes, stirring the purples around several times but keeping the bacon at the bottom. By the end of cooking time all the water should have evaporated.

Serve the purples with the onion mixed into them and the bacon on the top.

Rosemary, anchovies and olives also go well with lamb. Here I have used the fillet which is the long strip of boned-out meat from the neck. It can be difficult to find but some butchers will do it especially for you. If not, use chump chops instead, cut fairly thin.

Fillet of Lamb and Purple Sprouting

675-900g (1½-2 lb) fillet of lamb   60ml (4 tablespoons) lamb fat or
450g (1 lb) purple sprouting   25g (1 oz) butter
6 flat anchovy fillets   150ml (¼ pt) dry red wine
8 black olives   10ml (2 teaspoons) chopped
1 clove garlic, finely chopped   rosemary

Trim any excess pieces of fat from the lamb. Cut the fillets in half lengthways and then into pieces about 10cm (3 in) long. Cut each piece lengthways again into three. Break the purple sprouting into small heads and leaves. Pound the anchovies, olives and garlic together with a pestle and mortar. Heat the fat in a shallow, flameproof casserole on a high heat. Put in the pieces of lamb and brown them on both sides. (Do this in two batches so as not to overcrowd the pan and create too much moisture.) Remove the lamb and pour off all but a thin film of fat from the pan. Set it back on the heat, pour in the wine and bring it to the boil. Stir in the anchovy paste and the rosemary and replace the lamb. Put all the purple sprouting on top. Cover and set on a low heat for half an hour. Serve the lamb on a bed of purples with any juices from the pan spooned over the top. Cooked this way the purples will steam nicely on top of the lamb, picking up all its flavour but not overcooking as it does not come into direct contact with heat or moisture.

Like cauliflower, purple sprouting can also be made into cooked salads. For this one I have used the strong fairly hard-textured cheese that is made on the Isle of Islay, but you could also use Parmesan which is a little drier.

Chicken and Purple Sprouting Salad

1 cooked chicken weighing
* 1.5kg (3-3½ lb) before cooking*
450g (1 lb) purple sprouting
30ml (2 tablespoons) grated Isle
* of Islay Cheese*

90ml (6 tablespoons) olive oil
30ml (2 tablespoons) wine
* vinegar*
2 hard boiled eggs

Dice all the chicken. Break the purple sprouting into small heads and leaves. Put it into a saucepan with 2cm (½ in) water. Cover, and set it on a low heat for 20 minutes. Drain, refresh and drain again and let it cool completely. Mix the cheese, olive oil and vinegar together and mix half of the resulting dressing into the purple sprouting. Arrange the purples on a flat serving dish. Pile the diced chicken on top. Finely chop the eggs and mix them into the remaining dressing. Spoon this mixture evenly over the chicken.

Here are two good first courses using purples. The first is a little more extravagant than the second but when one of the ingredients is so cheap you can sometimes afford to spend a little more on the other.

Scallops and Purples

225g (8 oz) purple sprouting
4 scallops
50g (2 oz) butter

15ml (1 tablespoon) grated
* Parmesan cheese*
juice 1 lemon

Break the purple sprouting into small leaves and tiny flowers and break off most of the stems. Put it into a small saucepan with 2cm (½ in) water. Cover and set it on a low heat for 15 minutes. Cut each scallop from its shell and turn it over. Put a small dot of butter on each one. Preheat the grill to high, put under the scallops and grill them for two minutes on each side. Take the scallops off the shells and keep them warm. Lay a bed of the cooked leaves on each shell. Set a scallop on top and arrange the flowers around them. Heat the remaining butter in a small frying pan on a moderate heat. Let it just begin to brown and put in the cheese. Cook it for one minute and pour in the lemon. Let the sauce bubble and spoon it over the scallops. Serve them in the shells.

This recipe uses the springtime combination of purple sprouting, eggs and cheese.

Individual Broccoli Omelettes

For the cheese sauce:

25g (1 oz) butter	*50g (2 oz) grated Farmhouse*
15ml (1 tablespoon) flour	*Cheddar cheese*
275ml (½ pt) milk infused with 1	*10ml (2 teaspoons) English*
bayleaf, 1 blade mace, 1 slice	*Vineyard or other granular*
onion, 6 black peppercorns	*mustard*

For 4 omelettes:

450g (1 lb) purple sprouting	*40g (1½ oz) butter*
broccoli	*25g (1 oz) grated Farmhouse*
4 eggs	*Cheddar cheese*
16 small salad onions	

Make the sauce first. Melt the butter in a saucepan on a moderate heat. Stir in the flour and let it bubble. Take the pan from the heat and stir in first the mustard and then the milk. Set the pan back on the stove and bring the sauce to the boil, stirring. Simmer for two minutes. Beat in the cheese and keep the sauce warm. Cook the purple sprouting for 20 minutes and keep it warm. Beat each egg separately. Chop the onions. Melt 15g (½ oz) of butter in a frying pan on a low heat. Put in the onions and cook them until they are soft. Divide them into four and mix them into the eggs. Make a small, thin omelette with each egg using the remaining butter for frying. Lay some cooked purple sprouting on each one, spoon over 15ml (1 tablespoon) of the cheese sauce and fold each one in half. Lay them on a heatproof serving dish. Spoon over the rest of the sauce and scatter over the remaining cheese. Put them under a high grill to brown.

Spinach

It is difficult to put spinach into any category of vegetables when writing mainly from a cook's point of view. As we use its leaves, the obvious place would seem to be in the 'Leaves and Sprouts' section, but it is really a relative of the beetroot (we just use the other end of the plant) and so I am giving it a class of its own. In any case, it is usually so good as to deserve a little special treatment.

The common ancestor of spinach and beetroot is the wild plant that we now call sea-beet which was first brought under cultivation over two thousand years ago in the Middle East. Some strains were developed for their roots and some for their leaves and by the time they reached Europe spinach and beetroot were regarded as two completely different vegetables.

Sea-beet grows prolifically in some places round the flatter areas of our coast and on river estuaries, and if ever you find ordinary cultivated spinach difficult to track down in the shops and you do not grow it yourself, you can always use sea-beet instead if you know of a convenient source. I once lived near a river estuary and was lucky enough to have a constant supply which I found far more reliable than that provided by any shop.

The height of the pottage period was over when spinach was adopted as a garden vegetable in Britain and although all the old-established cabbages and pulses were still used in such a way a new vegetable deserved new treatment, and spinach was one of the first to be cooked and served alone. Savoury recipes for spinach were sometimes surprisingly simple for the times. One written in the late fourteenth century says that it should be boiled and then fried in oil and seasoned with a little spice, and this same basic idea was still used in the eighteenth century.

Plain boiled spinach was of course served hot with melted butter; and the boiled salads of the Elizabethan era were dressed with oil and vinegar or melted butter and vinegar and seasoned with a combination of various spices, sometimes given the sweet touch of currants and very often garnished with hard-boiled eggs.

The spices used in savoury spinach dishes (nutmeg, cinnamon and sometimes ginger) were the ones most often put into the sweet fillings for tarts, known in the sixteenth and seventeenth centuries as 'tartstuff', so using spinach as the basic ingredient was a natural extension of the idea. It was cooked and puréed in the same way as apples and other fruits and mixed with sugar or honey, spices, and later on candied orange and lemon peel. This idea was still employed in the eighteenth century, and there is one recipe of the time called 'To Make Fritters of Spinnedge', which uses a purée of cooked spinach mixed with spices, dates, currants, eggs and breadcrumbs to make small balls which are dipped in a beer batter and deep-fried. Hannah Glasse makes a pudding with eggs, cream and Seville oranges, and Eliza Acton in the nineteenth century gives basic instructions for cooking spinach and says that it can be served either with gravy as a savoury or with cream and sugar as a sweet.

Spinach juice has often been employed as a natural food colouring. It has heightened the colour of gooseberry creams, citron puddings, sweetmeats and cucumber soups, but its main use has been to colour Sage Derby Cheese. The sage gives all the flavour but the small amounts needed will only make the small dark green flecks that you can see in the cheese. The lighter green marbled effect is even now produced by using spinach.

As a vegetable, spinach is best in the spring and autumn. The early crop is drilled in September or October to be ready in April and May, and the later crop is drilled in the spring. You can still pick it during the summer months, but if the weather is very hot it will quickly go to seed. The leaves would then be small and it would take the pickers ages to fill just one crate. Some farms do grow beet spinach, or perpetual beet which can be sold as spinach or as a different vegetable. It is first drilled in March and once it is established can be picked throughout the year and will replenish itself with a fresh crop of leaves every time.

A field of spinach is not a really spectacular sight — just a mass of deep green leaves. Whatever the variety, it is always cut by hand and put into wooden crates, and either sent directly to market or first to the packhouse where it is put into bags in the same way as spring greens.

As spinach is not usually washed before it is sent out to the shops, it is very often dirty or sandy when you buy it; so always wash it very well to avoid getting a slightly crunchy purée! The centre stems cook down well so you can leave the whole leaves intact and just nick off the ends of the stalks.

Boiling spinach in large amounts of water tends to make the leaves tough and dull green and the flavour strong, but stewing it literally in its own juice preserves the best in texture, colour and flavour. Basically all you need do is put it in a saucepan with only the water that remains on its leaves after you have washed it. Cover the pan and set it on a moderate heat for 15 minutes, giving it the occasional stir so it all cooks evenly. When it is done, turn it into a colander or sieve and press it down to extract any excess moisture. If the spinach is to be served plain and alone and no further cooking or preparing is required, add a knob of butter to the pan as well. Flavour it with different chopped herbs, some chopped spring onions, or a sliced large onion that has been softened in the butter first.

There are few vegetables which can be cooked in the same pan as spinach as it requires such a short cooking time and its texture is so soft. Cabbage lettuce, however, is ideal. The combination gives a flavour quite different from either of the two cooked separately and brings both vegetables into the luxury class. The amounts here seem enormous when you chop them up, but they shrink considerably in the pot.

Spinach, Lettuce and Salad Onions

450g (1 lb) spinach
1 really large or 2 small cabbage lettuces
10 large salad onions

25g (1 oz) butter
30ml (2 tablespoons) chopped parsley

Wash the spinach and lettuces, drain them well and chop them. Chop the onions. Melt the butter in a saucepan on a low heat. Stir in the onions and let them cook for one minute. Stir in the spinach, lettuce and parsley. Cover and cook gently for 12 minutes, turning everything in the pan once for even cooking.

The spinach in this veal recipe is cooked as in the eighteenth century 'To Stew Spinach'.

Veal and Spinach

8 veal chops
grated rind and juice 1 lemon
freshly ground black pepper
675g (1½ lb) spinach
25g (1 oz) butter

8 large salad onions, chopped
6 flat anchovy fillets, finely chopped
freshly grated nutmeg

Bone the chops. Sprinkle the meat with the lemon rind and the pepper. Cook the spinach according to the basic recipe, without butter, for 15 minutes. Melt the butter in a large frying pan on a moderate heat. Put in the veal and cook it for 15 minutes, turning the pieces of meat frequently. Lower the heat, put in the onions and carry on cooking for a further five minutes. Remove the chops only and keep them warm. Put the spinach into the pan and grate over some nutmeg. Keep chopping the spinach with a sharp knife for one minute. Mix in the lemon juice and anchovies. Set the chops on top and keep the pan on a low heat for two minutes more.

Serve the chops on a bed of spinach.

This recipe was sparked off by the song 'A Frog he would A-Wooing Go' which has a chorus that begins 'With a roly poly gammon and spinach.' I'd just bought some gammon and quite by chance saw the first spinach of spring in the greengrocers. That's too much for any vivid imagination!

Roly-Poly Gammon and Spinach

For the roly-poly:

225g (8 oz) wholemeal flour
125g (4 oz) beef suet
pinch sea salt
freshly ground black pepper
8 large spinach leaves (from the
   total amount below)

900g (2 lb) spinach
4 gammon steaks (about 175g
   (6 oz) each)
15ml (1 tablespoon) pork
   dripping or lard
1 large onion, thinly sliced

Make the roly-poly first. Put the flour and suet into a bowl and season them well. Make a well in the centre and mix them to a stiff paste with cold water. Divide the dough into four pieces. Finely chop the eight spinach leaves. Roll each piece of dough into a rectangle about 0.5cm (¼ in) thick. Scatter the chopped spinach equally over each one. Roll them up and press the ends together. Wrap each one in butter papers and then tie all of them securely in a pudding cloth. (Either a piece of butter muslin or an old thin tea towel.) Bring a large saucepan of water to the boil, drop in your bundle and let it simmer for 50 minutes. Turn it over once during cooking to make sure the rolls all cook evenly.

For the gammon and spinach: wash and drain the spinach and cook it on a moderate heat for 12 minutes. Drain it well. Melt the dripping in a frying pan on a moderate heat. Put in the gammon steaks, two at a time, and fry them for five to ten minutes, depending on how much you like them done. Put in the onions with the last steaks so they can fry in the dripping until they are golden. Remove the gammon but keep the onions in the pan and spoon off all but 15ml (1 tablespoon) of the dripping. Keep the heat at moderate and put in the spinach. Chop it into the onions and mix them all together. Keep chopping and stirring for two minutes.

Arrange the spinach in a serving dish and set the gammon on top. Serve the roly-polys either on a separate plate or if there is room, round the edges of the dish.

In the next recipe the spinach forms the base on which to serve the sausages and it also makes the sauce and is chopped up and used like a herb. There is a good contrast between the taste of the plain spinach and the sauce and the sausages form the link in between.

Beef and Spinach Sausages

900g (2 lb) spinach
900g (2 lb) best quality minced
  beef
40g (1½ oz) butter
1 large onion, finely chopped

grated rind 1 lemon
freshly grated nutmeg
juice 1 lemon
1 carton (5 fl oz) natural yoghurt

Wash the spinach and break off the lower stems. Finely chop 225g (8 oz) and put the rest into a saucepan. Put the beef into a large bowl. Melt 25g (1 oz) of the butter in a frying pan on a low heat. Put in the onion and let it soften. Raise the heat to moderate and put in the chopped spinach. Stir it around until it wilts and put all the contents of the pan into the bowl with the beef. Grate in the lemon rind and some nutmeg and beat everything together well. Form the mixture into 16 small sausage shapes and put them aside to set into shape. Cook the spinach in the saucepan for 15 minutes and drain it well. Keep it warm. Preheat the grill to high and grill the sausages until they are brown all over. While they are cooking, take a quarter of the cooked spinach and chop it. Melt the remaining butter in a frying pan on a moderate heat. Put in the chopped spinach, grate in a little more nutmeg and cook, stirring for one minute. Mix in the lemon juice and yoghurt and just bring them to the boil. Remove the pan from the heat.

Arrange the plain, cooked spinach on a warm serving dish, put the sausages on top and spoon over the sauce.

Spinach, smoked fish and eggs are another well-tried combination. Here, just smoked fish and spinach make a light and slimming mould for a lunch dish or for a first course.

Spinach and Smoked Fillet Mould

450g (1 lb) spinach
10g (½ oz) gelatine

juice 1 lemon
225g (½ lb) smoked cod fillet

For cooking:
small piece onion
bouquet garni
1 blade mace
6 black peppercorns

30ml (2 tablespoons)
  mayonnaise plus
  extra mayonnaise for serving
tomatoes for garnish
lightly oiled 450g (1 lb) loaf tin
  or jelly mould

131

Cook the spinach according to the basic method for 15 minutes. Drain it well and chop it finely. Soak the gelatine in the lemon juice. Put the fish into a shallow pan with its cooking ingredients and cover it with water. Cover, bring it gently to the boil and simmer for three minutes. Lift it out with a perforated fish slice and flake it, removing all the skin and any bones. Put the spinach and fish into a blender and work them together to a smooth paste. Put in the mayonnaise and blend again. Turn the mixture into a bowl. Put the soaked gelatine into a small saucepan and set it on a very low heat to melt. Stir it quickly into the spinach mixture. Pour everything into the oiled tin or mould and leave it in a cool place to set. To turn it out, dip the bottom of the mould into hot water to just melt the edges. Arrange sliced tomatoes round the mould and serve the mayonnaise separately.

Here is a simple hot first course using Camembert which melts to make a creamy sauce.

Spinach with Camembert and Almonds

450g (1 lb) spinach
100g (4 oz) Camembert

50g (2 oz) almonds, blanched
and split

Trim and wash the spinach and cook it according to the basic recipe for 15 minutes. Drain it well. Cut the Camembert into thin slivers. Put half the spinach into a heat-proof serving dish and lay half the Camembert on top. Put in rest of the spinach and top with the remaining cheese. Preheat the grill to moderate. Put the dish under the grill for five minutes. Take out the dish and raise the heat to high. Scatter the almonds over the melting cheese and return the dish to the grill for them to brown.

Now use a good strong Farmhouse Cheddar to make a creamy soup.

Cream of Spinach and Cheese Soup

225g (8 oz) spinach
1 large onion, finely chopped
425ml (¾ pt) stock
425ml (¾ pt) milk infused with 1
   slice onion, 1 bayleaf, 1 blade

mace, 6 peppercorns
25g (1 oz) butter
15ml (1 tablespoon) flour
75g (3 oz) grated Farmhouse
   Cheddar cheese

Chop the spinach. Put it into a saucepan with the onion and stock. Bring them to the boil and simmer for 15 minutes. Work them together in a blender until they are smooth. Melt the butter in a saucepan on a low heat. Stir in the flour and blend in the infused milk. Raise the heat to moderate and stir until you have a thick bubbly sauce. Take the pan from the heat and beat in the cheese. Stir in the spinach mixture. Reheat, without boiling.

Pulse Vegetables

Broad beans and peas, the pulse vegetables, were once grown in this country so widely that they were the cheap fillers, used when cereals were scarce and before potatoes were introduced in pottages, puddings, bread and sometimes even beer. Different varieties were also used as winter fodder for animals when hay and straw became short.

Now, to use these beautiful, early summer vegetables for these purposes would be absolute sacrilege. They are grown on a far smaller scale than any cereal or potato, and although more peas than beans are grown most of them unfortunately go for canning and freezing.

Although freezing is a relatively new innovation, preserving certainly isn't and at one time both broad beans and peas were dried for winter use. These were boiled up with perhaps a little meat in the pottage pot to make a thick and filling stew, or sometimes they were boiled to a purée to make peas or bean puddings or to be served as we would now serve mashed potatoes. They were, in a way, the convenience foods of the day, used in the home and also taken in large quantities on board ship to be eaten with ships' biscuits.

Whereas cereal crops often failed the pulses never seemed to and so in years when there had been a bad harvest they were ground down into meal to be made into a coarse and rather bad-tasting bread, eaten mostly by the poor but sometimes, out of necessity, by the rich as well.

Gradually, pea and bean breads diminished in popularity but they were still made in the eighteenth century when wheat flour had to be imported at a cost that at times made it inaccessible to the poor. By the nineteenth century it was illegal to use anything but cereal flour but many bakers still sneaked in the odd pound or two of bean meal to make it go further. Nowadays, this is one thing that can't happen — the sheer cost and availability would make it impossible.

Today, fresh peas and beans should be treated with the utmost respect and cooked and prepared in different ways throughout their relatively short seasons to use all their qualities to the full.

Broad Beans

Broad beans are usually the first of the summer vegetables to arrive, heralding the start of a brand new season. Scarce as they are it is difficult to imagine now that broad beans were once one of the staples of the British diet, but until quite recently they were one of the most widely grown vegetables. Smaller varieties were first cultivated as a field crop in the Iron Age, and in Medieval times they rotated with cereal crops and a fallow year in the three-year system that was employed all over the country. Most were for human consumption, but a coarser kind called a horse-bean was also grown for animals.

Although broad beans were certainly eaten fresh in the summer, they were most often dried in some way for the winter. Methods of drying were many and varied and the beans could either be shelled first or left in the pods. Sometimes they were simply laid out in the sun, but to stop them from germinating the process had to be a little more complicated. 'Frizzled' beans were first boiled in their pods and then shelled and held over some form of heat in a metal spoon to dry them quickly or 'frizzle' them. Then you could get 'canebyns' which were first soaked in several changes of water for 48 hours, put in a low oven to dry really hard and then broken up with a hand-mill. Canebyns were boiled in pottages and broths and were also cooked with almond milk and sugar during Lent to make a sweet pottage.

Broad beans and bacon were always served together and the partnership has been immortalized in the words of a song which goes: 'broad beans and bacon and a pint of strong ale'. Most of the cottage pigs were killed in the autumn and their meat was salted and preserved for winter in as great a quantity in some houses as beans were dried. They were boiled up together to make a complete dish of pottage, or sometimes the beans were served separately in a form of pudding or purée. In the poorer houses when there wasn't even bacon to be had the beans were boiled in a broth that was thickened with oatmeal or breadcrumbs.

Dried beans went out of favour during the eighteenth century as potatoes became the main filling vegetable and more cereals were available for bread. Broad beans from then on were never so widely grown. In the eighteenth and nineteenth centuries fresh beans were boiled and buttered. Broad beans and bacon were still inseparable at the table but they were boiled separately for according to Hannah Glasse 'the bacon will spoil the colour of the beans'. Older beans were cooked, pureed with butter, tied in a cloth and boiled to make a pudding and sometimes they were made richer with egg yolks and cream and mixed with a few bread crumbs as well. Bean purées were also spread on toast and topped with scrambled eggs and bacon.

Beans were used in various early beauty treatments. The pods were steeped in wine and vinegar to make a form of skin tonic and a concoction of bean meal and milk was used on the face to give a soft complexion.

Nowadays, beans are not usually a permanent crop that is grown in the same place every year. On larger farms they are often sown to refresh the soil after several years of cereals. After they are harvested the bines are ploughed back in as green manure and then it is back to wheat or barley. Mostly now they are a market garden crop. They are sown either in November or December or at any time from March to early May. On the bigger farms, broad bean seeds can be sewn in a similar way to cabbage plants but on small plots all the work is done by hand. The market gardener I visited drew lines in the earth with a tractor, dropped in the beans and simply shuffled up the rows putting the earth back into the small trench and pressing it down with his feet.

The beans that are sown late in the year are ready at the end of May or very beginning of June. The ones sown in the spring follow quickly behind as they take a shorter time to grow, and the season usually lasts until August. The plants are usually about three feet high; a very awkward back breaking height to pick from. The stems are tough and hard to break and care has to be taken when you are picking beans that you don't pull up or damage the whole plant. It is a slow and laborious job which must be done by hand as they all mature at different times and a machine would grab them all from the plants at once without being discriminating. This is why the price of beans seems high and also because the earlier sown ones at least, take up the ground for all the year and only produce a small crop for a short time.

With broad beans, you have to buy quite a weight to get enough for a substantial dish, but this can be overcome in various ways, especially when they are young.

When they are really small and tiny, you can gently simmer them in their pods for 20 minutes and serve them whole. The furry inner coat melts away, leaving a small, tender vegetable that can be served as an accompaniment to the main course, or with melted butter and lemon juice as an unusual first course. You could also coat the beans in a dressing of oil and lemon juice while they are still warm, cool them completely and serve them as a salad sprinkled with Parmesan cheese. When you have cooked beans in their pods, be careful how you handle them as they easily spit open leaving you with a selection of stray beans and halves of pods.

Serving vegetables raw always makes them go further and tiny young beans can make superb additions to green salads or can be used as salads in themselves. Always let the beans stand for a quarter of an hour in the dressing before serving or adding the softer vegetables. Then they will absorb all the flavour.

Put broad beans with their traditional accompaniment, bacon, to make a first course salad.

Broad Bean, Bacon and Green Leaf Salad

450g (1 lb) broad beans weighed in their shells
100g (4 oz) lean bacon
12 dandelion leaves
6 large or 12 small sorrel leaves
15ml (1 tablespoon) chopped savory

For the dressing:

60ml (4 tablespoons) olive oil
30ml (2 tablespoons) white wine vinegar
10ml (2 teaspoons) Dijon
mustard
freshly ground black pepper
lettuce leaves for serving

Shell the beans. Grill the bacon until it is crisp, cool it and chop it

136

finely. Put the beans, bacon, sorrel and dandelions into a bowl. Mix all
the ingredients for the dressing together, and fold them into the salad.
Let them stand for 15 minutes. Arrange some lettuce leaves on four
small plates and pile the salad on top. Serve either as a first course or as
a side salad.

If you are going to cook shelled broad beans as the main vegetable of
the meal you will need 900g (2 lb) weighed in their shells for four
people. Put them into a saucepan with 25g (1 oz) of butter and 150ml
(¼ pt) stock or water and simmer them gently for 15 minutes at the
beginning of the season and 20 minutes towards the end. To vary the
flavour to go with your main dish, add different herbs such as parsley,
thyme or savory and use white wine or cider instead of stock.

If you are using the oven for cooking it can sometimes be economical
to cook the vegetables in the oven as well. Again you can vary your
liquid and your herbs. For this method use broad beans in the middle
of their season or towards the end. It would spoil the finer flavour of
the youngest beans.

Broad Beans in Cider

900g (2 lb) broad beans weighed   *150ml (¼ pt) dry cider*
in their shells   *30ml (2 tablespoons) chopped*
25g (1 oz) butter   *parsley*

Preheat the oven to 180°C (350°F)/Gas 4.
Shell the beans. Melt the butter in a small flameproof casserole on a
low heat. Stir in the beans, pour in the cider and add the parsley. Cover
the casserole and put it into the oven for 50 minutes.

Wild rabbits and beans are not traditional in the cookery books but no
doubt they were stewed up together in some way when the man of the
house in country districts came home with two furry ears protruding
from his poacher's pockets. You could use tame rabbit for this one, but
the flavour is never as good.

Rabbit, Beans and Mustard

1 wild rabbit   *25g (1 oz) butter or bacon fat*
900g (2 lb) broad beans weighed   *30ml (2 tablespoons) chopped*
in their shells   *thyme*
275ml (½ pt) stock
15ml (1 tablespoon) Dijon
mustard

Joint the rabbit, take all the meat from the bones and cut it into 3cm

137

(1 in) pieces. Shell the beans. Mix the stock and mustard together.
Heat the fat in a large frying pan or sauté pan on a high heat. Put in the
rabbit and brown it well, moving it around all the time. Pour in the
stock and mustard and bring them to the boil. Cover and set on a very
low heat for 30 minutes. Serve it with buttered new potatoes.

When I first made this rabbit recipe I cooked twice the amount I
needed. I hate to waste anything and so made it into a paté with some
bacon. It was really good — not like leftovers at all — and worth
making intentionally.

Rabbit and Bean Paté

*1 wild rabbit cooked as above
with broad beans
100g (4 oz) streaky bacon*

*15ml (1 tablespoon) chopped
thyme
50g (2 oz) softened butter*

Let the rabbit and beans cool. Trim the rinds from the bacon and grill
the rashers under a high heat until they are just cooked but not brown
or crisp. Put the cooked rabbit and beans and the bacon through the
fine blade of a mincer. Beat in the butter and the thyme. Pack the
mixture into an earthenware terrine or bowl and chill it until it is firm.

Towards the end of their season, large, fairly tough beans can be made
into patés and mixed into meat loaves.

Bean, Pea, Bacon and Egg Paté

*450g (1 lb) broad beans weighed
in their shells
450g (1 lb) peas weighed in their
shells
175g (6 oz) lean bacon
50g (2 oz) butter
1 small onion, finely chopped*

*30ml (2 tablespoons) double
cream
2 hard boiled eggs
juice ½ lemon
15ml (1 tablespoon) mixed
chopped savory and parsley*

Shell the beans and peas. Chop the bacon finely. Boil the beans in
salted water for 20 minutes. Drain them and remove the outer skins.
Melt 25g (1 oz) of the butter in a small saucepan on a low heat. Stir in
the peas, onion and bacon. Cover the pan and cook them gently for 20
minutes. Melt in the remaining butter and stir in the beans. Put all the
contents of the saucepan into a blender with the cream and work them
until you have a smooth paste. Put this into a large bowl. Chop the eggs
finely and beat them into the mixture with the herbs and lemon juice.

Press the paté into an earthenware terrine or bowl and chill it until it is firm.

Serve it either as a first course or as a cold summer lunch.

Lightly cooked broad beans are ideal for the cooked salads that were once so popular in this country. Shell them and cook them gently in simmering water for 15 minutes at the beginning of the season and 20 minutes towards the end. Drain them and let them steam dry and coat them while they are still hot in mayonnaise or French dressing. Then, as they cool, they absorb all the flavour.

Lambs tongues and beans here make a fairly cheap but very attractive and unusual cooked salad.

Lambs' Tongue and Broad Bean Ring

6 lambs' tongues

For boiling:

1 small onion
1 small carrot
1 small piece celery (if available)
6 black peppercorns
bouquet garni
15ml (1 tablespoon) white wine vinegar

900g (2 lb) broad beans weighed in their shells
4 firm tomatoes
15g (½ oz) gelatine
150ml (¼ pt) dry white wine
15ml (1 tablespoon) white wine vinegar
15ml (1 tablespoon) tomato purée

For dressing:

150ml (¼ pt) mayonnaise
15ml (1 tablespoon) tomato purée
15ml (1 tablespoon) chopped mint

lightly oiled 25cm (8 in) diameter ring mould

Put the lambs' tongues into a saucepan and cover them with water. Bring them to the boil, drain and refresh them. Put them back into the rinsed-out pan with the boiling ingredients. Bring them to the boil, skim and cover and simmer for 1¼ hours. Lift them out of the pan and skin them when they are still warm and moist, leaving them in the stock until you get to each one. If you let them dry too much they will be difficult to skin. Let them cool completely. Strain and skim the stock, and put it into a saucepan. Shell the beans. Bring the saucepan of stock to the boil, put in the beans and simmer them for 15 minutes. Drain them, reserving the stock again. Divide the beans into two portions.

139

Make the dressing by mixing the mayonnaise, tomato purée and mint and fold in one portion of the beans. Scald, skin and seed the tomatoes and cut them into strips. Dice the tongues. Soak the gelatine in the wine and vinegar. Take 275ml (½ pt) of the reserved stock and warm it in a saucepan. Mix in the tomato purée. Stir in the soaked gelatine and let it dissolve. Pour 45ml (3 tablespoons) of this liquid into the bottom of the oiled ring mould and put it into the 'fridge or into a cold place to set. Take the remaining portion of beans and put a circle of them around the set jelly with half the tomato strips. Arrange half the tongue on top, the remaining beans and tomatoes and the rest of the tongue. When the rest of the liquid in the saucepan is cool pour it into the mould and let the whole thing set. Turn out the jelly and fill the centre with the bean salad.

Here is another salad with cooked broad beans. Mild tarragon vinegar enhances the delicate bean flavour which penetrates the whole chicken as it cooks.

Chicken, Broad Bean and Apricot Salad

One 1.5kg (3-3½ lb) roasting chicken

900g (2 lb) broad beans weighed in their shells

2 bouquets savory

For boiling:

6 bean pods
1 small onion
1 small carrot

1 small stick celery
few black peppercorns

For the salad:

8 apricots
90ml (6 tablespoons) olive oil
60ml (4 tablespoons) tarragon vinegar

30ml (2 tablespoons) chopped savory

Put a bouquet of savory inside the chicken and truss it. Shell the beans and reserve four pods. Put the chicken into a saucepan with the boiling ingredients and the bean pods and cover it with water to just above the thighs. Bring it to the boil, cover and simmer for 50 minutes, putting in the beans for the last 20 minutes. Lift out the chicken and let it cool completely. Strain the stock, reserve all the beans and let them cool. Joint the chicken and dice it. Stone and slice the apricots and put them in a bowl with the chicken and beans. Blend the oil and vinegar together and mix them into the salad with the chopped savory.

140

If you have made the previous recipe and are wondering what to do with the stock make a broad bean soup. This one is unblended and uses tarragon again.

Broad Bean and Tarragon Soup

900g (2 lb) broad beans weighed
   in their shells
25g (1 oz) butter
1 medium onion, finely chopped
15ml (1 tablespoon) wholemeal
   flour

725ml (1¼ pt) stock
30ml (2 tablespoons) tarragon
   vinegar
15ml (1 tablespoon) chopped
   tarragon
150ml (¼ pt) dry white wine

Shell and finely chop the beans. Melt the butter in a saucepan on a low heat. Stir in the beans and onion, cover and let them sweat for seven minutes. Stir in the flour and then the stock. Bring them to the boil, stirring frequently. Add the vinegar and chopped tarragon and simmer, uncovered for 20 minutes. Pour in the wine and reheat to serve.

Peas

When broad beans have been in the shops for barely a week the first of the early peas arrive, a real seasonal treat. You can extol the virtues of the ever-available frozen ones as much as you like, but their flavour and texture is never the same and as a vegetable they are nowhere near as versatile.

One variety of green pea was first grown here by the Romans and in Anglo-Saxon and Medieval times three varieties were grown as field crops, alternating with cereals and the fallow year in the same way as beans. They too had the added advantage of having bines that could be ploughed back in as green manure. There were green and white peas for eating fresh or dried and larger, tougher grey peas for animal fodder.

The garden peas we know today were first developed in the fifteenth century by a French gardener called Michaux and they arrived in Britain in late Tudor times.

Early peas were nearly always put into the pottage pot partnering salt pork as broad beans did bacon. Both fresh and dried peas were used in this way and always they were simmered until they became a rich, thick, soupy purée which blended with the broth and the meat.

When no meat was to be had the pottage was given substance by bread crumbs and oatmeal. From here came the rhyme

'Peas pudding hot,
Peas pudding cold,
Peas pudding in the pot
Nine days old.'

One wonders what it must have been like!

Peas made a good substantial dish without meat and so they were used quite considerably during Lent and on fasting days throughout the year. White peas especially made a pottage in the religious and I should imagine the richer houses, that was flavoured with minced onions, sugar and honey and coloured with saffron.

During the fifteenth century green peas were also cooked as a distinguishable vegetable instead of being puréed. They were simmered in beef broth and flavoured with parsley, sage and savory.

Even in Tudor and Stuart times, however, pottage of peas was still a favourite dish, but then it took on a more solid form and was often mixed with flour and breadcrumbs and called 'peas porridge'. The new garden peas were prized for their sugar content and at first were made into sweet tarts with sugar, butter and spices, with the pastry top coated with icing.

During the eighteenth century dried peas were used less and less. Mostly they were eaten fresh and if they were preserved, they were bottled. Hannah Glasse gives an account of how 'to keep green peas till Christmas'. Boiling and buttering was inevitably one of the favourite cooking methods, but peas were also simmered in stock, either alone or with lettuce, and the resulting sauce was thickened with egg yolks.

In the nineteenth century they were boiled and buttered, and boiled and glazed with sugar or served in cream. They were also a favourite soup ingredient, again either alone or with lettuce, spinach or carrots.

Like beans, peas can either be sown at the end of the year or in the spring. The picking can be hot and laborious when done by hand but then so is picking, cutting or pulling any vegetable. Why, then, have so many of the larger pea-growers turned to picking mechanically for frozen food companies? In 1975 108 thousand acres of peas out of a total of 146,100 acres went for processing, and I am told this is because of public demand. Frozen peas are now as popular as peas pudding used to be and any demand, one farmer informed me, can be met if it is great enough.

If you have only eaten frozen peas during the past few years, try some fresh ones, and discover their flavour and texture all over again. This will at least encourage those growers who do provide us with fresh peas to carry on.

One of the best ways of cooking peas is to simmer 450g (1 lb) in 25g

142

(1 oz) of butter for ten minutes in a covered saucepan, stir in 150ml (¼ pt) double cream and 5ml (1 teaspoon) of honey and carry on simmering for a further five minutes.

The first few, sweet pickings of the season can, like beans, be served raw. With no dressing they have a tendency to bounce all over the place, so keep them under control with mayonnaise and pile them onto a bed of lettuce.

Here is a raw pea salad with eggs for a first course.

Raw Peas and Egg Salad

450g (1 lb) young, tiny peas weighed in their shells
60ml (4 tablespoons) fresh mayonnaise
15ml (1 tablespoon) tarragon vinegar
30ml (2 tablespoons) chopped mint
4 hard boiled eggs
1 small lettuce, shredded
2 boxes mustard and cress

Shell the peas. Mix the mayonnaise and tarragon vinegar together and stir in the peas and mint. Let them stand for 15 minutes. Cut the eggs in half lengthways. Mix the lettuce and cress together and arrange them on four small plates. Put the eggs on top, cut-side down. Spoon the peas and mayonnaise over the eggs.

Mixtures of summer vegetables can be simmered or braised together. They also make delicious mixed cooked salads.

Salad of Peas, Beans and Carrots

450g (1 lb) peas weighed in their shells
900g (2 lb) broad beans weighed in their shells
450g (1 lb) new carrots
6 pea pods
2 bean pods
2 sprigs mint
15ml (1 tablespoon) chopped chives
15ml (1 tablespoon) chopped mint
60ml (4 tablespoons) thick mayonnaise
15ml (1 tablespoons) Dijon mustard

Shell the peas and beans. Trim the carrots and cut them into 1.5cm (½ in) pieces. Bring a saucepan of lightly salted water to the boil. Put in the vegetables, pods and mint sprigs. Cook them gently for 20 minutes. Drain them and let them steam dry. Discard the pods and mint. Put them into a bowl with the herbs. Mix the mayonnaise and mustard together and fold them into the vegetables while they are still warm.

143

Leave them until they are quite cold. Mix them all around again just before serving.

Here is another cooked salad, this time making a complete meal.

Peas and Smoked Fillet Salad

900g (2 lb) smoked cod fillet

For cooking the fish:

1 bayleaf
1 slice onion
bouquet garni
6 black pepercorns
900g (2 lb) peas weighed in their shells
40g (1½ oz) butter
45g (3 tablespoons) chopped parsley

30ml (2 tablespoons) chopped chives
30ml (2 tablespoons) chopped lemon thyme or thyme
juice 1 lemon
60ml (4 tablespoons) double cream
freshly ground black pepper
1 lettuce for serving

Skin the fish and put it into a shallow pan with the bayleaf, onion, bouquet garni and peppercorns. Cover it with water, bring it to the boil and let it simmer for five minutes. Drain it well and flake it. Shell the peas. Melt the butter in a heavy saucepan on a low heat. Stir in the peas, cover them and cook for ten minutes. Add the flaked fish and herbs and mix them in well. Cover again and cook for a further five minutes, stirring occasionally. Mix in the lemon juice and cream and season with the pepper with the pan still on the heat. Turn it all out onto a plate to cool. Arrange the lettuce leaves in a serving bowl so they line it and just reach attractively over the top.

Pile the salad into the bowl so you have a dish of green and yellow. N.B. You could also serve this dish hot with brown rice.

Omelettes or baked egg dishes are ideal hot for supper or cold for lunch or to be cut into wedges and taken on a picnic. Although there are only four eggs in this one the peas make it quite substantial enough for four people. I have used coriander as it is a herb often put into pea and egg dishes in Spain. Use parsley or chervil if none is available.

Egg and Pea Bake

450g (1 lb) peas weighed in their shells
4 very large bulbous salad onions (or 8 smaller ones)
25g (1 oz) butter

15ml (1 tablespoon) chopped mint
15ml (1 tablespoon) tomato purée
5ml (1 teaspoon) paprika

1 sprig mint
4 eggs
15ml (1 tablespoon) chopped
   coriander

*little butter for greasing 25cm
(8 or 9 in) diameter pie plate
or flat oven-proof dish*

Preheat the oven to 200°C (400°F)/Gas 6.

Shell the peas and chop the onions. Melt the butter in a saucepan on a low heat. Mix in the peas and onions and tuck in the mint sprig. Cover and simmer for 15 minutes. Let them cool and remove the mint. Beat the eggs with the coriander, chopped mint, tomato purée and paprika. Mix in the peas and onions. Pour the mixture into a buttered oven-proof pie-plate or dish. Bake for 30 minutes.

For this next dish use fillet of lamb if you can find it, or if not, chump chops cut very thinly. It is best made with young, sweet peas as the cooking time is not long. Cooked in this way they maintain the fresh flavour of raw peas but have a soft texture.

Lamb with Peas and Turmeric

*675g (1½ lb) fillet of lamb
900g (2 lb) young peas weighed
   in their shells
25g (1 oz) butter*

*1 large onion, finely chopped
10ml (2 teaspoons) turmeric
150ml (¼ pt) dry white wine
60ml (4 tablespoons) sour cream*

Cut the lamb into strips about 4cm x 1.5cm (1½ in x ½ in). Shell the peas. Melt the butter in a large frying pan or skillet on a high heat. Put in the pieces of lamb and brown them well, moving them around constantly in the pan. Lower the heat and put in the onion, peas and turmeric. Continue to cook, stirring occasionally, until the onion is soft. Raise the heat again and pour in the wine. Bring it to the boil. Cover the pan and set it on a low heat for 20 minutes. Stir in the sour cream and let it bubble.

Serve it with buttered brown rice.

Green Peas and curd cheese make a simple summer paté that needs no other flavouring than mint which makes it really fresh tasting.

Paté of Green Peas

*225g (½ lb) peas weighed in their
   shells
25g (1 oz) butter
1 sprig mint*

*175g (6 oz) curd cheese
15ml (1 tablespoon) chopped
   mint*

Shell the peas. Melt the butter in a small saucepan on a low heat. Mix in the peas and add the mint sprig. Cover and cook very gently for 12 minutes. Discard the mint. Pound the peas and butter to a paste with a large pestle and mortar or with a wooden spoon in a bowl. Thoroughly mix in the cheese and chopped mint. Put the paté into four small ramequins or individual soufflé dishes and chill it until it is firm.

Serve it with brown toast.

Put young sweet peas into an unblended soup with chicken. This could be an extremely economical dish if for the stock you use the carcass and giblets of a chicken that you have jointed before cooking in another recipe. After boiling up the stock, scrape every piece of meat you can from the bones and gizzard and chop the heart very finely. Use these as the cooked chicken meat.

Chicken and Pea Soup

225g (½ lb) peas weighed in their shells
25g (1 oz) butter
1 large onion, finely chopped
15ml (1 tablespoon) wholemeal flour
125g (4 oz) cooked, shredded chicken
15ml (1 tablespoon) chopped mint
15ml (1 tablespoon) chopped tarragon

Shell the peas, reserving ten of the best pods. Melt the butter in a saucepan on a low heat. Stir in the onion and cook it until it is just turning golden. Stir in the peas. Stir in the flour and then the stock. Bring it to the boil, stirring. Lower the heat and put in the shredded chicken, pea pods, mint and tarragon. Simmer for 15 minutes and remove the pods just before serving.

146

Green Beans

The history of runner beans and French beans is something of a mystery. They were both discovered in South America in the sixteenth century, but it is not known when they reached Britain.

The small, delicate French beans were known here in the eighteenth century as Hannah Glasse gives just one recipe for them — boiling and buttering. Mrs Beeton gives them the same treatment, and so does Eliza Acton, but she also simmers them in a sauce of stock or cream which is then thickened with egg yolks and lemon.

Runner Beans

When runner beans come into the shops, it is a sure sign that summer is on its way to becoming full-blown.

They are larger, flatter and coarser than French beans and have a more savoury flavour. There are basically two kinds but they are so similar that they can be treated as one vegetable.

Ground beans are the first to arrive, usually in the middle of July. These are grown in bushy clumps and not trained up sticks or strings. As it grows, the trailing head is pinched out and the side shoots are allowed to develop. To do this successfully, the whole field has to be gone over every day, making them a time-consuming crop.

True runner beans, on the other

hand, are encouraged to grow upwards, and every plant has to be provided with a string or wire to climb up as soon as it is about 18cm (6 in) high. On a large acreage, this can be expensive, time consuming and they also have to be weeded by hand. Hence this type of bean is becoming more of a market garden crop whilst the ground beans are increasing in popularity with many of the bigger growers.

Of the two, ground beans are harder to pick as you have to bend right down to get at them. Bean plants produce both flowers and beans at the same time and so it isn't a question of taking up a whole plant and stripping it as you would with peas, but of methodically inspecting each one and carefully pulling off the largest beans.

Ground beans are always the earlier crop, but there are many who prefer to wait for the true runners as they believe they have more flavour. They are definitely straighter and so easier to prepare as they are allowed to hang straight down from the stems, whereas the ground beans, if they actually touch the ground as they grow, become curled or crooked.

Before you slice or chop these particular beans, the stringy outside edge must be cut away carefully. The traditional way of cutting beans for cooking is in thin, diagonal slices, but you can also chop them into squares or cut them into small julienne sticks about 4cm (1½ in) long and half the width of the bean wide.

Beans need very little liquid when you cook them as they have such a high moisture content. Put a pound of sliced or chopped beans into a saucepan with 25g (1 oz) butter, 60ml (4 tablespoons) water and a small pinch of salt. Cover them tightly and set them on a moderate heat for 20 minutes and they will cook perfectly in their own steam. You can add different herbs to the pan for flavour and use stock or cider instead of water. Another good idea is to soften an onion in the butter before you add the beans and liquid.

If you would rather not add butter to the pan, simply increase the amount of liquid to 90ml (6 tablespoons).

Green peppers and tomatoes are plentiful at the same time as runner beans. Make an English ratatouille with all three together. You can serve it hot as an accompanying vegetable or cold as a salad or a first course.

Green Bean Ratatouille

450g (1 lb) runner beans
1 large green pepper
60ml (4 tablespoons) olive oil
1 large onion, thinly sliced

1 large clove garlic, finely
chopped
225g (½ lb) firm tomatoes,
scalded, skinned and sliced

Slice the beans diagonally. Deseed and dice the pepper. Heat the oil in a frying pan on a low heat. Put in the onion and garlic, cover and cook them for ten minutes. Mix in the beans and pepper, cover again and cook for a further 20 minutes, adding the prepared tomatoes for the final two minutes so they just heat through.

Runner beans are a little tough to be served raw but they do make good cooked salads if they are simmered in the dressing for a short time so they stay slightly crunchy, and are then allowed to cool.

Runner Bean and Anchovy Salad

450g (1 lb) runner beans
45ml (3 tablespoons) olive oil
1 medium onion, thinly sliced
1 large clove garlic, finely
  chopped
6 flat anchovy fillets, finely
  chopped

15ml (1 tablespoon) chopped
  thyme
30ml (2 tablespoons) wine
  vinegar

Slice the beans diagonally. Heat the oil in a saucepan on a low heat. Put in the onion and garlic and cook them until the onion is soft. Stir in the beans, anchovies, thyme and vinegar. Cover the pan and keep it on the low heat for ten minutes, stirring once. Let the salad cool completely, and if it is a really hot day, serve it slightly chilled.

Put beans with fish and cockles to make a salad for a summer lunch or for a first course.

Bean and Fish Salad

450g (1 lb) runner beans
60ml (4 tablespoons) olive oil
1 large onion, thinly sliced
1 clove garlic, finely chopped
15ml (1 tablespoon) lemon
  thyme
juice 1 lemon
350g (¾ lb) coley or cod

little butter for greasing dish
125g (¼ lb) cockles
freshly ground black pepper
15ml (1 tablespoon) chopped
  lemon thyme
12 green olives, stoned and
  chopped
8 firm tomatoes, chopped

Slice the beans. Heat the oil in a saucepan on a low heat. Put in the onion and garlic, cover them and cook them gently for five minutes. Stir in the beans, 15ml (1 tablespoon) lemon thyme and the juice of ½ lemon. Cover and cook for ten minutes. Turn everything into a bowl to cool. Skin the fish and cut it into eight even-sized pieces. Lay them in a lightly buttered ovenproof dish. Grind over some pepper and scatter over the remaining lemon thyme. Add rest of lemon juice and let the fish stand for one hour. Preheat the oven to 190°C (375°F)/Gas 5. Cover the fish with foil and put it into the oven for 20 minutes. Cool the fish completely and flake it. Combine the beans, fish, cockles, tomatoes and olives in a large serving bowl.

Serve the salad with wholemeal scones.

Runner beans and eggs are here made into an attractive mould with the centre filled with a cooked bean salad. It is very filling and will easily make a cold meal for four people or a first course for six or even eight. Use a really good quality German salami from a delicatessen. Some of those made in this country taste synthetic and will spoil the dish.

Runner Bean Ring

450g (1 lb) runner beans
1 medium onion, finely chopped
15ml (1 tablespoon) chopped
   savory
60ml (4 tablespoons) water
10g (½ oz) gelatine
juice 1 lemon
4 hard boiled eggs

125g (4 oz) spicy salami
150ml (¼ pt) freshly made
   mayonnaise
30ml (2 tablespoons) olive oil
15ml (1 tablespoon) white wine
   vinegar
little oil for greasing 25cm (8 in)
   diameter ring mould

Dice the beans into 0.75cm (½ in) pieces. Put them into a saucepan with the onion, savory and water. Cover them and set them on a low heat for 15 minutes, stirring occasionally. Soak the gelatine in the lemon juice. Chop the eggs and salami and put them in a bowl. Mix in the mayonnaise and half the cooked beans. Dissolve the gelatine in a small pan on a low heat and quickly mix it into the egg mixture. Pour everything into the oiled ring mould and smooth the top, pressing down to make the mixture compact. Put it in a cool place or into the 'fridge to set. Mix the oil and vinegar into the remaining beans and cool them. Turn out the mould by first dipping the base into a bowl of hot water. Fill the centre with the bean salad.

This pork dish is also flavoured with a continental sausage which I have often found goes very well with runner beans — the Spanish Chorizo.

Pork with Chorizo Sausage and Runner Beans

1 piece lean end of the belly of
   pork weighing around 1.125kg
   (2½ lb)

1 clove garlic, finely chopped
pinch cayenne pepper
150ml (¼ pt) stock

10ml (2 teaspoons) paprika
675g (1½ lb) runner beans
piece Chorizo sausage the same
   length as the pork 100g
(3-4 oz)
15g (½ oz) pork dripping or lard
1 large onion, finely chopped

5ml (1 teaspoon) tomato purée
15ml (1 tablespoon) chopped
   savory
225g (½ lb) tomatoes, scalded,
   skinned, deseeded and
   roughly chopped

Preheat the oven to 160°C (325°F)/Gas 3.

Cut the rind and bones from the pork. Rub 5ml (1 teaspoon) paprika over the cut surface. Take five beans and cut them in half lengthways. Cut each piece into lengths the same size as the pork. Cut a lengthways strip from the piece of sausage, taking about one third of it. Then cut your strip into four lengthways pieces. Lay the lengths of beans and Chorizo on the pork. Roll up the joint and tie it with strong thread or fine cotton string. Dice the remaining beans. Melt the fat in a large, flameproof casserole on a high heat. Put in the pork and brown it all over. Remove it and set it aside. Lower the heat and stir in the onion, garlic, remaining paprika and cayenne pepper. Cook them until the onion is soft. Add the beans and mix everything together. Pour in the stock and add the tomato purée and savory. Bring them to the boil and replace the pork. Cover the casserole and put it into the oven for 1½ hours. Take out the meat and keep it warm. Put in the tomatoes and just heat them through. Carve the pork and arrange the slices on a warm serving dish. Put the beans down each side and spoon any juices left in the casserole over the pork.

The savoury flavour of runner beans is also brought out in this pie which is covered with a crumbly dripping pastry.

Runner Bean and Lamb Pie

For the pastry:

225g (8 oz) wholemeal flour
pinch fine sea salt
125g (4 oz) beef dripping
freshly ground black pepper
water to mix
milk or beaten egg for glaze

675g (1½ lb) runner beans
675-900g (1½-2 lb) lean boneless
   lamb cut from the shoulder

60ml (4 tablespoons) lamb fat or
   25g (1 oz) butter
2 medium onions, finely
   chopped
150ml (¼ pt) sherry
15ml (1 tablespoon) chopped
   thyme
15ml (1 tablespoon) chopped
   marjoram

Make the pastry and set it aside to chill. Preheat the oven to 200°C

(400°F)/Gas 6. Finely chop the beans. Dice the lamb into 2cm (¾ in) pieces. Heat the fat in a large frying pan on a high heat. Put in the lamb and brown it well, moving it around to drive away any moisture that may collect. Remove it and put it in a pie dish. Lower the heat and cool the pan a little. Stir in the beans and onions, cover the pan, and let them sweat for five minutes. Pour in the sherry and bring it to the boil. Add the thyme and marjoram. Tip all the contents of the pan into the pie dish with the lamb and mix everything together. Cover with the pastry and brush it with the beaten egg or milk. Bake the pie for 30 minutes.

For this soup, runner beans are put with tomatoes again, and it is made really special by the best tomato herb of all. If you haven't any basil, use thyme instead.

Runner Bean and Tomato Soup

675g (1½ lb) runner beans
450g (1 lb) ripe tomatoes
60ml (4 tablespoons) olive oil
1 large onion, finely chopped

575ml (1 pt) stock
30ml (2 tablespoons) chopped basil

Finely chop the beans. Scald, skin and chop the tomatoes. Heat the oil in a saucepan on a low heat. Stir in the beans, onions and garlic. Cover, and let them sweat for ten minutes. Mix in the tomatoes, cover again and cook for a further five minutes so they go thick and pulpy. Pour in the stock and add the basil. Simmer, uncovered, for ten minutes.

French Beans

French beans are easier and cheaper to grow than both ground and runner beans as no shoots have to be picked out, they don't have to be hoed by hand and no strings or frames are required for them to climb up. They are drilled in April, usually a certain amount of the acreage every two weeks, so they are ready for picking in late July and carry on until the middle of August. They are a tiring crop to pick as the plants are so low and the beans hide right underneath the large leaves, but as their season coincides conveniently with the beginning of the school holidays, when many of the older children are looking for something to do to earn them some pocket money, this difficulty is easily overcome and many farmers have found this an incentive to change from runner beans to French beans as the easier crop.

I saw a coach-load of children picking willingly and well, amidst a lot of happy chatter, lining the straight beans in the cardboard boxes in two even rows to be sent directly to market, and putting them into the crates to be sent off to the packhouse and put into bags.

French beans, as well as being easy to grow and no trouble to get picked, are also easy to prepare for the pot. All you have to do is break off each end and they are ready. Cook them whole or, if they are quite long, snap them in half.

153

Like runner beans, French beans have a high moisture content and need little water or liquid added while they cook. Put 450g (1 lb) into a saucepan with some chopped herbs (thyme, marjoram or savory are the best) and 3cm (1 in) of water and set them on a low heat for 20 minutes, by which time they will be just tender. To give them an attractive glaze and make them even better to eat add 15g (½ oz) butter or 30ml (2 tablespoons) of olive oil to the pan as well.

For extra flavour, soften an onion in the butter first, and for a special dish add 100g (4 oz) lean, diced bacon.

French beans are one of the most popular vegetables in many Italian restaurants, so give them a Mediterranean flavour with green peppers and olives.

French Beans and Green Peppers

450g (1 lb) French beans
2 medium sized green peppers
45ml (3 tablespoons) olive oil
1 clove garlic, finely chopped
15ml (1 tablespoon) tomato
  purée

10 green olives (stoned and
  quartered)
15ml (1 tablespoon) chopped
  thyme
75ml (⅛ pt) stock

Top and tail the beans. Core and slice the peppers. Heat the oil in a saucepan on a low heat and stir in the garlic and tomato purée. When they are well-blended, mix in the beans, peppers, olives and thyme. Pour in the stock and bring it gently to the boil. Cover and simmer for 20 minutes.

For this salad, as the beans cook in the oil and vinegar, they absorb all the vinegary flavour and leave the oil for the dressing, which will be creamy and almost set, like scrambled eggs. The salad will be bright green and yellow, flecked with thyme, and topped with the chopped white. Serve it with cold meat or as a first course.

French Bean and Egg Salad

225g (8 oz) French beans
60ml (4 tablespoons) olive oil
30ml (2 tablespoons) white wine
  vinegar
15ml (1 tablespoon) chopped
  thyme

1 clove garlic, finely chopped
freshly ground black pepper
4 eggs

Top and tail the beans and break them into 3cm (1 in) pieces. Put them into a saucepan with the oil, vinegar, thyme, garlic and pepper. Cover,

154

and set them on a low heat for 20 minutes, turning them occasionally. Soft boil the eggs. Put the yolks into a bowl and chop the whites. Lift the beans from the saucepan and cool them. Gradually beat any oil, vinegar and thyme left in the saucepan into the egg yolks. Mix the dressing into the beans and put them in a bowl. Scatter the chopped whites over the top.

If you can't find any chilles for this recipe, use Tabasco sauce (5-10ml (1-2 teaspoons) according to taste) and one small green pepper. Three chilles will make a really hot dish, two a medium-hot, and one will give just a touch of hotness. Use as many (or as few) as you like.

Hot French Bean and Tomato Salad

225g (½ lb) French Beans
1-3 green chilles
175g (6 oz) ripe tomatoes
30ml (2 tablespoons) olive oil
1 clove garlic, finely chopped

5ml (1 teaspoon) paprika
225g (8 oz) firm tomatoes
30ml (2 tablespoons) chopped
* chervil or parsley if there is no*
* chervil available*

Top and tail the beans. Deseed and finely chop the chilles (don't lick your fingers!). Scald, skin and roughly chop the ripe tomatoes. Put the beans, chilles and ripe tomatoes into a saucepan with the oil, garlic and paprika. Cover the pan and set it on a moderate heat for 20 minutes. Turn everything into a bowl and cut the beans into 3cm (1 in) lengths. Let everything get quite cold. Scald, skin and deseed the firm tomatoes and slice them. Add the to the salad with the chervil. Let the salad stand for 30 minutes before serving for all the flavours to blend.

This dish with ham can be served as a first course or as part of a main meal with poached or fried eggs, a slice of quiche or an omelette.

French Beans and Ham

450g (1 lb) French beans
350g (12 oz) lean ham (cut from
* the bone or home-cooked)*
25g (1 oz) butter
1 large onion, thinly sliced
1 clove garlic, finely chopped

150ml (¼ pt) stock
15ml (1 tablespoon) chopped
* savory*
15ml (1 tablespoon) grated
* Parmesan cheese*

Top and tail the beans. Dice the ham. Melt the butter in a saucepan on a low heat. Put in the onion and garlic and cook them until the onion is soft. Mix in the beans, ham and savory. Pour in the stock. Cover the pan and keep it on the low heat for 25 minutes. Move everything around occasionally for even cooking. Serve with the Parmesan cheese sprinkled on the top.

Cooked with neck of lamb, French beans add flavour to the stock and themselves pick up the richness of the meat. The simple sauce coats everything and brings the dish together well, and it is clear, so it doesn't mask the colour of the beans.

French Beans and Lamb in the Pot

*1.125kg (2½ lb) neck of lamb
  (scrag end)*

For boiling:

stock to cover
6 black peppercorns
*1 small onion, cut in half but not
  peeled*
1 small carrot
*1 stick of celery and a few leaves
  (if available)*

bouquet garni

450g (1 lb) French beans
15ml (1 tablespoon) flour
*15ml (1 tablespoon) chopped
  thyme*
juice ½ lemon

Put the lamb into a large saucepan with the boiling ingredients. Set them on a moderate heat, bring them to the boil and skim. Cover and simmer for 1¼ hours. Top and tail the beans and put them into the saucepan for the final 15 minutes. Lift the lamb and beans from the pan. Strain the stock into a bowl and let it cool so the fat almost sets on top. Take all the meat from the bones and cut it into 2cm (¾ in) dice. Chop the beans into 3cm (1 in) lengths. Skim all the fat from the surface of the stock and put 15ml (1 tablespoon) into a saucepan. Measure off 275ml (½ pt) stock for the sauce. Heat the fat in the saucepan on a low heat. Stir in the flour and gradually mix in the stock. Bring the sauce to the boil, stirring, add the thyme and simmer for two minutes. Add the lemon juice and fold in the lamb and beans. Reheat gently but don't cook for any longer than half a minute or they will become overcooked.

The beans in this salad should be only just cooked and the chicken made moist by mixing it into the hot dressing.

Chicken, French Bean and Lemon Salad

*1 small cooked chicken (1.125-
  1.5kg (2½-3 lb) before
  cooking)*
450g (1 lb) French beans

*15ml (1 tablespoon) chopped
  lemon thyme (or thyme if
  none is available)*
grated rind and juice 1 lemon

156

60ml (4 tablespoons) olive oil
1 large onion, thinly sliced
1 clove garlic, finely chopped

Dice all the meat from the chicken. Top and tail the beans and if they are long ones break each one in half. Heat the oil in a large saucepan on a moderate heat. Stir in the beans, onion, garlic and lemon thyme. Cover, and cook them for 15 minutes, stirring occasionally. Add the lemon rind and juice and let the juice bubble. Take the pan from the heat and mix in the chicken. Turn the salad into a bowl to cool.

Seed Filled Vegetables

The technical name for this family of vegetables is curcurbitacea, and it includes, marrows, courgettes, pumpkins, cucumbers, melons and squashes. They all have a high water content and a delicate flavour, and their centres are filled with flat seeds. Under this section I have included only the first three, as apart from cucumbers, none of the others are commercially grown in this country to my knowledge. Cucumbers are grouped with salad vegetables.

Pumpkins and marrows have little part in traditional British cooking, and courgettes none at all. Pumpkins, the golden fruits of autumn, were grown here earlier than the rest but were carried away by the Pilgrim Fathers to take their place in American kitchens. Marrows were a later arrival and have probably been more popular in the country than in the towns.

In recent years we have had courgettes, small and tender and not so pippy. They have become just as popular, if not more so, than the enormous varieties.

Pumpkins are also beginning to make a small comeback, so now we have all three. Each has its own specific qualities so we can cook them all differently and make the most of them.

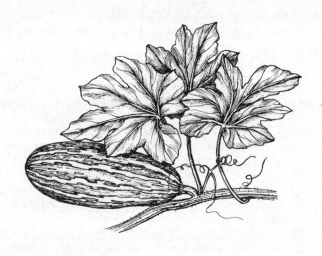

Marrows

Marrows are a relatively recent addition to our list of vegetables, but despite this in the nineteenth and certainly twentieth centuries they have been quite popular, particularly in country districts where a few plants could conveniently fill a small corner.

Although marrows were around in Roman times, they were unknown after this until the late eighteenth century, when they seem to have been used more for sweets than for savoury vegetable dishes. They were always referred to then as 'vegetable marrows' so as to avoid confusion with the bone marrow that had been used in sweet and savoury dishes since Medieval times. Often they were made into pies or puddings with spices or candied fruits. Hannah Glass gives a marrow pudding recipe that uses the vegetable chopped and mixed with cream, egg-yolks, sugar, brandy, sack and orange-flower water all baked in a case of puff pastry. The blandness of flavour and the slightly melon-like texture of marrow later made it an ideal ingredient in sour-sweet chutneys (often as a cheaper substitute for mangoes), and also in sugary jams. Marrow and ginger jam was and still is a great favourite.

Marrow can be rather tasteless if it is plainly boiled, but this did not deter the nineteenth century boilers and butterers and boilers and mashers. Sometimes slices were boiled, dipped in crumbs and deep-fried, and Mrs Beeton goes to all the trouble of cutting it up before cooking into sugar-loaf shapes, boiling them and then standing them upright in a dish to be coated with white sauce. She also makes a soup which sounds equally tasteless in which the marrow is boiled in stock, sieved, and then mixed with cream, with no other seasonings or flavourings.

Stuffed marrow, in later years, has provided many a poor country family with a mid-week meat substitute. Filled full of forcemeat, or if you were lucky, with sausage meat it was baked whole like a chicken or goose and served with brown gravy and potatoes, and any other seasonal vegetables.

Light, delicate marrows aren't robust enough to be used alone for wine, but there are several recipes for marrow rum in which the vegetable is used really more as a container than as an ingredient. It is hollowed out, stuffed full of Demerara sugar with sometimes some dried fruit, and then hung up and left to drip. One marrow will only make just over a pint and this was often kept as a Christmas treat and served mulled with spices.

Marrows have never been a large farm crop, being mostly grown in gardens and many of those that reach the shops now are grown on market gardens and the smaller farms.

Marrow seeds can be set directly in the field or they can be raised first in pots or trays, which are kept either in greenhouses or under cloches or polythene outside.

Cutting marrow isn't really difficult but it is awkward as they are large and cumbersome. They are put into wooden crates and sent off to shops and markets with no other forms of wrapping or packing being necessary.

Marrows are versatile in that they can be served hot or cold, which is just as well with our crazy British summer when sometimes we never know how to cook to get the better of the weather. We can eat them in the heat of the July or August sun, and in the cool of the early autumn.

You can buy two kinds of marrow now — the long cylindrical ones which can get really huge and weigh 2.5kg (5 lb) or more, and the smaller, round ones which are not so common. If you are going to chop them up in any way, either will be suitable, and for a large family the long ones are better for stuffing. When I can get them, I tend to favour the medium-sized round ones as they are easy to hollow out, will stand upright in the oven and look extremely attractive when you serve them. If you can buy the really tiny round ones, you can serve a complete half to each person instead of having to cut them into quarters and have all the stuffing fall out.

Boiling marrows is never a good idea as they tend to become sloppy and tasteless. Steaming, however, is a much better proposition and for this you can cut them into chunks or slices or hollow them out and steam them whole, or cut lengthways in half. Use a vegetable steamer or a colander covered with foil placed over a saucepan of simmering water and tuck in a mint sprig for extra flavour. Chopped marrow or one that has been cut into two needs 15 minutes in the steamer. A whole one will need 20 minutes — ten minutes for each side if you turn it over half way through.

Chopped, steamed marrow can be mixed with butter and herbs to be served hot, or with different dressings to make it into a salad. Try a yoghurt dressing with chopped mint or a pinch of curry powder.

Marrow rings can be baked alone, either in dripping or butter. Put them in a moderate oven for 45 minutes and turn them over once during cooking. Scatter over some chopped herbs just before you serve them, or, if you are using butter, some grated Parmesan cheese.

Usually, if you stuff a marrow with sausage meat you bake it in the oven for a fairly long time, but what do you do if you are in a hurry? Cut a long marrow into slices and steam them first. If you only have an open wire grill-rack, cover it with foil for this recipe.

Quick-Stuffed Marrow

16 2cm (¾ in) thick slices from a long marrow
2 sprigs mint
16 small salad onions
900g (2 lb) good butcher's sausage meat
30ml (2 tablespoons) tomato purée
10ml (2 teaspoons) dill seeds
8 firm tomatoes
15ml (1 tablespoon) grated Parmesan cheese

Peel and core the marrow slices. Steam them with the mint for 15 minutes, turning them once. Chop the salad onions. Put the sausage meat into a large bowl and mix in the onions, tomato purée and dill. Lay the marrow rings on a flat surface and pack the sausage meat mixture inside them. Preheat the grill to high, lay the stuffed rings on the rack and grill one side until it is brown. Turn them and brown the other side. Slice the tomatoes each into four and lay two on each marrow ring. Scatter the cheese over the tomatoes. Put the pan back under the grill until the tomatoes are hot and the cheese is beginning to brown.

Steamed marrow can provide a form of edible container for all kinds of dishes. Choose one that weighs around 900g (2lb) and is fairly even-shaped. Peel it, cut in in half lengthways and scoop out the seeds. Put a mint sprig inside the two halves and steam them for 15 minutes. Lift them out carefully, remove the mint and drain them well.

Hot, they can be filled with scrambled eggs for a lunch-time meal or with any cooked vegetables that are in season at the time, such as carrots, broad beans and peas in July and runner beans in August and September. If you leave your steamed marrow halves to get quite cold

161

you can fill them with cooked salads or tomato salads, or salads of cottage or curd cheese.

Marrows of course can be stuffed whole. How you actually prepare a marrow for stuffing depends on the filling. If it is something that will cook quickly or is already cooked, then steam the marrow first. Cut the top off and hollow out the seeds with a long spoon. Then peel both the top and the marrow. Do it this way round as if you peel it first it will be too slippery to handle! Put a sprig of mint inside it and steam it for 20 minutes, turning it once. Steam the cap as well. Fill it with the stuffing and anchor the top back on with cocktail sticks. If you are going to cook the stuffing in the marrow for a long time, then all you need do is hollow it out and peel it. If your marrow is a long one, prop the cap end up when it is in the oven on a wedge of bread or a long potato, so all the stuffing stays inside.

Here is a recipe for a steamed stuffed marrow. The cheese and the sauce should make the amounts sufficient for four, but if you have hearty appetites, use a larger marrow and increase the stuffing in proportion, leaving the sauce the same.

Marrow Stuffed With Smoked Fish and Cheese

1 marrow weighing around 900g (2 lb)

1 sprig mint
450g (1 lb) smoked cod fillet

Flavourings for fish and milk:

2 slices onion
2 bayleaves
2 blades mace

2 bouquets garnis
12 black peppercorns

For the sauce:

25g (1 oz) butter
15ml (1 tablespoon) flour
275ml (½ pt) milk

50g (2 oz) grated Farmhouse
Cheddar cheese

For the filling:

50g (2 oz) grated Farmhouse
Cheddar cheese
15ml (1 tablespoon) chopped
parsley

15ml (1 tablespoon) chopped
thyme
2.5ml (¼ teaspoon) ground mace

For cooking:

Little melted butter

For finishing:

15ml (1 tablespoon) browned
granary bread crumbs

15ml (1 tablespoon) grated
Parmesan cheese

162

Cut the top off the marrow, scoop out the seeds and peel it. Steam it for 20 minutes, turning once. Skin the fish and put it into a shallow pan with half the flavourings. Cover it with water, Bring it to the boil and simmer for five minutes. Drain it well, remove the bones, flake it and keep it warm. Infuse the milk with the remaining flavourings. Melt the butter for the sauce in a small saucepan on a low heat. Stir in the flour and let it bubble. Stir in the flavoured milk, bring it to the boil, stirring, and simmer for two minutes. Take the pan from the heat and beat in the 50g (2 ozs) cheese. Keep the sauce warm. Mix the flaked fish with the remaining cheese, parsley, thyme and ground mace. Pack the mixture into the marrow. Put on the cap and secure it with the cocktail sticks. Lay the marrow on a heat proof dish and brush it with melted butter. Preheat the grill to high. Put the marrow under the grill and brown it. Turn and brown the other side. Pour over the sauce and scatter over the crumbs and Parmesan cheese. Put the marrow back under the grill and brown the top again.

Here are some traditional flavours to bake inside a marrow. This turns out like a hot, savoury terrine surrounded by a shell of marrow. If you have any left, it is ideal served cold with mustard. The marrow will keep it fresh, but if you don't like the idea of cold roasted marrow, throw it away the next day and just serve the middle.

Marrow Stuffed with Pork, Sage and Onion

1 fairly large marrow weighing 1.125-1.5kg (3-3½ lb)
350g (12 ozs) belly of pork
100g (4 oz) streaky bacon
350g (12 oz) good butcher's sausage meat

freshly ground black pepper
40g (1½ oz) bacon fat or dripping
2 medium onions, finely chopped
12 chopped sage leaves

Preheat the oven to 180° 350°F) Gas 4.
  Cut the top of the marrow. Scoop out the seeds and peel the main part and the cap. Put the pork and the bacon through the fine blade of the mincer. Mix them with the sausage meat and season with the pepper. Melt 15g (½ oz) of the dripping in a frying pan on a low heat. Put in the onion and cook it until it is soft. Mix it into the pork with the sage. Press all the filling into the marrow. Secure the cap with cocktail sticks. Put the remaining dripping in a roasting tin and put it into the oven to melt. Put the marrow in the tin with the cap end propped up, and baste it well. Put it into the oven for 1¼ hours, basting several times. Serve it with the following sage and onion sauce handed separately.

This is a good, dark brown sauce which isn't too thick. The stuffed marrow isn't by any means the only thing you can serve it with. Pour it over plain, steamed marrow, or over new potatoes, or in the winter serve it with parsnips and potatoes baked in their jackets. It also goes with plain grilled sausages or roast beef.

Sage and Onion Sauce for Stuffed Marrow

25g (1 oz) pork dripping
1 medium onion, finely chopped
15ml (1 tablespoon) wholemeal
   flour
275ml (½ pt) stock

grated rind and juice 1 lemon
15ml (1 tablespoon)
   Worcestershire sauce
12 chopped sage leaves

Melt the dripping in a saucepan on a low heat. Put in the onion and let it brown. Stir in the flour and brown it. Stir in the stock and bring it to the boil. Add the lemon rind and juice, Worcestershire sauce and sage. Cover and simmer for 30 minutes.

This salad recipe can conveniently be served either hot or cold and it is equally good in each case.
   Savory is not a herb often associated with marrow, but with dill it makes a fresh green salad that is excellent with pork.

Marrow, Dill and Savory Salad

1 small marrow, weighing
   around 900g (2 lb)
60ml (4 tablespoons) olive oil
1 large onion, thinly sliced
1 clove garlic, finely chopped

5ml (1 teaspoon) dill seeds
30ml (2 tablespoons) white wine
   vinegar
30ml (2 tablespoons) chopped
   savory

Peel the marrow. Cut it in half lengthways and scoop out the seeds. Cut each half into 0.75cm (¼ in slices). Heat the oil in a large saucepan on a low heat. Put in the onion, garlic and dill, cover and cook them gently for five minutes. Stir in the marrow, cover again and cook for ten minutes more. Stir in the vinrgar and savory. Let the vinegar bubble and take the pan from the heat. Either serve the salad hot or turn it all into a bowl and let it cool completely.

Steamed marrow is made more tasty by a mint sprig, so put the two together for a light and quickly-cooked dish with fillet of lamb.

Lamb Marrow, Mint and Mustard

675-900g (1½-2 lb) fillet of lamb
1 small marrow weighing around
   675g (1½ lb)

150ml (¼ pt) dry white wine
25g (1 oz) butter
1 large onion, thinly sliced

10ml (2 teaspoons) Dijon
  mustard

15ml (1 tablespoon) chopped
  mint

Cut the meat into small, thin slivers. Peel the marrow, cut it in half lengthways and remove the seeds. Cut each half lengthways again and chop it into slices about 0.75cm (¼ in thick). Mix the mustard and wine together. Melt the butter in a large frying pan or sauté pan on a high heat. Brown the pieces of lamb, moving them around most of the time. Remove them and set them aside. Lower the heat, cool the pan a little and put in the onion. Cook it until it is soft. Mix in the marrow. Pour in the wine and mustard, raise the heat to moderate and bring them to the boil, scraping in any residue in the bottom of the pan. Stir in the mint and replace the lamb. Cover and cook on a very low heat for 20 minutes.

Marrow soups can be uninteresting without the addition of various spices and herbs. This one, flavoured with ginger, has a creamy texture and is light, creamy green in colour.

Marrow and Ginger Soup

1 marrow weighing about 900g
  (2 lb)
25g (1 oz) butter
1 large onion, thinly sliced
1 clove garlic, finely chopped
10ml (2 teaspoons) ground
  ginger

850ml (1½ pt) stock
Bouquet garni
30ml (2 tablspoons) mango
  chutney
15ml (1 tablespoon) chopped
  mint

Peel and core the marrow and chop it into small, thin pieces. Melt the butter in a large, heavy saucepan on a low heat. Stir in the marrow, onion, garlic and ginger. Cover and cook them gently for five minutes. Pour in the stock and bring it to the boil. Add the bouquet garni, cover, and simmer for 15 minutes. Cool the soup a little, remove the bouquet garni and work it in a blender until it is smooth. Put the chutney into the blender. (Try not to use the great big pieces that you sometimes get in the jar.) Work the soup for about 15 seconds more. Return it to the pan and reheat it gently. Pour it either into a large tureen or into individual serving bowls and scatter the chopped mint over the top.

Courgettes

Courgettes or baby marrows have only been grown in this country for a very short time, but sometimes, in the nineteenth century, larger varieties were cut while they were still small. Eliza Acton recommends that you should gather marrows 'when not larger than a turkey's egg'. That sounds more like a courgette-size than a marrow. She boils them in their skins and peels and deseeds them afterwards. Then she either serves them, buttered, on toast, deep fries them in crumbs, or stews them in butter, gravy or sauce.

Actual courgettes were first grown in Britain in the 1950s by enterprising gardeners, eager to find something new to fill their greenhouses and their cooking pots; and gradually, as more foreign and then unusual food found its way into our more cosmopolitan cities, the demand for them began to increase. Although still not grown on an exceptionally large scale, they are generally successful and can yield around six tons an acre; and during July, August and September at least, we can keep ourselves well-supplied.

They are a heat-loving vegetable, and as such have to be raised from seed under glass early in the year and transplanted outside during April being set by machine or hand.

As with most of the summer vegetables, cutting courgettes can be thirsty and tiring work, particularly if the weather is hot, but the ladies that I saw out in the fields in bikini tops and rolled-up jeans seemed to be enjoying it. Each one took charge of a row and stooped to inspect every plant and cut off all the courgettes that were ready with a small, sharp knife. They put them into baskets first and, when they were full, emptied them into large plastic crates that were taken off by a tractor to the packhouse. Here, they were put into 10 pound boxes, covered by a window wrapper to make them look attractive, and put into a small cold store to keep them fresh until they went to market.

If courgettes are regularly cut, the plants go on producing fruit rapidly and so every day throughout the season the work is the same.

Most of the courgettes that I saw being cut were even-sized, on average about 15cm (6 in) long and 3-4cm (1-1½ in) in diameter, giving about six to the pound. This is just about perfect for all kinds of recipes, and if you fancy courgettes for dinner but are not quite sure what you are going to do with them, get them this size and you won't go far wrong. They are neither too large for slicing nor too small for stuffing.

Unlike marrows, the skin of courgettes becomes soft and tender when you cook them, so there is no need at all for peeling. Just give them a quick wipe with a damp cloth. Then you can cut them and cook them in all manner of ways.

Slice them into rounds about 0.5cm (¼ in) thick and sauté them either alone or with sliced onions until they are golden. Just before serving them, sprinkle them with some Parmesan cheese or some chopped thyme.

You can also cut them into lengthways halves or slices, brush them with melted butter, and grill them.

Grilled Courgettes with Lemon Butter

6 small courgettes
25g (1 oz) softened butter
grated rind 1 lemon
15ml (1 tablespoon) chopped
    parsley

1 clove garlic, very finely
    chopped

Wipe the courgettes and cut off the stalks. Cut them in half lengthways. Beat the butter, lemon rind, parsley and garlic together. Preheat the grill to high. Lay the courgettes on the grill-rack, cut-side down and spread half the butter on the rounded sides. Grill them for five minutes. Turn the courgettes over and spread over the rest of the butter. Put them back under the grill for a further five minutes.

You can take a leaf out of Eliza Acton's book and cook courgettes whole. If you buy very small ones about 10cm (3 in) long and 1.5-2cm (½-¾ in) in diameter, they are absolutely delicious if you simmer them whole in butter.

Wipe them and trim away the stalk. Use 25g (1 oz) butter to 450g

(1 lb) courgettes. Melt it in a wide-based saucepan on a very low heat. Turn the courgettes in it, cover them and simmer for 20 minutes, turning them several times during cooking. Serve them plain with any butter left poured over them. Be careful not to be too eager, for they hold their heat for some time!

A way of cooking medium sized courgettes whole that preserves all their flavour is to wrap them in oiled foil and bake them. If the oven is set at 180°C (350°F)/Gas 4, you will need to cook them for 45 minutes if you are going to serve them plain. If, however, you are going to hollow them out and stuff them, they will only need half an hour as in this case you need to keep the outsides fairly firm.

As an alternative to serving courgettes hot as an accompaniment, have them cold as a light summer first course.

Cold Courgettes Stuffed with Cheese

4 medium sized courgettes   *grated rind and juice 1 lemon*
little oil for greasing   *15ml (1 tablespoon) chopped*
175g (6 oz) curd cheese   *fennel*

Preheat the oven to 180°C (350°F)/Gas 4.
   Wrap the courgettes in oiled foil and bake them for 30 minutes. Leave the stalks intact and cut them in half lengthways. Let them cool completely. Scoop out the flesh and chop it finely. Mix it in a bowl with the cheese, lemon rind and juice and fennel. Pile the mixture back into the shells and chill very lightly.

The mild, subtle flavour of courgettes makes them the perfect accompaniment to chicken.

Chicken and Courgettes with Lemon and Cheese Sauce

One 1.5kg (3-3½ lb) roasting   *100g (4 oz) button mushrooms,*
  chicken, jointed   *thinly sliced*
25g (1 oz) butter   *150ml (¼ pt) dry white wine*
1 small onion, finely chopped   *grated rind and juice 1 lemon*
1 clove garlic, finely chopped   *150ml (¼ pt) double cream*
450g (1 lb) courgettes, cut in   *15ml (1 tablespoon) Parmesan*
  0.5cm (¼ in) slices   *cheese*

Melt the butter in a large sauté pan or shallow, flameproof casserole on a moderate heat. Put in the chicken joints, skin-side down first and brown them on both sides. Remove them and set them aside. Lower the heat and stir in the onion and garlic. Cook them until the onion is soft. Stir in the courgettes and mushrooms and let them get well-

168

coated with the butter. Pour in the wine and bring it to the boil. Add the lemon rind and juice. Replace the chicken joints and cover them with the courgettes. Cover the pan and set it on a low heat for 25 minutes. Lift out the chicken and courgettes with a perforated spoon and put them on a serving dish. Pour the cream into the casserole and stir it around on a moderate heat for two minutes. Stir in the cheese and take the pan from the heat as soon as it has melted. Pour the sauce over the chicken to serve.

If stewing beef is cooked with white wine, it can also make a light-tasting summer dish. It usually needs long cooking, which would be too much for the courgettes, so add them half way through and brighten up the appearance at the last minute with tomatoes.

Casserole of Beef and Courgettes

900g (2 lb) lean stewing beef
60ml (4 tablespoons) olive oil
1 large onion, thinly sliced
1 large or 2 small cloves garlic,
* finely chopped*
150ml (¼ pt) dry white wine
150ml (¼ pt) stock

4 flat anchovy fillets, pounded to
* a paste*
30ml (2 tablespoons) mixed
* chopped thyme, marjoram*
* and savory*
450g (1 lb) small courgettes
4 firm tomatoes

Preheat the oven to 180°C (350°F)/Gas 4.
Cut the beef into 3cm (1 in) cubes. Heat the oil in a heavy flameproof casserole on a high heat. Put in the beef and brown it well, in two batches if necessary. Remove it and set it aside. Lower the heat, stir in the onion and garlic and cook them until the onion is soft. Pour in the wine and stock and bring them to the boil, stirring in any residue from the bottom of the pan. Stir in the pounded anchovies, replace the meat and add the herbs. Cover the casserole and put it into the oven for 45 minutes. Cut the courgettes into 0.5cm (¼ in) slices. Add them to the casserole and put it back for a further 45 minutes. Scald, skin and deseed the tomatoes and add them to the casserole for the final two minutes of cooking so they just heat through.

Serve this salad as a first course.

Egg and Courgette Salad

450g (1 lb) courgettes
12 medium sized salad onions
* (white and green parts)*
60ml (4 tablespoons) olive oil
1 large clove garlic, finely
* chopped*

30ml (2 tablespoons) chopped
* parsley*
30ml (2 tablespoons) wine
* vinegar*
4 hard boiled eggs

169

Slice the courgettes thinly. Chop the onions into 3cm (1 in) lengths. Heat the oil in a frying pan on a low heat. Mix in the courgettes, onions and garlic. Cover the pan and keep it on a very low heat for ten minutes, moving everything around once. Add the parsley. Pour in the vinegar and let it bubble. Take the pan from the heat and turn the salad into a bowl to cool. Chill it slightly. Slice the eggs into rounds. Either use one serving bowl or four small ones. Put in half the courgettes, arrange all the egg slices on top, and then finish with all the remaining salad. Serve it with brown bread and butter or pumpernickel.

At the beginning of the season, before the seeds get too large, you can put thinly sliced raw courgettes into salads. They are perfect in a simple dressing of olive oil.

Raw Courgette Salad

350g (12 oz) courgettes
60ml (4 tablespoons) olive oil
1 large onion, thinly sliced
1 clove garlic, finely chopped

225g (½ lb) firm tomatoes
15ml (1 tablespoon) chopped
basil

Slice the courgettes thinly. Heat the oil in a frying pan on a low heat. Put in the onion and garlic and cook them gently until the onion is soft. Mix in the courgettes and when they are well coated with oil, take the pan from the heat. Halve and slice the tomatoes and mix them into the salad with the basil. Turn the salad into a bowl to cool completely. The courgettes just absorb the oil enough to be succulent but stay firm. The tomatoes and basil together provide all the sharpness needed without having to use vinegar.

Pumpkin

There seem to be more and more of these once rare vegetables around these days as their potential has been realized in both sweet and savoury dishes, and their popularity has encouraged growers to increase their crop.

Pumpkins were introduced from France in the sixteenth century and then they were called 'pompions' or 'pompians'. The poor hollowed out all the seeds and pith, stuffed the space with apples and spices, resealed the outside, and baked the pumpkin whole. It must have taken a good long time but the pulpy, spicy result must have been worth it.

In the kitchens of the well-to-do, pumpkin was put into pies with herbs, spices, sugar, beaten eggs and dried fruits. These sometimes took the form of raised pies, filled with alternative layers of pumpkin, apples and currants.

During the eighteenth century the pumpkin for some reason went out of fashion. It was occasionally grown in country gardens and the poor in some orchard counties used still to mix it with chopped apples and put it into pasties and pies to make the meat or bacon go further. Pumpkins were little used in the nineteenth century and were regarded as a particularly American vegetable, used mainly for their thanksgiving pies.

171

Now, most pumpkins are grown on market gardens or on very small areas in the corners of fields, and they usually find their way into local wholesalers or direct to nearby greengrocers.

The seeds can be set outside like marrows, or they can first be raised under cover. The seeds are set in pots in greenhouses early in the year, and the small plants are put outside at the end of May or the beginning of June. From then on they get quite rampant and trail all over the place. There are usually about three pumpkins on each plant and they sit amongst the big leaves getting larger and larger and more and more golden until the time comes to cut them either at the end of September or beginning of October.

Usually, pumpkins are sold whole, but some shops do cut off thick slices and sell them by the pound. They keep well in a cool place and will probably last for a week, and every day a slice can be cut off and used for something different.

A slice of pumpkin that weighs about 450g (1 lb) before the seeds and rind are removed will give you about 350g (¾ lb) of raw pumpkin. For some dishes, the pumpkin has to be puréed first. To get 575ml (1 pt) of purée you need 675-725g (1½-1¾ lb) of chopped raw pumpkin. Simmer it gently in a covered saucepan with 0.75cm (½ in) of water until it is thick and pulpy.

You can bake pumpkin very plainly in dripping or butter, either in 3cm (1 in) slices or in 3cm (1 in) cubes. It needs 30 minutes at a temperature of 200°C (400°F)/Gas 6, or you can roast it round the joint at a lower temperature for 45 minutes.

Boiled pumpkin is not to be recommended. Like marrow, it becomes tasteless and rather soggy. Here again, steaming is much the better way. Cut the pumpkin into slices about 1-2cm (½-¾ in) thick rather like a melon, remove the seeds, but keep the rind on. Put the slices into a vegetable steamer (or a colander covered with foil) and cook them over lightly simmering water for 12 minutes, turning them once. When they are done, you can make them sweet or savoury. For a sweet, pour over melted honey flavoured with cinnamon. The following recipe is for a savoury first course.

Steamed Pumpkin with Bacon and Anchovy Sauce

4 slices of a large pumpkin or 8
from a small one cut 1-2cms
(½-¾ in) thick
4 collar rashers bacon
4 flat anchovy fillets

45ml (3 tablespoons) olive oil
1 clove garlic, finely chopped
15ml (1 tablespoon) wine
vinegar

Cut the seeds from the pumpkin slices, but leave on the rind. Steam them for 12 minutes, turning them once. Grill the bacon rashers until they are crisp. Chop them finely. Chop the anchovies. Heat the oil in a small frying pan on a moderate heat. Put in the garlic and brown it. Pour in the vinegar and bring it to the boil. Put in the bacon and anchovies. Swirl them all around and pour the sauce over the slices of pumpkin.

Pumpkin makes a delicious creamy base for a curry when it is puréed, or it can be flavoured with curry powder and cooked only long enough to let the pieces soften. Then it can be served as an accompaniment to curry or as a vegetable with any plain meat dish, sausages, cold ham or even bacon and eggs. This next recipe also goes well with a wedge of strong cheese for lunch.

Curried Pumpkin and Lemon

675-900g (1½-2 lb) pumpkin
  weighed before removing
  seeds and rind
25g (1 oz) butter
1 large onion, thinly sliced
15ml (1 tablespoon) chopped
  thyme

15ml (1 tablespoon) curry
  powder
juice ½ lemon
1 bayleaf

Chop the pumpkin into small, thin pieces. Melt the butter in a frying pan on a low heat. Put in the onion and cook it until it is soft. Stir in the pumpkin, thyme, curry powder and lemon juice. Tuck in the bayleaf. Cover tightly and keep the pan on a low heat for 15 minutes, stirring occasionally.

Cooked in stews and casseroles, thinly sliced pumpkin purées down to make a thick, creamy sauce. Use paprika again, and make a goulash with carraway seeds and gherkins.

Pumpkin Goulash

900g (2 lb) lean stewing beef
24 small button onions
25g (1 oz) lard
15ml (1 tablespoon) paprika
10ml (2 teaspoons) carraway
  seeds

150ml (¼ pt) dry white wine
275ml (½ pt) stock
450g (1 lb) chopped pumpkin
2 pickled Hungarian gherkins,
  very finely chopped

Preheat the oven to 180°C (350°F)/Gas 4.
  Dice the beef into 3cm (1 in) pieces and peel the onions. Heat the lard in a flameproof casserole on a high heat. Put in the beef and brown it all over. Remove it and set it aside. Lower the heat, put in the onions

173

and cook them until they begin to look transparent. Stir in the paprika and carraway seeds, wine and stock. Bring them all to the boil, stirring. Add the pumpkin and the beef. Cover and put the casserole into the oven for 1½ hours. Put in the chopped gherkins and return it to the oven for a further 15 minutes.

This is a spicy-hot dish using minced beef in which the pumpkin is used to make just a small amount of tasty sauce.

Hot Spiced Beefburgers with Pumpkin Sauce

For the burgers:

900g (2 lb) best quality minced beef
25g (1 oz) butter
1 medium onion, finely chopped
1 large or 2 small cloves garlic, finely chopped

2.5ml (½ teaspoon) ground allspice
15ml (1 tablespoon) Worcestershire sauce
12 chopped sage leaves

For the sauce:

15g (½ oz) butter
1 medium onion, finely chopped
275ml (½ pt) pumpkin purée
2.5ml (½ teaspoon) ground allspice
15ml (1 tablespoon) Worcestershire sauce

15ml (1 tablespoon) tomato purée
10ml (2 teaspoons) molasses or black treacle
15ml (1 tablespoon) wine vinegar

Put the beef into a mixing bowl. Melt the butter in a frying pan on a low heat. Put in the onion and garlic and cook them until the onion is soft. Tip all the contents of the pan into the beef and mix them in well. Beat in the Worcester sauce, allspice and sage. Form the mixture into 16 small burgers about 10cm (2½ in) across and 0.75cm (½ in) thick. Set them on a flat plate in a cool place for half an hour to take shape. To make the sauce, melt the butter in the frying pan on a low heat. Put in the onion and let it brown. Stir in the pumpkin purée and all the rest of the ingredients and bring them to the boil. Keep the sauce warm. Preheat the grill to high and grill the burgers as close to the heat as possible until they are well-browned on each side. Serve each burger with a blob of sauce on top.

Here we have the well-tried partnership of apples and pumpkin. The apples give the sharpness and the pumpkin the creaminess, and both combine to make a sauce for pork chops.

Pork Chops with Pumpkin and Apple Sauce

4 loin pork chops
1 large clove garlic
2.5ml (½ teaspoon) fine sea salt
10ml (2 teaspoons) finely
chopped rosemary
30ml (2 tablespoons) pork fat or
15g (½ oz) butter

1 large onion, thinly sliced
1 large cooking apple, peeled,
quartered, cored and sliced
350g (¾ lb) chopped pumpkin
(from a 450g (1 lb) slice)
150ml (¼ pt) dry cider

Crush the garlic, salt and rosemary together and rub them into the surface of the chops. Heat the fat or butter in a large frying pan on a moderate heat. Put in the chops and brown them on both sides. Remove them and set them aside. Lower the heat, put in the onion and cook it until it is soft. Stir in the apple, pumpkin and cider and bring them to the boil. Replace the chops, cover, and set the pan on a low heat for 30 minutes, stirring occasionally. Take out the chops and put them on a warm serving dish. Keep them warm. Rub all the rest of the contents of the pan through a sieve. Put the resulting sauce into a small saucepan and reheat it gently. Spoon it over the chops to serve.

Pumpkin purée and curd cheese seem an unusual combination but this cheese-on-toast with a difference makes a delicious lunch-time snack.

Pumpkin and Cheese on Toast

25g (1 oz) butter
1 large onion, thinly sliced
275ml (½ pt) pumpkin purée
225g (8 oz) curd cheese
juice ½ lemon

2.5ml (½ teaspoon) ground
allspice
2.5ml (½ teaspoon) ground mace
8 small or 4 large slices buttered
brown toast

Melt the butter in a frying pan on a low heat. Put in the onion and cook it until it is golden. Stir in the pumpkin, cheese, lemon juice and spices and heat them through. Pile the mixture onto the toast.

Put pumpkin with eggs, cheese and tomatoes to make a light and fluffy-textured first course for four or a lunch dish for two.

Pumpkin, Cheese and Tomato Savoury

225g (8 oz) chopped pumpkin
2 eggs, beaten
1 small onion, finely chopped
100g (4 oz) grated Farmhouse
Cheddar cheese
30ml (2 tablespoons) chopped
chervil (or parsley)

5ml (1 teaspoon) Tabasco sauce
5ml (1 teaspoon) paprika
225g (½ lb) tomatoes
thickly buttered 28cm (8 in)
diameter pie plate or flat
oven-proof dish

Preheat the oven to 200°C (400°F)/Gas 6.

Put the pumpkin into a saucepan with 0.6cm (¼ in) of water. Set it on a low heat for 20 minutes until it is thick and pulpy. Put the eggs into a bowl and mix in the pumpkin, chopped raw onion, chervil, 75g (3 oz) of the cheese and the Tabasco sauce. Pour the mixture into the buttered dish. Cut the tomatoes into rounds and lay them on top. Sprinkle over the remaining cheese and then the paprika. Bake in the centre of the oven for 25 minutes.

Pumpkin, like root vegetables can be made into soups without having to be thickened with milk or flour. This one would be quite expensive during the winter when the price of tomatoes is high, but at the beginning of the pumpkin season they are still quite cheap and plentiful. Together, they make a creamy, golden-orange soup, slightly tangy and flavoured with herbs.

Creamy Pumpkin and Tomato Soup

25g (1 oz) butter
1 medium onion, finely chopped
350g (12 oz) chopped pumpkin
450g (1 lb) tomatoes, scalded,
  skinned and roughly chopped

575ml (1 pt) stock
30ml (2 tablespoons) chopped
  mixed herbs

Melt the butter in a saucepan on a low heat. Put in the onion and cook it until it is soft. Mix in the pumpkin and tomatoes. Cover and simmer gently for ten minutes. Stir in the stock, bring it to the boil and simmer for ten minutes. Work the soup in a blender until it is smooth. Return it to the pan and stir in the herbs. Reheat to serve.

Mushrooms

Unless we consider such exotic and expensive things like truffels and morrels, mushrooms are certainly in a class of their own, as they are the only fungus that we use regularly as a vegetable. There are many edible varieties growing wild in Britain, including the famous ceps and chanterelles, but in Britain only field mushrooms and horse mushrooms are accepted, any others being regarded as 'toadstools' and not to be picked.

Mushrooms were eaten by the ancient Greeks and also by the Romans who served them as a small appetizer at the beginning of the meal. They were certainly growing wild in Britain at the time of the Roman occupation and probably even before. A recipe for a mushroom and leek soup appears in a cookery book written in 1390, but they were never really widely used in later Medieval times, being scarce and surrounded with mystery because they are able to grow in the dark and the fact that there are quite a number of poisonous varieties. At the time, they were more often put into medicines and potions.

In the seventeenth and eighteenth centuries mushrooms increased in popularity. They were very often pickled and used to flavour meat dishes and gravies and to garnish salads. The big, flat dark ones were slowly stewed with vinegar and spices to make ketchups.

Nowadays, we don't have to rely on the autumn crop of wild mushrooms. Cultivated mushrooms are grown all the year round under controlled conditions in specially built sheds. Cultivation was attempted in a few country homes in the eighteenth century, but I couldn't say with what success. Hannah Glasse's method is so amusing that I can't resist quoting it. 'To raise mushrooms. Cover an old hot-bed three or four inches thick with fine garden mould, and cover that three or four inches thick with mouldy long muck of a horse muck-hill, or old rotten stubble; when the bed has lain some time thus prepared, boil any mushrooms that are not fit for use, in water, and throw the water on your prepared bed; in a day or two after, you will have the best small button mushrooms.' I wonder!

Since the last war, more and more mushroom farms have been set up in this country, making mushrooms one of the most reliable vegetables on the market.

You can buy button mushrooms, ones that are just open known as cups and the really dark flat ones called flats. The buttons are best for slicing raw into salads, for braising whole and for garnishing. The cups can be cooked whole or sliced, and can be put into stews and soups. The flats are good for frying, grilling or baking whole.

Never peel mushrooms as most of their goodness lies just under the surface. The flavour is far better, too, if you leave them intact. Never, either, scrape away the brown gills as this also takes away flavour. I must confess, I never even wash them, but if you like dip them quickly into cold water.

Flat mushrooms are the most flavoursome of them all and are often the better for being simply cooked. Here is a delicious way of baking them.

Mushrooms Baked with Lemon

8 really large flat mushrooms
40g (1½ oz) butter
juice 1 lemon

30ml (2 tablespoons) browned
granary or wholemeal bread
crumbs

Preheat the oven to 200°C (400°F)/Gas 6.

Put the butter into a large, flat ovenproof dish and put it into the oven to melt. Take the stalks from the mushrooms and reserve them. Put the caps, black side down, in the butter to coat them, and then turn them over. Roll the stalks in the butter and leave them beside the mushrooms. Pour over the lemon juice and put the dish into the oven for ten minutes. Scatter over the crumbs and put it back for a further five minutes.

Slice up open or flat mushrooms and cook them in butter. Add lemon again for flavour or perhaps a little spicy mustard.

Mushrooms and Mustard

350g (12 oz) dark, flat
* mushrooms*
40g (1½ oz) butter

10ml (2 teaspoons) English
Vineyard (or other granular
white wine) mustard

Slice the mushrooms. Melt the butter in a frying pan on a low heat. Stir in the mustard and then the mushrooms. Cover the pan and set it on a low heat for 15 minutes, stirring the mushrooms around once or twice.

The versatility of mushrooms is clearly demonstrated by cooking them

178

with other vegetables in various ways. With aubergines, they can be served in bowls as a first course or they can accompany a curry.

Curried Mushrooms and Aubergines

2 medium sized aubergines
10ml (2 teaspoons) fine sea salt
125g (4 oz) mushrooms (flat
  ones)
40g (1½ oz) butter
10ml (2 teaspoons) curry powder

2.5ml (½ teaspoon) ground
  cumin
2.5ml (½ teaspoon) ground
  coriander
juice 1 lemon

Slice the aubergines into rounds 0.75cm (¼ in) thick. Put them into a colander, sprinkle them with the salt, and leave them to drain for 30 minutes. Wash them and pat them dry with kitchen paper. Thinly slice the mushrooms. Melt the butter in a frying pan on a low heat. Stir in the mushrooms and aubergines and mix in the curry powder, cumin and coriander. Pour in the lemon juice. Cover the pan and keep it on a very low heat for ten minutes.

Braise button mushrooms and button onions together for an attractive dish to serve with roasts, grills and egg dishes.

Casserole of Button Mushrooms and Button Onions

225g (½ lb) button mushrooms
225g (½ lb) button onions
25g (1 oz) butter
150ml (¼ pt) stock

15ml (1 tablespoon) chopped
  thyme
15ml (1 tablespoon) chopped
  parsley

Preheat the oven to 190°C (375°F)/Gas 5.
  Leave the mushrooms whole. Peel the onions. Melt the butter in a flameproof casserole on a moderate heat. Put in the mushrooms and onions and let them brown, turning them frequently. Pour in the stock and add the herbs. Cover the casserole and put it into the oven for 45 minutes. Serve the vegetables in the rich brown sauce that they make for themselves.

N.B. If you are cooking anything else in the oven that requires a lower temperature (around 180°C (350°F)/Gas 4) cook the mushrooms with them for one hour.

Mushrooms and eggs can make a cheap but tasty and effective first course.

Buttered Mushrooms and Eggs

3 hard-boiled eggs
100g (4 oz) flat mushrooms
50g (2 oz) butter
30ml (2 tablespoons) chopped
 parsley

5ml (1 teaspoon) made English
 mustard
juice ½ lemon

Finely chop the eggs and mushrooms. Melt the butter in a frying pan on a moderate heat. Put in the mushrooms and cook them for three minutes. Keep the pan on the heat and stir in the eggs, parsley, mustard and lemon juice. Press the mixture into four small soufflé dishes or ramekins and chill it until it is firm. Serve them with brown toast.

Skirt of beef is one of my favourite cuts as it is tender, has very little, if any, fat, and is fairly cheap. It is also very manageable and can be slit open into pockets to be filled with tasty stuffings. I first made this recipe with wild forest mushrooms, but it works just as well with dark, flat cultivated ones.

Skirt Stuffed with Mushrooms

900g (2 lb) beef skirt cut 2cm
 (¾ in) thick

For the stuffing:

25g (1 oz) butter
1 medium onion, finely chopped
175g (6 oz) dark, flat
 mushrooms, finely chopped
50g (2 oz) granary breadcrumbs
2.5ml (½ teaspoon) ground mace
2.5ml (½ teaspoon) ground
 cloves

30ml (2 tablespoons) mixed
 chopped marjoram and thyme
30ml (2 tablespoons) chopped
 parsley
30ml (2 tablespoons) sherry

For cooking:

25g (1 oz) beef dripping
15ml (1 tablespoon) wholemeal
 flour
150ml (¼ pt) sherry minus the

30ml (2 tablespoons) taken
 out for the stuffing
175ml (7 fl oz) stock

Cut the skirt into four even-sized pieces. Using a sharp knife, carefully slit each piece to make a pocket, still joined on three sides. For the stuffing, melt the butter in a frying pan on a low heat. Put in the chopped onion and cook it until it is soft. Raise the heat to moderate. Stir in the mushrooms and cook them for two minutes. Take the pan from the heat and work in the breadcrumbs, spices and herbs. Bind the stuffing with the sherry. Stuff the pockets of skirt with this mixture. Melt the dripping in a large sauté pan or shallow flameproof casserole. Put in the pockets and brown them on both sides. Remove them and set them aside. Stir in the flour and cook it, stirring all the time, until it is a good russet brown. Stir in the sherry and stock and bring them to the boil. Replace the pockets, cover the casserole, and set it on a low heat for 50 minutes, turning the beef once so it cooks evenly.

Here are two ways of making mushrooms into a sauce.

Whiting with Mushroom Sauce

4 whiting
butter for greasing dish
juice 1 lemon
225g (8 oz) button mushrooms
40g (1½ oz) butter
40g (1½ oz) flour
625ml (¾ pt) milk infused with 1 bayleaf, 1 small slice onion, 1 blade mace, 4 black peppercorns

10ml (2 teaspoons) made English mustard
100g (4 oz) grated Farmhouse Cheddar cheese

Preheat the oven to 180°C (350°F)/Gas 4.
 Fillet the whiting. Lay the fillets on a lightly buttered oven-proof dish. Pour over the lemon juice, cover the fish with a butter paper, and bake them for 15 minutes. Make the sauce while the fish is cooking. Thinly slice the mushrooms. Melt the butter in a small saucepan on a low heat. Put in the mushrooms, cover them, and cook them gently for five minutes. Stir in the flour and let it bubble. Take the pan from the heat and stir in the milk. Bring it to the boil, stirring, and simmer for two minutes. Beat in the mustard and 75g (3 oz) of the cheese. Take the whiting from the oven and lay them on a heatproof serving dish. Strain any juices from the cooking dish into the sauce and mix them in well. Pour the sauce over the whiting and scatter the remaining cheese over the top. Put the dish under a high grill for the cheese to brown.

Lamb Chops with Mushroom and Dill Sauce

8 small lamb chops
30ml (2 tablespoons) olive oil
1 clove garlic, crushed with a pinch of sea salt

freshly ground black pepper

For the sauce:

40g (1½ oz) butter
175g (6 oz) flat mushrooms,
  finely chopped
10ml (2 teaspoons) paprika

10ml (2 teaspoons) dill seeds
625ml (¾ pt) stock
grated rind and juice 1 lemon
parsley sprigs for garnish

Mix the oil, pepper and garlic together and brush them over the chops. Let them stand while you make the sauce. Melt the butter in a small saucepan on a low heat. Add the mushrooms, cover them and simmer gently for five minutes. Stir in the paprika and dill seeds, cover again and cook for a further two minutes. Stir in the flour and then the stock. Bring it to the boil, stirring. Simmer the sauce gently for two minutes. Add the lemon rind and juice and reheat. Preheat the grill to high. Put under the chops and grill them to your liking. Arrange them on a warm serving dish, pour over the sauce and garnish with parsley sprigs.

Mushroom soups are always popular, so here is a good substantial one with bacon and cider.

Bacon and Mushroom Soup

100g (4 oz) dark, flat mushrooms
100g (4 oz) lean collar rashers
  bacon plus the rinds
1 medium onion, finely chopped
15ml (1 tablespoon) flour

575ml (1 pt) stock
275ml (½ pt) dry cider
10 chopped sage leaves
1 bayleaf

Finely chop the mushrooms. Finely chop the bacon and put it into a saucepan with the rinds and no other fat. Set it on a low heat and let it cook gently until it is cooked but not brown and there is enough fat in the pan to cook the mushrooms. Take out the rinds. Stir in the onion and mushrooms. Cover the pan and cook them gently for ten minutes. Stir in the flour and then the stock and cider. Bring them to the boil, stirring. Add the bayleaf and sage, and simmer, uncovered for 15 minutes. Remove the bayleaf before serving.

Asparagus

The luxurious vegetable, asparagus, is a native of Italy and Mediterranean France, and although a little may have been grown in the gardens of English Roman villas, its first real introduction to this country was in Elizabethan times. Even then it was only grown on a very small scale. It was boiled and served with melted butter and put both cooked and raw into salads. It was considered to stimulate the appetite and so was often served at the beginning of the meal.

Samuel Pepys is said to have loved asparagus, and throughout the seventeenth century its cultivation increased. There were many variations of the name at this time including 'sperage', 'sparage', 'sparagrass' and the most appealing of them all, 'sparrowgrass'.

Asparagus tongs were invented in 1815, but there were never any real changes in the way this superb vegetable was cooked, or any unusual and elaborate dishes made up around it. Asparagus, simply boiled, with butter or perhaps Hollandaise sauce remained the order of the day.

The elegant appearance, sweet flavour and almost creamy texture of asparagus all contribute to giving it the luxury status it most definitely deserves, but there are other, more practical reasons why it has for so long remained one of our most scarce and expensive crops.

Some asparagus is grown from seed, but most often the prospective grower buys the large root mass called the crown. I have never actually seen one of these, but I was told by one market gardener that it looks 'like an octopus with lots of legs'. Trenches about 15cm (6 in) deep are dug across the fields usually about 1 metre (3 ft) apart, and the crowns are laid in by hand at 50cm (18 in) intervals. They are covered over and in some cases earthed up so the field or plot is covered with ridges. Then comes the first clue as to why asparagus is so expensive — a two year wait before any crop at all can be gathered and any profit made.

All that can be seen of asparagus when it is growing are the soft green tender shoots poking straight out of the ground with no leaves or side shoots at all. Glancing at an asparagus bed is like looking for elusive wild orchids! To be of top-quality, asparagus spears must have tightly packed heads. If they are left for too long they will start to open out, and so however large or small the field, someone has to walk up and down the rows of plants every day inspecting each one closely, and cutting all those that are ready with a sharp knife about 6cm (2 in) below the surface. On days when the crop is fairly large, this could be quite productive, but the time taken is exactly the same when you can only find one or two boxes. Here, then, are two more reasons for the cost and scarcity: the time involved in cutting and the relative skill that is needed to insert the knife in the right place.

Another reason is the shortness of the season. There are many vegetables that can be picked or lifted over a period of months, but asparagus is only available in May and June and even then the yield per acre is very small. Then, too, the cost of cleaning, trimming, sorting and packing must be taken into consideration.

Usually I like to cook vegetables in as many different ways as possible. Boiling and buttering can in many cases be improved upon, but not with asparagus. By boiling, though, I don't mean simply immerse the whole spear under gallons of rapidly bubbling water.

The tenderest, freshest asparagus needs no more preparation than just a quick trim of the ends, but towards the end of the season you will need to gently scrape the stringy surface away from the lower part. Then tie the spears up in bundles with thread. Usually, you can allow 450g (1 lb) for four people and make 100-125g (4 oz) bundles and tie them separately so everyone gets a fair share. To prevent the tender tips from disintegrating or over-cooking, keep them always above the surface of the water, so choose a tall, narrow saucepan, and fill it to about 9cm (3 in) below the top of the spears. Salt it lightly and bring it to the boil first, then put in your bundles of asparagus, cover them, and simmer them very gently for 15 minutes. If you find the tips poke out of the top, don't jam them down with the saucepan lid, but cover the pan with foil, raising it up as high as the tips. When the asparagus is ready, lift it out and drain it and lay it on warmed plates, and serve it as a first course so you can appreciate it alone. Serve it with a dish of melted butter; or vary it a little by adding a very little finely chopped parsley and a squeeze of lemon juice to the dish as well. You can also brown the butter first, adding a little grated Parmesan to the pan just as it changes colour. In this case, pour it over the asparagus before serving. Hollandaise, or some other thickened butter sauce can also be served with plainly boiled asparagus. In the following recipe, soft-boiled eggs and lemon make one that is really creamy and light in flavour.

Asparagus with Egg and Lemon Sauce

450g (1 lb) asparagus	*grated rind and juice 1 lemon*
2 eggs	*75g (3 oz) butter*

Trim the asparagus and scrape the ends if necessary. Tie it into four separate bundles. Soft-boil the eggs. Put the yolks into a bowl and chop the whites. Mix the lemon rind and juice into the yolks and put the bowl into a saucepan of water. Set it on a low heat and keep stirring until the yolks begin to thicken. Add the butter, in small pieces, and stir until the sauce is really thick, without letting the water in the saucepan boil. Mix in the chopped whites and keep the sauce warm while you cook the asparagus for 15 minutes according to the basic method. Lay the cooked asparagus on four small plates and spoon the sauce over the top.

A good way of cooking green peas is to simmer them in cream. As the flavour of asparagus is in many ways similar, try it in the same way to make it even more extravagant.

Asparagus in Cream

450g (1 lb) asparagus   *150ml (¼ pt) double cream*
40g (1½ oz) butter   *freshly ground black pepper*

Trim the asparagus and scrape the lower ends if necessary. Choose a large saucepan or casserole with a large base big enough to take the asparagus without having to bend it too much. An oval bourgignon-type casserole is ideal. Melt the butter in the pan on a low heat. Put in the asparagus and turn it over in the butter. Cover it tightly and keep it on the heat for 15 minutes, turning it once or twice. Pour in the cream, season with the pepper, cover again and simmer for a further five minutes. Serve the asparagus on four separate plates with the cream poured over it. Accompany it with fresh granary or wholemeal bread (no butter) so you can mop up any spare cream from the plate.

If a more substantial first course is called for, cook asparagus in white wine with small but thick slices of ham — home cooked if you have it, but in any case unpressed and cut from the bone.

Asparagus and Ham

450g (1 lb) asparagus   *150ml (¼ pt) dry white wine*
25g (1 oz) butter   *15g (½ oz) kneaded butter*
350g (12 oz) ham cut in 8 small,   *30ml (2 tablespoons) chopped*
* thick slices*   * parsley*

Trim the asparagus and scrape the lower ends if necessary. Choose a saucepan or casserole as in the previous recipe. Melt the butter on a low heat. Put in the asparagus and turn it in the butter. Lay the pieces of ham on top. Pour in the wine, cover, and simmer gently for 15 minutes. Lift out the asparagus and ham and arrange them on four small plates. Whisk the kneaded butter into the wine and stir in the parsley. Simmer the sauce for one minute. Spoon it over the ham but not the asparagus.

If asparagus were cooked with a strong-flavoured meat it might be overpowered, but with white meats such as chicken or veal it is perfect. This next recipe is a good way of using up the tips of older asparagus towards the end of the season when the stems may be too tough.

Veal Escalopes with Asparagus

4 veal escalopes each weighing
   around 175g (6 oz)
25g (1 oz) butter
150ml (¼ pt) dry white wine
grated rind and juice ½ lemon
15ml (1 tablespoon) chopped
   lemon thyme (or thyme)
15ml (1 tablespoon) chopped
   parsley

tips only from 450g (1 lb)
   asparagus
60ml (4 tablespoons) double
   cream
15ml (1 tablespoon) grated
   Parmesan cheese

Melt the butter in a large frying pan on a high heat. Put in the escalopes and brown them on both sides. Remove them and set them aside. Pour in the wine and bring it to the boil, stirring in any residue in the bottom of the pan. Add the lemon juice and rind and herbs. Replace the veal and put the asparagus tips on top. Cover the pan and set it on a low heat for 30 minutes. Remove the veal and asparagus and arrange them on a warm serving dish. Raise the heat under the pan to moderate and stir in the cream. Let it bubble, still stirring, and mix in the cheese. Take the pan from the heat as soon as the cheese has melted. Pour the sauce over the veal and asparagus.

The thinnest asparagus is called in the trade 'sprue' and it is ideal for chopping up raw into salads. Keep the ingredients simple so that you can appreciate the sweetness of its flavour.
   Serve this one either as a first course or with cold beef.

Asparagus and Black Grape Salad

225g (8 oz) asparagus 'sprue'
225g (8 oz) black grapes
60ml (4 tablespoons) olive oil
30ml (2 tablespoons) tarragon
   vinegar

1 clove garlic crushed with a
   pinch of fine sea salt
15ml (1 tablespoon) chopped
   tarragon

186

Discard the tough ends of the asparagus and scrape away any stringy pieces from the rest of the stems. Chop the stems and tips into 3cm (1 in) pieces. Halve and deseed the grapes and put them into a bowl with the asparagus. Mix the oil, vinegar, garlic and tarragon together and stir them into the salad.

Salad Vegetables

Although the pottage pot was for a long time the final destination of many vegetables, raw salads have been prepared and eaten in Britain since Roman times. Then, many vegetables we now associate with salads (cucumbers, lettuce, endive and some of the roots) were served with heavily seasoned sauces which were the forerunners of the later, more simple salad dressing.

In medieval times, salads were complex and consisted of mixtures of up to 20 or more of the smaller herbs which grew in great profusion in nearly every garden. They were carefully matched to provide contrasts in flavours and colours and were often garnished with flowers. The first salad recipe was written in 1393: 'Salad. Take parsley, sage, garlic, chibols, onions, leek, borage, mints, porray, fennel and garden cresses, rue, rosemary, purslain; lave and wash them clean; pick them, pluck them small with thine hand, and mingle them with raw oil. Lay on vinegar and salt and serve it forth.' Many of these ingredients are familiar flavourers today, but they also used a whole range of other herbs which now are looked on as wild flowers, or even weeds. Alexanders was a favourite plant of which the buds were used in salads, and dandelions, red nettles, rocket and ramsons were also included. Favourite flowers were violets, primroses, cowslips and borage.

These attractive mixtures carried on into Tudor and Stuart times when they became even more elaborate. Cucumbers were reintroduced and they were soon included, sometimes alternating as a flavourer with thinly sliced lemons or other raw fruits. All kinds of flowers, including daisies and marigolds were used for garnishing, and the most popular were clove gilliflowers which were used fresh in the summer and were also pickled in wine or vinegar, or candied in sugar, for winter use. Onions, leeks, shallots and chives were used as flavourers, but by this time garlic, which had been popular in Medieval salads, had fallen from favour and was only used occasionally and in very small quantities. Dressings were simple ones: Oil, vinegar and sugar were the standard ingredients, and there were many who favoured just plain vinegar.

188

In Elizabethan times, salads began to include hard-boiled eggs, and during Lent and on other fasting days these were replaced by winkles and whelks. These salads were usually served as first course dishes and suppers.

In the seventeenth century the smaller plants, known then as 'salading' or 'small salad' were still used, mixed with the new additions such as spinach, celery, cucumbers, and lettuce, which had hitherto been pottage vegetables. Salads became very grand affairs, and as well as eggs they included cold meats, fish and poultry, and were garnished with anchovies, pickles, flowers, small colourful fruits such as barberries, redcurrants and grapes, and sometimes slices of orange or lemon. One of the most popular concoctions was called 'Salmagundy' (later corrupted to Solomongundy) which was basically an egg and herb salad, with sliced cold roast capon and anchovies.

Dressings for these main-course dishes were of the mayonnaise type, made with oil and vinegar and the yolks of hard-boiled eggs. There were also more simple side-salads consisting of one or two vegetables dressed with vinegar, oil and sugar, or vinegar alone.

In the eighteenth century, flowers were no longer popular. The only one used was the nasturtium which had been lately introduced from the West Indies. Pickles were used in all dishes at this time and those of cucumbers, broom-buds, mushrooms, ash-keys, red cabbage and beetroot were all included in salads.

Gradually, the old 'saladings' and small herbs were dropped and by the nineteenth century the most used salad vegetables were lettuce, cucumber, beetroot, radishes, chicory, mustard and cress and celery. Salads remained mixed dishes, with eggs, cold meats and fish. They were attractively arranged on a base of shredded vegetables, and the whole was coated with a creamy-textured dressing, sometimes made with olive oil and eggs, and sometimes with milk or cream.

One can see, looking at the basic ingredients, how the twentieth century standard salads consisting of a few lettuce leaves, sliced cucumbers and tomatoes, and some chopped beetroot evolved, but now, as more and more people are becoming aware of how good raw vegetables can be, salads of all kinds are being served as first courses, side dishes and main meals.

Lettuce

Lettuces these days usually mean salads but with so many of them about, why not make more of them? Base a salad on the flavour of lettuce, cook them whole, or chopped with another vegetable, or make them into soups.

Lettuces were brought to Britain by the Romans who cooked them and made them into a purée mixed with oil, wine, vinegar and herbs. They considered raw lettuces indigestible unless they had a really highly spiced dressing which included in its ingredients cumin, ginger, rue, pepper, honey and vinegar.

The most popular way of using lettuces in medieval times was to put them as flavourings into the pottage pot together with dandelions, marigolds, daisies, red nettle, chives, leeks and radishes. Several types were listed in a garden book written in 1440, but the most common was the long Cos. There was also a variety called 'lop-lettuce' which never hearted.

By the sixteenth century, lettuce was more often put with spinach and other leaves into salads, and the stalks of bolted lettuce were candied like angelica.

Lettuce has never been considered particularly special and few recipes have been written for it specifically. In the seventeenth and eighteenth centuries it was popular for soups. It was finely chopped and added to clear consommes with celery, onion and vermicelli. Later it was made into thicker soups with spinach or peas.

Eliza Acton uses the hearts to garnish a chicken and mayonnaise salad, and she also makes what she calls a 'Suffolk Salad' using shredded lettuce, minced ham, hard-boiled eggs and thin slices of chicken or veal.

Mrs Beeton says lettuces should be 'nicely blanched and eaten young', or stewed with butter, gravy or lemon juice. I have a recipe for stuffed lettuces which is probably also nineteenth century which recommends that they should be boiled for 15 minutes, opened out and filled with force-meat. Then tied up, stewed (probably in butter but it doesn't say), dipped in batter, deep-fried, sprinkled with bread crumbs and covered with white sauce. Could you, I wonder, possibly know that you were eating lettuce after such a complicated procedure?

At one time lettuce was only a warm-weather vegetable, but now, with modern methods of growing, we can buy English-grown ones for most of the year with only a small break in November and December. Not an enormous amount is grown in the winter as the process is expensive, needing controlled, glass-house conditions. Very often, in the larger nurseries, the same glass-houses are used that later house cucumbers and tomatoes, as watering and heating for all these vegetables is similar. The ground in the houses is sub-soiled, rotavated and cultivated, and the lettuces sown in December. Then they are treated with hot steam which makes them grow rapidly so they are ready for cutting in January. At the time of writing, it costs the grower 10p to produce one lettuce using this method, so no wonder they are expensive when they reach the shops.

The first outdoor lettuces that you buy in April are usually the August-sown ones which have been growing slowly but surely all through the winter. These are followed in succession by those sown in spring and early summer. On one farm that I visited, four kinds of lettuces were growing in different coloured strips in one field. There were bright green cabbage lettuces, darker green, round Webbs and long Cos, and fresh green Densities.

Each type of lettuce has its own flavour and qualities. The winter ones are soft and delicate and are best for side-salads. The round and cabbage vareties that are grown outside have fairly soft-textured leaves and a flavour which blends well with milder salad dressings and which, when cooked has a suprisingly pleasant savoury quality. Then you have the firmer and crisper round Webbs which is a good universal lettuce for all kinds of salads, and the long, crisp Cos which can go with stronger-flavoured dressings and can also be braised. In appearance, the Density is rather like a cross between a Webbs and a Cos. It is longer than it is round, but not quite as long as a Cos and slightly more opened out. The outer leaves are crisp and slightly crinkly, and the yellow heart firm and tightly-packed. It is ideal for all kinds of salads, and its outer leaves make an extremely attractive base for cold dishes or chopped meat, or eggs or flaked fish. It is also superb braised whole or cut in half and simmered on top of the stove.

Here is an example of each of these methods. If you can't get hold of densities for the first one, use the inner hearts of two Cos.

When you braise lettuce, you can vary the flavour by using all wine or all stock, adding a herb of your choice, or mixing in a little tomato pureé. Serve it as a vegetable with any kind of meat or with white fish.

Braised Density Lettuce

2 small, firm density lettuces or
   the inner hearts of 2 Cos
25g (1 oz) butter
1 medium onion, thinly sliced

75ml (⅛ pt) dry white wine
75ml (⅛ pt) stock
Bouquet garni
freshly ground black pepper

Preheat the oven to 180°C (350°F) / Gas 4.
Trim the brown part of the stalk and floppy outer leaves from the lettuces. Melt the butter in a large flameproof casserole on a low heat. Stir in the onion and cook it until it is soft. Turn the lettuces over on top of the onion until the outer leaves begin to wilt. You may have to do this one at a time as before they are cooked they take up a fair amount of room. Pack them both in when they are ready. Pour in the

wine and stock, season with the pepper and add the bouquet garni. Cover the casserole and put it into the oven for 30 minutes. To serve, cut the lettuces in half lengthways and trim away the tougher, lower end of the stalk, keeping the rest in tact. Lay the halves in a warm serving dish and spoon over all the onion and a little of the stock and wine sauce.

Cook lettuces on top of the stove to make a first course for four people. If you cannot find any Densities, use one whole Cos. Cut it in half lengthways and then cut each piece across to give four pieces. Take care to keep all the leaves of the top halves together as they cook as they will have no stem to anchor them.

Lettuces Cooked With Bacon and Cheese

2 small Density lettuces or 1 Cos
25g (1 oz) butter
1 large onion, thinly sliced
175g (6 oz) lean bacon, diced

10ml (2 teaspoons) granular mustard
100g (4 oz) grated Farmhouse Cheddar cheese

Cut away the lower stems from the lettuces and remove any wilted outer leaves. Cut each one in half lengthways. Melt the butter in a large frying pan on a low heat. Put in the onion and bacon and cook them until the onion is soft. Put in the lettuces, cut-side down. Cover the pan and cook them for five minutes. Turn them over, spread over the mustard and scatter the cheese over the top. Cover the pan again and cook for another five minutes. Serve the lettuce halves in a warm serving dish with the onion and bacon scattered on top.

N.B. Many of the amounts given for cooking lettuces may seem enormous when you are chopping them up, but they have a high water content and do diminish considerably in the pot.

If you cooked lettuce in a casserole for a considerable time, it would practically disappear, but it does have a savoury flavour that you can use like a herb, so add it to the pot for the last stages of cooking.

This beef stew has a lovely light flavour, ideal for the cooler, drearier days of summer when you feel you want to be warmed a little, but don't fancy anything too rich and heavy.

Beef Stew with Lemon and Lettuce

900g (2 lb) lean stewing beef
12 allspice berries or 2.5ml (½ teaspoon) ground
12 black peppercorns or 2.5ml (½ teaspoon) ground

15ml (1 tablespoon) wholemeal flour
425ml (¾ pt) stock
30ml (2 tablespoons) chopped parsley

192

4 cloves (or pinch ground)	grated rind and juice 1 lemon
25g (1 oz) butter	1 large Density or 1 Cos lettuce
2 medium onions, thinly sliced	
1 large or 2 small cloves garlic,	
finely chopped	

Preheat the oven to 160°C (325°F) / Gas 3.

Cut the beef into 2cm (¾ in) dice. Crush the spices together with a pestle and mortar. Melt the butter in a flameproof casserole on a high heat. Put in the beef (in two batches if necessary) and brown it well. Remove it and set it aside. Lower the heat and cool the pan a little. Put in the onions and garlic and cook them until the onions are soft. Stir in the flour and blend in the stock. Bring it gently to the boil, stirring, and add the spices, parsley and lemon rind and juice. Replace the beef and put the casserole into the oven for 1¼ hours. Cut the lettuce in half lengthways and slice it into 1.5cm (½ in) pieces. Stir it into the casserole and put it back into the oven for a further 30 minutes.

Cabbage lettuces are usually the first of the outdoor ones to arrive in the shops. They make an unusual hot vegetable cooked whole with a sprinkling of herbs.

Whole Cabbage Lettuce with Fennel

25g (1 oz) butter	30ml (2 tablespoons) chopped
2 large cabbage lettuces	fennel

Trim away any limp or ragged leaves from the lettuces and cut off the browned end of the stalks. Wash them well under running water, gently prising the leaves apart. Find a saucepan just big enough to take the two lettuces tightly packed together. Put in the butter and melt it on a low heat. Put in the lettuces, stalk-end down and scatter the fennel over the top. Cover and cook gently for ten minutes.

For another first course, stuff Cos lettuce hearts with a creamy filling of cheese that contrasts superbly with the sweet and savoury salad.

Stuffed Lettuce Salad

inner hearts of 2 Cos lettuces	15ml (1 tablespoon) tomato
and the outer leaves of 1	purée
100g (4 oz) Demi Sel Cheese	1 clove garlic, crushed with a
30ml (2 tablespoons) olive oil	pinch of sea salt
30ml (2 tablespoons) white wine	freshly ground black pepper
vinegar	30ml (2 tablespoons) currants

Slit the lettuce hearts in half lengthways. Cut out the tender inner leaves, leaving a case about two leaves thick. Chop the leaves from the centre. Cream the cheese in a bowl and work in the chopped leaves. Fill the cases with this mixture. Chop the outer leaves. Mix together the oil, vinegar, tomato purée, garlic and pepper. Coat the outer leaves in the dressing and mix in the currants. Serve the lettuce hearts on a large serving plate, surrounded by the salad.

Eggs for a first course again. In this simple salad, the heart of the lettuce is used like a herb. The chive flowers are a special touch, inspired by the Elizabethan flower salads. They turn simple eggs and lettuce into a summer garden of purple flowers.

Lettuce and Poached Egg Salad

4 eggs
30ml (2 tablespoons) wine
   vinegar
1 medium sized Density or 1
   small Cos lettuce
90ml (6 tablespoons)
   mayonnaise

juice ½ lemon
30ml (2 tablespoons) chopped
   chives
in May or early June — 8 open
   chive flowers

Put the vinegar into a saucepan with 6cm (2 in) water. Just bring it to the boil and soft-poach the eggs in it. Lift them out with a perforated spoon and set them aside to cool. Wash the outer leaves of the lettuce and arrange four on each of four small plates. Finely chop the hearts and mix them into the mayonnaise with the lemon juice and chives. Put the cold eggs on the lettuce and spoon over the mayonnaise mixture. Set two chive flowers on each one.

This not only looks attractive, it is delicious as well, as when you cut open the eggs the yolk combines with the mayonnaise dressing to coat the lettuce leaves.

This side-salad with peaches can be served with cold chicken or eggs. I have used a Webbs lettuce for this one, but any of the cabbage lettuces would be equally suitable.

Lettuce and Peach Salad

1 Webbs lettuce
4 small firm peaches
60ml (4 tablespoons) olive oil
juice 1 lemon
5ml (1 teaspoon) Dijon mustard
30ml (2 tablespoons) chopped
   chives

15ml (1 tablespoon) chopped
   fennel
in late May and early June — 8
   chive flowers

Wash and shred the lettuce and put it on a serving plate. Stone and slice the peaches and arrange them on top. Mix together the oil, lemon juice, mustard and herbs and spoon them over the peaches. Garnish with the chive flowers.

Lettuce has for many years been popular for summer soups. This one turns out a bright, fresh green. Adding the salad onions after blending makes it attractive to look at and interesting to eat.

Lettuce Soup

1 Webbs lettuce
850ml (1½ pt) stock
freshly ground black pepper
pinch fine sea salt
25g (1 oz) butter

8 large or 12 small salad onions,
  finely chopped
15ml (1 tablespoon) flour
60ml (4 tablespoons) sour cream

Chop the lettuce and put it into a saucepan with the stock and seasoning. Bring it to the boil on a moderate heat, cover and simmer for ten minutes. Cool the soup slightly and work it in a blender until it is smooth. Heat the butter in a saucepan on a low heat. Put in the onions and cook them until they are soft. Stir in the flour and then the blended lettuce. Bring them to the boil, stirring, and simmer for two minutes. Stir in the sour cream and reheat without boiling.

Cucumbers

The fresh smell of cucumbers always reminds me of high summer, with salads on the lawn and freshly-cut sandwiches, and this very thought really shows that we have not been using this vegetable as imaginatively as we might over the past few years. So often, cucumbers are thinly pared and put on the side of a mixed plate of salad, but they have all sorts of other uses as well.

At one time you could only get them in the summer months as they are a heat-loving vegetable, but now, as with lettuce you can buy them all year round, and English ones from February to autumn. Make the most of them at all times of the year, both in salads and in cooked dishes.

Cucumbers were first brought to Britain by the Romans who grew them in their villa gardens, but after the occupation they seem to have been unknown. A few were grown in the fifteenth century, but probably more as a garden curiosity than as a vegetable. A garden book of the time says, 'Cucumber, it beareth apples', and in fact early illustrations do show cucumbers to be pear-shaped or nearly round.

With the upsurge in gardening in the sixteenth century cucumbers began to be more popular and at this time they were grown for the flower and herb salads, that were dressed simply in oil and vinegar and often garnished with hard-boiled eggs. In the seventeenth and eighteenth centuries, cucumbers were used most of all for pickling, and there are numerous recipes 'to pickle cowcumbers' or 'cucombers' or even 'cowcombers'. They were used as a garnish for salads, served with cold meats, and chopped into sauces.

In the nineteenth century, cucumbers were still put into salads, but they were just as often used as cooked vegetable. They were boiled as a garnish for steak, simmered with onions and stock, stewed in gravy or served in a white sauce. If we take a leaf from all these books think of the dishes we could concoct.

Cucumbers are grown in glasshouses in which the temperature regulates how fast the cucumbers will grow. Ideally, this has to be 90°F during the day and 75°F at night, and at the farm I visited this was achieved by two enormous boiler rooms which looked more like the engine-room of a ship than a cucumber farm.

The tiny cucumber plants are set in the glasshouse in rows of banked-up earth with the heating and watering pipes running all the way down. At the beginning of the season, it takes eight weeks for the cucumbers to be ready for picking, but as the weather gets warmer, this is gradually lessened to four. As the stem grows, it has to be wound by hand up a seven-foot string, and when it reaches the top, four shoots, all of which will bear fruit, are allowed to hang down. In the first shed I went into the plants were half-grown and the main job at this stage is to go round to every plant and pluck off the unwanted side-shoots and the small, lower cucumbers. This concentrates all the growth in the head of the plant so it can grow as quickly as possible up the string.

The cucumbers were cut from the stems with small, sharp knives and packed into the crates which could then be moved easily along to the next plant without any hard lifting to be done.

The white crates full of green cucumbers were loaded onto the back of small white tractors and taken off from the glasshouse to the packing shed. Sometimes they are simply boxed before being sent out to the shops, but on this particular farm, they were put through a rhythmically clicking stretch-wrapping machine which gave them close-fitting, shiny polythene coats. I personally would rather buy my cucumbers naked, but I was told that this method of packing does preserve what is known as their 'shelf life'.

Cucumbers can be put into cold salads and hot salads. They can be quickly stir-fried in the Chinese way or simmered with butter and herbs. You can make them into a sauce for meat or fish or cook them in the same pot; or make a tasty soup for winter or summer.

In most dishes, cucumbers are best with the peel left on. It adds to the flavour of salads and in cooked dishes it keeps the cubes or slices fairly firm.

Yoghurt makes a good dressing for cucumber and you can either use it as it is or beat in 30ml (2 tablespoons) of olive oil to the carton to make it a little thicker. Flavour it with curry powder, Tabasco sauce, or lemon juice, and add some crushed garlic and chopped chives, fennel or mint.

Cucumber and cheese, chopped into dice, mixed with mayonnaise and sprinkled with thyme make a good lunch-time salad.

For a special meal, hollow out a cucumber and fill it with fresh crab.

Crab and Cucumber Salad

1 large crab or 225g (8 oz) crab   *1 medium sized cucumber*
   meat

For the dressing:

225g (8 oz) ripe tomatoes   *30ml (2 tablespoons) chopped*
15ml (1 tablespoon) olive oil   *chervil or parsley*
5ml (1 teaspoon) paprika

Take all the meat from the crab and mix the white and brown meats together. Cut the cucumber in half lengthways and discard the small stalk end. Cut each piece in half crossways. Hollow out the seeds, stopping 0.75cm (¼ in) from the ends of each piece. Discard them. Hollow out the flesh of the cucumber so you have four fairly deep boats. Reserve it and chop it finely. Put each cucumber boat on a small serving plate and fill it with crab. Each one should take about 15ml (1 tablespoon). Mix the remaining crab with the chopped cucumber and put a pile of this onto each plate. Scald and skin the tomatoes. Deseed them and rub the pips through a sieve to obtain the juice. Cut away the woody cores and roughly chop the flesh. Put them in a blender with the juice, oil and paprika and work them until you have a smooth sauce. Mix in the chopped chervil and spoon the sauce over the stuffed cucumber boats and the heaps of crab and cucumber.

Here is another cucumber and cheese first course in which the cucumber is heated but stays crunchy. Use smoked cheese that comes in a round sausage shape, just a little smaller in diameter than the cucumber.

Cucumber Rarebit

1 small cucumber
175g (6 oz) smoked cheese
up to 15ml (1 tablespoon)

English Vineyard or other
granular mustard

Cut the cucumber into slices 0.5cm (¼ in) thick, six slices per person. Cut the cheese into an equal number of slices. Lay the cucumber on a flat, ovenproof dish so the slices don't overlap. Put them under a high grill for two minutes. Turn the slices over and lay a piece of cheese on each one. Spread over a little mustard. Put the dish back under the grill for a further two minutes.

Hot salads can be served at all times of the year. Basically, the cucumber is cooked for a very short time (about two minutes) in hot oil, and vinegar or lemon juice and other flavourers to complete the dressing are added at the last minute. Hot cucumber salads and other dishes using a similar method (usually adding wine instead of vinegar) are best served immediately as they can go a little watery. This could be a little inconvenient at a dinner party, but the cooking is so quick that it is possible to nip out quickly and do it between courses without anyone ever knowing.

Cumin and lemon give a light and refreshing taste, to a hot salad which is ideal with curry and also with chicken or fish.

Cucumber with Cumin and Lemon

1 large cucumber
60ml (4 tablespoons) olive oil
1 clove garlic, finely chopped

5ml (1 teaspoon) ground cumin
juice 1 lemon

Cut the cucumber into quarters lengthways and each piece lengthways again. Chop the lengths into pieces 3cm (1 in) long. Put the oil and garlic into a frying pan and set them on a high heat. Cook the garlic until it is brown and frizzly. Put in the cucumber and sprinkle in the cumin. Stir them around for two minutes. Pour in the lemon juice and bring it to the boil. Serve immediately.

Here is a simple way with cucumbers that makes a dish suitable for serving with rich, spicy dishes. If it is to be served with fish use chopped fennel instead of parsley.

Cucumber and Salad Onions

1 large cucumber
16 salad onions
25g (1 oz) butter

75ml (⅛ pt) stock
30ml (2 tablespoons) chopped
* parsley*

Peel the cucumber and cut it into quarters lengthways. Remove the seeds and cut each piece lengthways again. Cut the long pieces into 5cm (1½ in) lengths. Chop the salad onions into pieces the same size. Melt the butter in a saucepan on a moderate heat. Stir in the cucumber and onions and cook until the cucumber is just beginning to brown. This will take about ten minutes. Pour in the stock, raise the heat, and let the stock reduce to a sticky glaze. Mix in the chopped parsley and serve as soon as you can.

Cucumber is sometimes put into the Spanish soup called Gazpacho. This sauce for skate is very similar.

Skate with Cucumber and Tomato Sauce

2 wings skate weighing
  approximately 450g (1 lb) each
350g (12 oz) ripe tomatoes
5ml (1 teaspoon) paprika
30ml (2 tablespoons) white wine
  vinegar

1 medium sized cucumber
40g (1½ oz) butter
1 medium onion, finely chopped
1 clove garlic, finely chopped
30ml (2 tablespoons) chopped
  parsley

Scald, skin and deseed the tomatoes. Roughly chop them and put them into a blender with the paprika and wine vinegar. Work them until you have a smooth sauce. Wipe the cucumber, cut it in quarters lengthways and remove the seeds. Chop it finely. Cut each skate wing into two pieces. Melt half the butter in a large frying pan on a moderate heat and fry the pieces of skate until they are golden on each side. Do this one or two at a time, depending on the size of your pan and use more butter as you need it. Put the fish on a serving dish and keep it warm. Lower the heat and put the onion, garlic and cucumber into the pan. Cook them until the onion is soft. Pour in the tomato mixture and bring it to the boil. Add the parsley, and pour the sauce over the skate to serve.

Cucumber and yoghurt salad is often served with curry, and here you have the hotness, the cucumber and the yoghurt all together. Use two chillies if you like your curries mild, four for a medium one, and six if you like it really hot.

Fillet of Lamb with Cucumber and Chillies

675g (1½ lb) fillet of lamb (or
  chump chops cut very thin)
2-6 green chillies to taste
60ml (4 tablespoons) lamb fat or
  25g (1 oz) butter

5ml (1 teaspoon) ground
  coriander
75ml (⅛ pt) stock
1 small cucumber
juice ½ lemon

1 large onion, finely chopped
1 large or 2 small cloves garlic,
   finely chopped
5ml (1 teaspoon) ground cumin

1 carton (5 fl oz) natural yoghurt

Cut the lamb into small pieces about 3cm by 5cm (1 in x 2 in) and 0.5cm (¼ in) thick. Remove the seeds from the chillies and chop them finely. Heat the fat in a large frying pan or sauté pan on a high heat. Put in the pieces of lamb and brown them well. Remove them and set them aside. Lower the heat and cool the pan a little. Put in the onion, garlic, cumin and coriander and cook them until the onion is soft. Pour in the stock and bring it to the boil. Replace the lamb and put in the chillies. Cover the pan tightly and set it on a very low heat for ten minutes. Wipe and dice the cucumber and add it to the pan with the lemon juice. Cover again and cook for a further 15 minutes. Add the yoghurt and reheat.
    Serve it with brown rice.

When I was talking to the people picking cucumbers in the glass-house, they all recommended cucumber soup. Peeled, and cooked with large onions, cucumbers can make a soup that is pale and uninteresting but keep the peel and use salad onions with long tails and you will have a lovely pale green one.

Green Cucumber Soup

1 small cucumber
75g (3 oz) salad onions, green
   and white parts
25g (1 oz) butter

850ml (1½ pt) stock
125g (4 oz) curd cheese
10ml (2 teaspoons) dill seeds

Dice the cucumber without peeling. Chop the spring onions. Melt the butter in a saucepan on a low heat. Stir in the cucumber and onions, cover them and cook gently for seven minutes. Pour in the stock and bring it to the boil. Simmer for five minutes, uncovered. Cool the soup slightly and work it in a blender until it is smooth. Put the cheese in the saucepan and gradually stir in the blended soup. Add the dill seeds and reheat gently, without boiling.

Tomatoes

Tomatoes were discovered in Mexico by the Spanish explorers, and by the middle of the sixteenth century they were being cultivated all over southern Europe, and soon became the standard ingredient in many traditional and regional recipes.

It was difficult to grow them in Britain except during high summer, and those that were raised were usually for decoration or for their supposed aphrodisiac qualities. A plant was reputedly given to Elizabeth I by Sir Walter Raleigh, but whether for the former or latter purpose I do not know! Certainly, the most common name for tomatoes at the time was 'Apples of Love', but the origins of this are obscure. Tomatoes probably travelled to Italy via Morocco and so became known as 'pomi de Mori' (apple from the Moors) which became pomodori, or golden apples. In France, they could have been called 'Pommes d'amour' as a corruption of this or because they were red, and red was the colour of love. In Britain, there were two varieties, red and yellow, love apples and golden apples.

But whatever the colour, and however strong their reputed aphrodisiac powers tomatoes were certainly not popular as a vegetable in Elizabethan Britain. People disliked the smell of the plant and the yellow stain it left on the fingers; and because it was related to nightshade the fruit was mistrusted. These prejudices weren't actually overcome until the late eighteenth century.

When tomatoes were first cooked, they were usually made into soups, and into sharp, vinegary pickles and sauces; and at the beginning of the nineteenth century they were candied and made into jam.

By this time they were called 'tomatas' and gradually they came to be baked, and stuffed and served as a vegetable. But even so, most of the written recipes of the time are for chutneys 'catsups' (ketchups) and sauces.

Early tomatoes were larger than those we know today. John Gerard in 1597 describes them as being 'the bignesse of a goose egg or a large pippin' and in appearance 'chamfered, uneven and bunched out in many places'. In the late 1880s market garden cultivation of tomatoes began under glass, and from then on varieties were developed and altered to give the smooth-skinned, even-sized ones that are so common today although at what sacrifice to flavour it is impossible to say.

Fifty years ago tomatoes were rare and expensive but now English grown ones are available from May to October. They are usually grown under glass in an area of anything between ten foot square and thirty acres. The very small growers sell at the door, the ones in the middle usually supply local shops, and the really large ones grow on the whole for the supermarket trade. The grower who gave me all my information is a local supplier with half an acre of glass, providing a crop lasting from mid-June to the end of September.

He sows from bought seed, but there are others who propagate their own and who also buy the plants. To be ready in June, the seeds are set

201

in trays between Christmas and the middle of January and are raised in a propagating frame, ideally at a temperature of 65°F. When they are still quite small, they are set individually into small pots of compressed compost which are usually made on the premises. A trailer-load of earth is treated with steam to sterilize it, and then mixed with peat, sand and fertilizer. This is all fed into a machine which makes it into hard, pot-shaped blocks with a round hole in the top for the plant to be set inside. When the plant is big enough, the whole thing is set in the ground. This does away with the need for expensive pots and gives the plant a good growing medium.

As the tomato plants grow, the temperature in the greenhouse has to be between 58° and 63°F at night and 70° and 75°F during the day. The problem and expense of heating decreases as the warmer weather comes, and on the hottest days there may even be a problem of too high a temperature. If it rises over 75°F the plants will start to wilt.

All the plants are looked over once a day and all the side-shoots are taken off, and they are trained clockwise round strings or canes. Careful watering is essential.

The day before the first tomatoes are picked, all the lower leaves are taken off to let the sun give the fruits a final ripening. Once the season has started, a crop is gathered every day or every other day. Apparently few people buy more tomatoes when prices are really low. One greengrocer told me that he actually sells more at Christmas than at the height of the summer. Then they are an expensive luxury, but in July and August they are within everybody's reach for every possible culinary purpose, so buy a few extra and see what you can do.

Tomatoes, if you are going to eat them raw, need no more preparation than a quick wipe with a damp cloth, and then either chopping or slicing.

For some recipes they need to be skinned. The best way is to put them into a bowl, pour boiling water over them, and leave them for ten seconds. Pour all the water away and the skins should peel off easily. Very ripe tomatoes will need barely ten seconds in the water and very firm, greener ones will need longer, but ten seconds is about average. Don't leave the tomatoes standing once they are out of the water as the skins will dry on again; and don't leave them in the water for too long or they will become soft and partly cooked.

To deseed tomatoes cut the tomato in half lengthways and gently squeeze it so all the pips come out. If you would like to keep the juice that comes out with the pips, place a sieve over a bowl and squeeze the pips into this. Then rub them with a wooden spoon so it all drips through.

Scalded and deseeded tomatoes can be cut into strips and used to add to the flavour and appearance of many hot and cold dishes, and

202

the general rule is always do it at the last minute. If they are cooked for long they will become a thick purée, which is excellent if you want a tomato flavoured sauce but not if you want some firm pieces of distinguishable tomato. Put them into stews and casseroles and use them to garnish soups. Mix them into other cooked vegetables such as cabbage, cauliflower or leeks; or put them into salads with other soft-textured ingredients such as raw mushrooms or with grated root vegetables.

Tomato salads are always best if they are kept fairly simple. Too strongly flavoured or too heavy and creamy dressings can easily spoil the flavour of sweet English tomatoes. Use fairly simple French dressings with not too much vinegar, or perhaps just a carton of natural yoghurt, and take your pick of all the herbs of summer. Tabasco sauce and paprika are also good flavourers and the colours blend so well.

The best herb for tomatoes is basil. With this herb alone, all you need is a little olive oil. It has its own kind of pungent sharpness so no vinegar is necessary. It is, however, usually difficult to grow. Try instead coriander, savory, fennel or the nutty-flavoured chervil. If you have any basil use it instead of any of the herbs in the following salads.

When tomatoes are plentiful, use the riper ones to make a fairly thick-textured but light and refreshing flavoured salad dressing. Take 225g (½ lb), scald, skin and deseed them and extract the juice from the seeds. Put the flesh and juice into a blender and work them to a purée that will form the base of the dressing. Add to it 15ml (1 tablespoon) of either wine vinegar, Worcestershire sauce or lemon juice; mix in half a carton of natural yoghurt; or thicken it with 30ml (2 tablespoons) of olive oil. For a more creamy dressing add to it double cream, sour cream, or mayonnaise.

This recipe uses double cream. Serve it with fish, eggs or pork.

Creamy Tomato and Fennel Salad

350g (12 oz) ripe tomatoes
90ml (6 tablespoons) double
  cream
45ml (3 tablespoons) chopped
  fennel

1 clove garlic, crushed with a
  pinch of sea salt
450g (1 lb) firm tomatoes

Scald, skin and deseed the ripe tomatoes and extract the juice from the seeds. Cut out the hard cores and put the rest into a blender with the juice and cream. Work them until you have a smooth dressing. Put it into a serving bowl and mix in the fennel and garlic. Chop the firm tomatoes and mix them into the dressing just before serving.

The same basic purée of tomatoes can also be made into a sauce for fish. Here the tomatoes are actually cooked with the mackerel first so all the flavours blend together. These amounts are for a first course for four people but you can easily double them for a cold main course.

Mackerel with Tomato and Lemon Sauce

2 small mackerel	1 small onion, thinly sliced
15ml (1 tablespoon) chopped lemon thyme	225g (½ lb) tomatoes
	5ml (1 teaspoon) paprika
15ml (1 tablespoon) chopped parsley	5ml (1 teaspoon) soft brown sugar
grated rind and juice ½ lemon	lettuce leaves for serving

Preheat the oven to 180°C (350°F)/Gas 4.

Fillet the mackerel, cut each fillet in half cross-ways and lay the pieces flat in a lightly oiled oven-proof dish. Sprinkle over the chopped herbs and the lemon rind. Scatter the onion over the top. Roughly chop the tomatoes and put them over the onion. Sprinkle over the paprika and sugar and pour in the lemon juice. Cover the dish with foil and put it into the oven for 20 minutes. Let everything in the dish get completely cold, leaving the foil in place. Lay a base of lettuce leaves on four individual serving plates. Carefully brush all the pieces of onion and tomato from the mackerel leaving any herbs in place. Lay two pieces of fish on each plate. Rub all the contents of the dish through a sieve and spoon the resulting sauce over the mackerel.

In the winter and spring, cooking tomatoes to serve as the only vegetable with the meal can be expensive and so all we very often have is the precious half (or sometimes even two halves!) to garnish grilled steak or chops or sometimes the breakfast bacon and eggs. Make the most of them in summer. Serve a whole dish of grilled tomatoes, each with a different herb or flavouring sprinkled over them before they are put under the heat. Spread over different kinds of mustards or a mixture of mustard and tomato purée; a thin layer of cream or curd cheese, some grated cheese or a little paté. Put a small piece of bacon on some of them, or some finely chopped onion or salad onion.

If you are having a roast dinner or a casserole, an economical way of cooking tomatoes is to bake them. You can either leave the skins on and cut them in half and bake them in a lightly buttered dish for ten minutes; or you can bake them whole in the following way.

Baked and Crumbed Tomatoes

8 small firm tomatoes	15ml (1 tablespoon) chopped thyme
60ml (4 tablespoons) dried granary bread crumbs	25g (1 oz) butter

Preheat the oven to 180°C (350°F)/Gas 4.

Scald and skin the tomatoes. Mix the thyme and breadcrumbs together and roll the tomatoes in the mixture to coat them. Put the butter in an ovenproof dish and put it into the oven to melt. Put in the tomatoes and baste them. Bake them for ten minutes.

Cheese and tomatoes are an ideal lunch-time snack and they can be combined very simply to make vegetable dishes and first courses as well. If visitors suddenly descend and you only have a little meat but there are tomatoes and cheese in the cupboard, then you can't go far wrong. A quick supplement dish can be made by slicing up the tomatoes and grating the cheese, layering them in an ovenproof dish and putting them into a hot oven until the cheese melts. Most of the hard English cheeses are suitable for this, but blue cheese makes it extra good. If the oven isn't on, then put the dish under the grill under a moderate heat, so it all heats through fairly slowly.

Kipper patés are often flavoured with tomato purée, but how much nicer to use fresh ones.

Kipper and Tomato Paté

3 kipper fillets
25g (1 oz) softened butter
4 small tomatoes, weighing
together 125-150g (4-5 oz)

1 small pickled dill cucumber
15ml (1 tablespoon) chopped
parsley
freshly ground black pepper

Put the kipper fillets into a shallow pan and cover them with water. Bring them to the boil on a moderate heat and simmer for two minutes. Lift them out and drain them well. Skin the fillets, remove the tail and fin bones and flake the flesh. Beat the butter in a mixing bowl until it is light and fluffy and gradually beat in the kippers, pounding them well to make a smooth mixture. Scald, skin and deseed the tomatoes and work them in a blender until they are mixed to a purée. Finely chop the pickled cucumber. Beat the tomato pulp, cucumber and parsley into the kippers and season with the pepper. Press the mixture into a small terrine or bowl and chill it until it is firm. Serve it with brown toast as a first course.

N.B. If you have no blender, flake the kippers and put them into a bowl. Cook the prepared tomatoes in the butter on a low heat until they are pulpy and beat the lot into the kippers. Then carry on as above.

This beef casserole relies solely on tomatoes to provide the liquid for its spicy sauce. Use an oven-to-table casserole if you have one, and serve it straight from the dish.

Beef, Onion and Tomato Casserole

900g (2 lb) lean stewing beef
675g (1½ lb) firm tomatoes
350g (¾ lb) onions
15ml (1 tablespoon) chopped
  thyme

30ml (2 tablespoons) chopped
  parsley
freshly ground black pepper
15ml (1 tablespoon) paprika
2 bayleaves

Preheat the oven to 180°C (350°F)/Gas 4.

Cut the beef into 3cm (1 in) cubes. Scald and skin the tomatoes and slice them into rounds. Slice the onions into rings. Put a layer of tomatoes in the bottom of the casserole, then some herbs, a layer of onion rings and then beef. Grind over some pepper and sprinkle over some paprika. Carry on layering, ending with tomatoes and tucking in the bayleaves on the way. Cover the casserole and put it into the oven for 1½ hours.

Soups made with tomatoes must be some of the most popular, so here is one more to add to the collection. This is a chilled one — just right for hot August days.

Chilled Cheese, Tomato and Yoghurt Soup

450g (1 lb) tomatoes, scalded,
  skinned and chopped
25g (1 oz) butter
1 medium onion, finely chopped
1 clove garlic, finely chopped
575ml (1 pt) stock
bouquet garni

50g (2 oz) cream cheese
1 carton (5 fl oz) natural yoghurt
15ml (1 tablespoon) chopped
  fennel
15ml (1 tablespoon) chopped
  mint

Scald, skin and roughly chop the tomatoes. Melt the butter in a saucepan on a low heat. Put in the onion and garlic and cook them until the onion is soft. Add the prepared tomatoes, cover and simmer for five minutes. Pour in the stock and bring it to the boil. Add the bouquet garni, cover and simmer for ten minutes. Leave the soup until it is just warm and remove the bouquet garni. Put the soup into a blender with the cheese and yoghurt and work until they are smooth. Chill the soup and serve it from a big tureen or bowl with the fennel and mint scattered on top.

N.B. If you have no blender, work the cheese and yoghurt together in a bowl. Rub the soup through a sieve and beat it into the cheese mixture a little at a time.

Cresses

The tiny-leaved but nutritious cresses have been included in pottages and raw salads at least since the tenth century and probably before. There are references in Anglo-Saxon to 'tun-cerse' or garden cress, and there were varieties growing in kitchen gardens soon after the Norman conquest. They were probably not at first actually cultivated as such but if a good crop were found growing wild it was picked carefully and nurtured for future use.

From the thirteenth century, cress was put more into salads than into pottages along with all the other herbs that grew so prolifically in every garden.

In Tudor and Stuart times, garden cress was included in the popular mixed salads of flowers and herbs, and later still in the more complex meat salads and Salmagundies.

Garden cress isn't to my knowledge grown commercially now. All we have are boxes of delicate flavoured salad cress, which we more commonly call mustard and cress, and the darker, stronger watercress. Between them they can supply us all year with salads, and they can be used in smaller quantities for flavouring in exactly the same way as parsley or thyme. Garnishes that are attractive and good to eat can be made from cresses, and watercress can also be cooked as a small but delicious vegetable.

Watercress

The Greeks were the first to actually cultivate watercress and to recognize its health-giving properties. 'Eat cress', they said 'and get more wit.' Watercress grows wild in Britain in rivers and streams which are supplied by fresh water springs, and it was this wild variety that was put into pottages and salads alongside garden cresses. Beds of wild watercress were obviously kept clear over the years and encouraged to spread, but the first actual man-made watercress beds were laid down as late as 1808 by William Bradbury at Springhead in Kent. At about this time and all through the nineteenth century it was sold first thing in the mornings in the town markets to provide a breakfast for the industrial workers.

To grow watercress successfully, you need fresh, uncontaminated spring water to run through the beds at a rate of half a million gallons per acre per day; and this comes bubbling up through the chalk belt that stretches through Dorset and Hampshire, through the Home Counties and up to Lincolnshire. Watercress cultivation is centred now mainly in these counties, but there are small beds in Devon, Surrey, Sussex and Kent as well. In all, there are about three hundred acres.

The watercress season lasts from October to May, with usually a break of about two months in the middle of winter when the weather is really cold and frosty. All the cutting is still done first thing in the morning so the cress can arrive in shops and markets on the same day.

Watercress needs little preparation for salads or for cooking, although sometimes it is best to cut away the thicker ends of the stems that have small, straggly roots on them, especially if you want an attractive garnish. One or two can be thrown away, but if you have stems from a whole bunch, save them and put them into a soup. Remove any slightly yellow leaves, and if the cress is to be put into a salad, chop it or break it into short lengths. Enormous stalks can be quite tricky to eat with a knife and fork! If for any reason, your bunch of cress is wilting a little, stand it upside down in a jar or bowl of water for 15 minutes and it should come up as good as new.

You can, if you like, cook large-leaved, thick-stemmed watercress very simply in butter. It maintains its strong flavour but not its hotness and is a lovely bright green. It tends to cook down quite a lot, though, so don't use it as the sole vegetable. Treat it more like a cooked garnish. It goes particularly well with roast lamb or lamb chops.

Buttered Watercress

25g (1 oz) butter   *2 bunches watercress*

Melt the butter in a saucepan on a low heat. Put in the watercress with all the stems facing in the same direction, and turn it over in the butter. Cover tightly and keep on the low heat for five minutes.

Fresh watercress salads are welcome at any time. Serve this one as a side-salad with a fairly plain meat or with quiches and soufflés.

Watercress and Mushroom Salad

1 bunch watercress   *10ml (2 teaspoons) tarragon*
175g (6 oz) button mushrooms   *mustard*
60ml (4 tablespoons) olive oil
30ml (2 tablespoons) white wine
    vinegar

Chop the watercress and thinly slice the mushrooms and put them

208

together in a bowl. Beat the oil, vinegar and mustard together and stir them into the salad.

Cheesy dips can often make refreshing first courses, especially if you use curd cheese which has a tangy flavour. Chop the watercress very finely in this one and mix it into the cheese to give an effect rather like the herbs in Boursin.

Watercress and Lemon Dip

175g (6 oz) curd cheese
1 carton (5 fl oz) natural yoghurt
1 bunch watercress
grated rind and juice ½ lemon

15ml (1 tablespoon)
Worcestershire sauce
225g (½ lb) carrots

Blend the cheese and yoghurt together. Finely chop the watercress and mix it into the cheese with the lemon rind and juice and Worcestershire sauce. Cut the carrots into sticks or into long thin slices. Divide the dip between four small bowls and arrange the carrot pieces round it, leaving plenty of room for them to be picked up and dipped in easily. Have some bran crispbreads and brown bread to dip in as well.

Watercress is used more like a herb in this recipe to make the ideal slimming meal. It has no butter, oil or flour and yet is appetising and extremely attractive.

Cod with Egg and Watercress Topping

900g (2 lb) cod fillet (the thick
end if possible)
juice 1 lemon
freshly ground black pepper

2 hard-boiled eggs
15ml (1 tablespoon) Dijon
mustard
1 bunch watercress

Skin the cod and cut it into even-sized serving pieces. Put it on a plate, pour over the lemon juice and grind over the pepper. Leave it to stand for two hours at room temperature. Finely chop the eggs and watercress and mix them with the mustard. Preheat the grill to high. Lay the pieces of fish on the rack and grill them as close to the heat as possible for four minutes. (Three minutes if you have the thinner end.) Spread the egg and watercress mixture over the top and put the fish back under the grill for the tops to brown.

Watercress and Orange Beefburgers

900g (2 lb) best quality minced
beef

1 bunch watercress, finely
chopped

25g (1 oz) butter
100g (4 oz) onions, finely
  chopped
grated rind and juice 1 medium
  orange (Spanish if it is
  available)

60ml (4 tablespoons) grated
  horseradish
pinch fine sea salt
freshly ground black pepper

Put the meat into a large bowl. Melt the butter in a frying pan on a low heat. Put in the onions and cook them until they are soft. Tip the onions and butter into the beef and beat them in with all the rest of the ingredients. Divide the meat into 16 equal portions and make each one into a round, flat burger about 1.5cm (½ in) thick. Put them onto a flat board or several flat plates and put them into a cool place to set into shape. Preheat the grill to high and cook the burgers as close to the heat as possible for two minutes on each side.

Serve them with a watercress and orange salad.

Added to meat dishes during the last few minutes of cooking, watercress makes a bright green and tasty addition to the sauce.

Pork Chops and Watercress

4 pork chops
12 black peppercorns
1 large clove garlic
pinch fine sea salt
30ml (2 tablespoons) pork fat or

15g (½ oz) butter
5ml (1 teaspoon) honey
150ml (¼ pt) stock
1 bunch watercress, chopped

Crush the peppercorns, garlic and salt together with a pestle and mortar and rub them into the surface of the chops. Heat the fat or butter in a frying pan on a moderate heat. Put in the chops and brown them on both sides. Lift them out and set them aside. Pour the stock into the pan and bring it to the boil. Stir in the honey. Replace the chops, cover the pan and set it on a very low heat for 20 minutes. Add the watercress, cover again and cook for five minutes more.

Watercress and cheese, as I said at the beginning, are a perfect combination. Make them into a creamy soup.

Watercress and Cheese Soup

1 bunch watercress
25g (1 oz) butter
1 large onion, finely chopped
15ml (1 tablespoon) wholemeal
  flour

850ml (1½ pt) stock
1 bayleaf
100ml (4 fl oz) double cream
100g (4 oz) grated Farmhouse
  Cheddar cheese

Finely chop the watercress and set aside 30ml (2 tablespoons) for garnish. Melt the butter in a saucepan on a low heat. Stir in the onion and cook it until it is soft. Stir in the flour and then the stock. Bring it to the boil, stirring, and add the bayleaf. Cover and simmer for ten minutes. Stir in the watercress and simmer for a further five minutes. Cool the soup slightly and remove the bayleaf. Work the soup in a blender until it is smooth. Rinse out the pan. Put in the cream and cheese and warm them very gently together, stirring, until the cheese has melted. Gradually stir in the soup and reheat without boiling. Serve in individual bowls with the reserved watercress floating on the top.

Mustard and Cress

Mustard and cress is the only vegetable that we buy that is still growing, and so every scrap of flavour and goodness are still there until it gets chopped into the pot or salad bowl.

It is available all the year round and this is probably why it is so often taken for granted and rarely made the most of. It may look flimsy and uninteresting, but it can be used in many different ways, not only for garnishes as is so often the case.

Mustard and cress is most welcome during the cold months in the middle of winter when there is no watercress to be had and lettuces are expensive, small and not very robust.

Whatever the weather, I always like to have a salad somewhere in the meal, very often, in the winter, as a first course before something hot and substantial. Cress can make ideal first-course salads, so here are two suggestions.

Brie always goes well with fruit, usually though at the end of the meal with pears or apples. With grapefruit and cress it makes a first course.

Piles of Grapefruit, Cress and Brie

2 large grapefruit   *2 boxes mustard and cress*
175g (6 oz) soft but not too
    runny Brie

Peel each grapefruit and cut them crossways in half. Cut each half into three crossways slices. Lay each of the four biggest slices on a small plate. Cover them with slices of Brie and then put on some cress. Carry on with grapefruit, Brie and cress and top with the smallest piece of grapefruit. Use one box of cress between the layers. Garnish the plates with the remaining box of cress.

I always like to play around with the names of things. If it is called mustard and cress, why not add mustard to the salad as well? Mustard seeds in salads add tiny amounts of savoury hotness that come as surprises in every mouthful.

Chicken, Mustard and Cress Salad

225g (8 oz) diced cooked
  chicken
2 boxes mustard and cress
60ml (4 tablespoons) olive oil
30ml (2 tablespoons) cider
  vinegar

5ml (1 teaspoon) mustard
  powder
10ml (2 teaspoons) mustard seed
1 small lettuce for serving
2 hard-boiled eggs

Put the chicken and cress together in a bowl. Blend first the oil and then the vinegar into the mustard powder and stir in the mustard seed. Mix the dressing into the chicken and cress. Line either one large or four small bowls with lettuce leaves and pile the salad on top. Cut the eggs into quarters, lengthways and garnish the salad with these.

When cress is cooked, it has a savoury flavour. You would need about ten boxes to serve it as a single vegetable, but put it with something more substantial and it can add just a little bulk and a good deal of flavour.

Crunchy Celery with Carraway and Cress

1 small head celery
30ml (2 tablespoons) olive oil
1 clove garlic, finely chopped
10ml (2 teaspoons) carraway
  seeds

75ml (⅛ pt) dry white wine
2 boxes mustard and cress

Chop the celery. Put the oil, garlic and carraway seeds into a large heavy frying pan or paella pan and set it on a high heat. When the garlic is just beginning to brown, put in the celery and stir it around for two minutes. Pour in the wine and cut in the cress. Let the wine bubble until it has nearly all reduced and serve as soon as possible.

Still playing around with the name, here is a cabbage recipe using mustard seeds again, and putting in the cress at the last minute to make a bright contrast in appearance and texture. It makes a light-tasting vegetable dish that is good with hearty beef stews or richly sauced game.

212

Cabbage, Mustard and Cress

1 small green winter cabbage
   weighing about 450g (1 lb)
25g (1 oz) butter
1 medium onion, thinly sliced

15ml (1 tablespoon) mustard
   seed
120ml (8 tablespoons) water
2 boxes mustard and cress

Shred the cabbage. Melt the butter in a saucepan on a low heat. Put in the onion and cook it until it is soft. Stir in the cabbage and mustard seed and add the water. Cover and keep the pan on the low heat for 20 minutes. Cut in the mustard and cress and just heat it through.

Here is another first course, not a salad this time, but one which uses the savoury flavour of cooked cress as a herb.

Cockles and Cress in Red Wine

225g (8 oz) cockles
25g (1 oz) butter
1 small onion, thinly sliced

1 clove garlic, finely chopped
2 boxes mustard and cress
60ml (4 tablespoons) red wine

Wash the cockles to remove any grit. Melt the butter in a small saucepan on a low heat. Put in the onion and garlic and cook them until the onion is brown. Stir in the cockles and cress and cook them for half a minute. Pour in the wine and bring it to the boil. Immediately put it into four small bowls so the cress doesn't wilt. Serve it hot with brown bread and butter.

Watercress and orange are often used together in salads or as a garnish. When Seville oranges are in the shops in January and February watercress may be scarce, use mustard and cress instead.

Lamb with Two Oranges

675-900g (1½-2 lb) lean boneless
   lamb, cut from the shoulder
60ml (4 tablespoons) lamb fat or
   25g (1 oz) butter
1 large onion, thinly sliced
grated rind and juice 1 Seville
   orange

15ml (1 tablespoon) chopped
   thyme
2 medium sized Spanish oranges
2 boxes mustard and cress

Cut the lamb into 2cm (¾ in) dice. Heat the fat or butter in a large frying pan or sauté pan on a high heat. Put in the lamb and brown it well, moving it around most of the time. Remove it and set it aside. Lower the heat and cool the pan a little. Put in the onion and cook it until it is soft. Replace the lamb and add the Seville orange rind and juice and thyme. Cover the pan tightly and set it on a low heat for 30 minutes. Cut away the rind and pith from the sweet oranges. Slice them thinly and cut each slice into quarters. When the lamb is done, mix in the oranges and cut in the cress and heat them through.

Serve with buttered brown rice.

Use cress like a herb to make a light and fluffy soufflé with cottage cheese, which is just flavoured but not made hot by the mustard.

Mustard and Cress Soufflé

15g (½ oz) butter
10ml (½ tablespoon) wholemeal
  flour
150ml (¼ pt) milk infused with 1
  bayleaf, bouquet garni, 1 slice
  onion, 1 blade mace, 4 black
  peppercorns
10ml (2 teaspoons) made English
  mustard

125g (4 oz) cottage cheese
4 eggs, separated
2 boxes mustard and cress
butter and crumbs for preparing
  a 20cm (7 in) diameter soufflé
  dish

Preheat the oven to 190°C (375°F)/Gas 5.

Melt the butter in a saucepan on a moderate heat. Stir in the flour and let it bubble. Stir in the milk and bring it to the boil. Keep stirring until the sauce is thick and bubbly. Take the pan from the heat and stir in the mustard. Let the sauce cool slightly and beat in the cheese, egg yolks and cress. Stiffly whip the whites and fold them into the mixture with a metal spoon. Quickly pile the mixture into a prepared soufflé dish and bake in the centre of the oven for 35 minutes.

Radishes

Radishes are really our smallest root vegetable, but as they have nearly always been eaten raw their rightful place is in the salad section. Although they are available from late March, their flavour is always reminiscent of summer gardens, especially when they are hot and slightly crunchy.

They were brought to Britain by the Romans remaining here after the occupation because they flourished better in our cooler climate than in Italy. The Anglo-Saxons found them an easy and convenient vegetable to grow in small plots, and ever since there have been few country gardens without a radish patch.

214

In both early and later Medieval times the leaves were put into the pottage pot, but radishes were one of the earliest vegetables to be eaten raw with only a hint of any other flavouring. In the eleventh century, they were recommended with a little salt and vinegar as a cure for indigestion. It wasn't a great culinary happening, but at least the value of raw vegetables in some form or other in the diet had been recognized.

Few actual recipes for radishes have been written, probably because they were so common as to have been included as a matter of course in some way in nearly every cold dish. The leaves were still being used in the sixteenth and seventeenth centuries. They were put with the red roots in the mixed salads and Salmagundies; and sometimes the pods of seeded radishes were pickled for salads.

Apart from the early inclusions in pottages, radishes were rarely cooked until the nineteenth century, and then only occasionally. Inevitably they were boiled and buttered or served with a white sauce, and Eliza Acton recommends that boiled radishes should be served on toast, like asparagus. Mrs Beeton puts them mainly into summer salads but warns, 'They do not agree with people except those who are in good health, and have active digestive powers'!

Pulling radishes is done by hand, measuring the exact size of the bunches by experience of feeling where the fingers meet round the leaves. Radishes grown on a small scale may be put straight into wooden crates and sent off the the shops as they are and some may be washed first. On the large farms some are put directly into crates and sent through a washing system all packed, and in other cases all the bunches are put into sacks in the field and washed before being crated.

On the farm I visited, half the radishes they grew were sent out washed and packed twelve bunches to a box and the other half were sent through a trimming machine that stripped off all their leaves by means of a system of rapidly revolving hungry rollers. The round red roots bounced into a large bin at the end and were sent off to yet another complicated machine to be graded, picked over, and packed into plastic trays.

This is all very convenient, and it does mean that you don't get any rotten ones, but in the early part of the season at least, it's a pity to miss out on the leaves. At the end of the season they are too tough to use, but in late March and all through April you can use them in salads like watercress. Buy your radishes by the bunch then, and when you get them home trim them and wash them and store the roots and leaves in separate polythene bags in the bottom of the 'fridge; or better still use them immediately. Young radishes only have small leaves, so in salads either use the leaves of two bunches or add to the amount of green by using a bunch of watercress as well. After about three weeks, the leaves are still tender but there are more of them so you only need one bunch. In the middle of May they become too tough to use.

Here is a salad in which you can taste all the goodness that the fresh leaves provide. It practically zings with health. Try it with pork or with good, herby sausages.

Spring Radish Salad

1 bunch radishes
10 sorrel leaves
large handful of dandelion
  leaves
½ bunch watercress
30ml (2 tablespoons) cider
  vinegar

30ml (2 tablespoons) olive oil
1 large clove garlic, crushed
  with a pinch of sea salt
freshly ground black pepper

Slice the radishes. Remove the stalks from the radish leaves. Chop the leaves, sorrel, dandelion leaves and watercress and put them into a bowl with the radishes. Mix the vinegar, oil, garlic and pepper together and mix this dressing into the salad.

Fresh radishes come in varying degress of hotness. Spice them up even more with mustard seed and horseradish to make a superb salad for serving with beef.

Fiery Radish Salad

2 bunches radishes (roots only)
60ml (4 tablespoons) olive oil
30ml (2 tablespoons) malt
  vinegar

15ml (1 tablespoon) grated
  horseradish
15ml (1 tablespoon) mustard
  seed

Slice the radishes. Mix together the oil, vinegar, horseradish and mustard seed and mix this dressing into the radishes.

Radishes can be thinly sliced and cooked quickly to make hot salads. Put radishes and cheese together here for a spicy first course salad or cheese-course savoury.

Hot Radish and Cheese Salad

1 large bunch radishes
60ml (4 tablespoons) olive oil
1 clove garlic, finely chopped
175g (6 oz) Farmhouse Cheddar
  cheese, diced

15ml (1 tablespoon) white wine
  vinegar
15ml (1 tablespoon)
  Worcestershire sauce

Slice the radishes. Chop the radish leaves, removing all the stalks. Heat the oil in a heavy frying pan on a moderate heat. Put in the garlic and radishes and cook them for two minutes. Quickly mix in the cheese and chopped leaves and move them around in the pan for not more than half a minute so the leaves just begin to wilt but the cheese stays firm. Add the vinegar and sauce, let them bubble, and serve.

Here is a salad for a first course that is quick and easy to prepare but very effective as the cheese is an unusual one. The colours are attractive, too. You have red and white radish slices with red and cream cheese in a pure white dressing with bright green lettuce leaves for contrast.

Radish and Red Windsor Salad

1 bunch radishes (roots only)
175g (6 oz) Red Windsor Cheese
1 carton (5 fl oz) natural yoghurt
1 clove garlic, crushed with a
   pinch of sea salt

freshly ground black pepper
1 small lettuce

Slice the radishes and dice the cheese. Put them together in a bowl. Mix the garlic and pepper into the yoghurt and stir it into the radishes and cheese.

Arrange a bed of lettuce leaves on four small plates and pile the salad on top.

Cooking radishes brings out an earthy but nevertheless delicate quality that you never discover when you eat them raw. You can simmer them gently in lightly salted water for 15 minutes and serve them tossed with butter and parsley; or better still, cook them whole, just covered with stock, with a knob of butter on a fairly low heat for 20 minutes. Add some chopped parsley just before you serve them. You will need two bunches for four people, 275ml (½ pt) stock and 25g (1 oz) butter.

In this recipe with pork, the radishes pick up the slightly sharp quality of the cider and go a delicate pink colour.

Pork Chops and Radishes

4 pork chops
1 bunch radishes
30ml (2 tablespoons) pork fat or
   15g (½ oz) butter

1 large onion, thinly sliced
1 clove garlic, finely chopped
275ml (½ pt) dry cider

Trim any excess fat from the chops. Slice the radishes and chop about 90ml (6 tablespoons) of the leaves. Heat the fat in a large frying pan on a moderate heat. Put in the chops and brown them on both sides. Remove them and set them aside. Lower the heat and put in the onion, garlic and radishes. Cook them until the onion is soft. Pour in the cider and bring it to the boil. Stir in the chopped leaves and replace the chops. Cover and set on a low heat for half an hour.

Serve the chops with the radishes and any juices left in the pan spooned over them. Have a green salad for contrast in colour.

Radishes make a soft pink, delicate-flavoured soup, that is just made creamy with Demi Sel Cheese.

Radish Soup

1 bunch radishes (roots only)
1 medium onion, thinly sliced
850ml (1½ pt) stock
bouquet of sage
freshly ground black pepper

small pinch sea salt
15g (½ oz) butter
10ml (½ tablespoon) flour
100g (4 oz) Demi Sel Cheese

Thinly slice the radishes. Put them into a saucepan with the onion, stock, and sage. Season, and bring them to the boil. Cover and simmer for 15 minutes. Cool slightly and remove the sage. Work everything in a blender until you have a smooth liquid. Melt the butter in a saucepan on a moderate heat. Stir in the flour and let it bubble. Stir in the blended liquid, bring it gently to the boil and simmer for one minute. Cream the cheese in a bowl and gradually work in half the soup. Stir the resulting mixture back into the saucepan and reheat the soup gently, without boiling.

Celery

Crisp, crunchy white sticks of celery with strong cheese, celery and nuts in winter salads, the gentle taste of cooked celery in stews and warming soups and the soft succulence of celery braised alone — one could go on and on, for there is no vegetable more versatile than this.

All sorts of wild herbs went into the early pottage pot, and among these was one called smallage, now more commonly known as wild celery. It had a similar flavour to the celery we use today but was far more bitter. Cultivated celery was developed from this plant in the late sixteenth century in Italy, probably, according to Charles I's botanist, John Parkinson, around Venice, as he first saw it growing in Britain in the early seventeenth century in the garden of the Venetian ambassador in Bishopsgate. At this time, wild plants were becoming neglected and vegetable gardening was increasing, and it wasn't long before smallage in pottages had been completely replaced by the new 'sweet smallage' or celery.

Right from the start, both the leaves and the stalks were put raw into mixed salads; and raw celery was still popular in Victorian times, served in a tall, specially made celery glass to accompany the cheese at the end of the meal, with the ends of the stems cut in thin slivers to make them curl.

When pottage disappeared from the table and was replaced by the thinner, more delicate, clear broths and consommes in the seventeenth century, finely shredded celery was used in these for both flavour and garnish

In the eighteenth and nineteenth centuries, celery was probably as often served cooked as it was raw, suffering the same boiling and buttering fate as most of our vegetables. Boiled celery was also made into fritters and deep fried, or simmered in various sauces, in a simple broth thickened with flour, or with a rich concoction of cream and egg yolks. Celery soups were favourites then, too; and since then celery has been chopped up into many a homely stew to add substance and flavour.

Until fairly recently, the most popular celery in this country was the kind that had to be earthed up to keep the stems white. It grew best in the rich, black earth around Lincolnshire and the Fens and was usually only available during the autumn and the first part of the winter. Now we have a self-blanching kind which costs less to grow and is available for most of the year, with only a small gap in late spring. For me, there is no substitute for the blanched celery, but more and more growers are turning to the self-blanching types. There is also a green celery which is just beginning to catch on. It was developed in America and has nowhere near the flavour of the other two.

All kinds of celery are sown in boxes and raised under glass at a temperature ideally of around 70°F. When they have germinated and are 3cm (1 in) high, each tiny plant is picked out individually and set in small, compressed peat pots or flower pots in the same way as tomato plants. They stay in these, usually still under glass, until they are 12cm (4 in) high when they are ready for transplanting. The celery that has to be blanched is picked out into pots in the spring and is usually put out into the fields in June. The stems have to be kept completely covered with earth as they grow, and the heads are ready for cutting in late August or early September. The self-blanching kinds can be raised much earlier and set under glass, so the first crop can be cut in May. Outside cutting starts in July and carries on until November. After this,

219

there will be more coming on under glass again that will last till the spring.

Celery is cut from the base of the hard, nutty root with sharp butcher's knives. The self-blanching kinds are laid in plastic trays and sprayed clean, and each is packed in a polythene sleeve before being sent in boxes to markets and supermarket depots.

I do tend to prefer blanched celery, sold shining translucent white through the sooty earth: it takes a little messy time and effort to wash, but as long as you do this as soon as you get your celery home and not just before you want to use it, it will be no inconvenience. Separate all the sticks and give them a good scrub in cold water, and if there are any brown patches, cut them away. Sometimes the very ends of the sticks can be slightly wilted, in which case cut them off to where the celery is really crisp and fresh, and save them for the stock-pot. Keep the leaves as well. You can use them like a herb, chopped and sprinkled over soups and stews, or mixed into salads and omelettes, or put into bouquets garnis, especially if they are to flavour fish or ham. If you can resist eating the crunchy root part while you are preparing the rest, save it for salads, particularly ones with nuts and apples. Keep all the cleaned parts of the celery separately in the bottom of the 'fridge or the crisper drawer, so they will be ready and waiting whenever you need them.

In salads, celery goes best with the crunchy things — carrots, nuts, celeriac, small pieces of green pepper, white cabbage and apples. Dress it with mayonnaise or with oil and different vinegars and various combinations of herbs and spices.

Here is an apple salad to go with pork, with a dressing made of ripe bananas.

Celery, Apple and Banana Salad

8 small or 4 really large sticks
 white celery
2 large cooking apples

2 ripe bananas
90ml (6 tablespoons) cider
 vinegar

Chop the celery. Quarter, core and slice the apples without peeling, and put them in a bowl with the celery. Mash the bananas and work them to a smooth dressing with the vinegar. Stir it into the celery and apple.

N.B. Do not leave the salad standing for long as although the taste will still be the same, it may go dark brown in colour and not very appealing.

Hot salads are always good in winter-time when you need something fresh but don't fancy a cold meal.

With prawns, a hot celery salad makes a light first course for four, which is especially good served before a rich, heavy meaty meal.

Hot Celery and Prawn Salad

4 large or 8 small sticks celery, chopped
175g (6 oz) shelled prawns
30ml (2 tablespoons) white wine vinegar
5ml (1 teaspoon) Tabasco sauce

10ml (2 teaspoons) tomato purée
5ml (1 teaspoon) paprika
60ml (4 tablespoons) olive oil
1 large clove garlic, finely chopped

Blend the vinegar, Tabasco sauce, tomato purée and paprika together. Heat the oil in a frying pan on a high heat. Put in the garlic and just let it start to brown. Put in the celery and stir it around on the heat for one minute. Put in the prawns and heat them through quickly. Pour in the vinegar mixture and let it bubble. Serve the salad immediately.

Cooked celery, very often in most people's minds, means braised celery, but there are many more ways of serving it as a vegetable. If you have to prepare a meal in a hurry, there is nothing like a quick fry-up which often ends up as tasty and effective as something over which you have taken a deal of time and trouble.

Take equal parts of sliced celery and onion and fry them up in butter with a chopped clove of garlic until they are golden. Just before they are ready add some sliced, flat mushrooms, some peeled and chopped tomatoes (or just chopped) and, if you have it, some sliced green pepper.

Celery can be cooked fairly quickly in a covered saucepan on top of the stove, with different herbs and flavourings. It needs less liquid than most vegetables as it produces a lot of moisture of its own. Use about 90ml (6 tablespoons) of stock to a small head of chopped celery and 15g (½ oz) butter or 30ml (2 tablespoons) olive oil. Flavour it with sage, parsley or thyme, or add a little mustard or tomato purée.

This recipe uses Soy sauce for a slightly Chinese flavour.

Celery with Soy and Onion

1 small head celery
30ml (2 tablespoons) olive oil
15ml (1 tablespoon) Soy sauce

90ml (6 tablespoons) stock
1 medium onion, thinly sliced
1 clove garlic, finely chopped

Cut the celery into 3cm (1 in) squares. Combine the oil, sauce and stock in a saucepan. Mix in the celery, onion and garlic. Cover the saucepan and set it on a low heat for 25 minutes.

221

Braised celery hearts appearing on restaurant menus have made cooked celery seem like a luxury vegetable. It may taste that way, but it doesn't have to be expensive. Use the stems as well and the effect will be just as good.

Here the celery is cut into sticks and flavoured lightly with bacon.

Braised Celery and Bacon

1 small head celery
25g (1 oz) bacon fat or pork
  dripping
1 medium onion, thinly sliced

100g (4 oz) lean bacon, diced
150ml (¼ pt) stock
bouquet garni which includes
  sage

Preheat the oven to 180°C (350°F)/Gas 4.

Cut the sticks of celery into 7cm (2½ in) lengths and cut the wide ends in half lengthways. Melt the fat or dripping in a flameproof casserole on a low heat. Put in the onion and bacon and cook them until the onion is soft. Put in the celery and mix it around with the bacon and onion. Pour in the stock and tuck in the bouquet garni. Cover the casserole and put it into the oven for one hour.

Nearly any casserole or stew will benefit from the flavour of celery. If you are using a bouquet garni, tie in a small stick or a sprig of the leaves with the herbs; or use chopped or diced celery as one of the main vegetable ingredients.

Here, pickled walnuts give a final, spicy contrast in flavour.

Braised Beef and Celery in Beer

900g (2 lb) best quality braising
  steak
350g (12 oz) celery
45ml (3 tablespoons) seasoned
  wholemeal flour
40g (1½ oz) beef dripping

1 large onion, thinly sliced
275ml (½ pt) strong light ale
150ml (¼ pt) stock
bouquet garni including celery
  leaves
4 pickled walnuts

Preheat the oven to 180°C (350°F)/Gas 4.

Cut the beef and the celery into pieces 2cm by 6cm (¾ in by 2 in). Coat the beef in the seasoned flour. Melt 25g (1 oz) of the dripping in a flameproof casserole on a high heat. Put in the pieces of beef and brown them well. (Do this in two batches.) Remove the beef and set it aside. Lower the heat and cool the pan a little. Put in the remaining dripping. Stir in the onion and cook it until it is soft. Stir in the ale and stock and bring them to the boil. Put in the celery and bring them to the boil again. Replace the beef and add the bouquet garni. Cover the casserole and put it into the oven for one hour and 20 minutes. Finely chop the walnuts. Take out the bouquet garni and stir in the walnuts. Put the casserole back into the oven for a further ten minutes.

Add herrings to braised celery towards the end of cooking time to make another casserole-type dish.

Herring, Celery and Apple Casserole

4 herrings
6 large or 12 small sticks celery
2 large cooking apples
50g (2 oz) lean bacon
25g (1 oz) dripping or bacon fat

1 large onion, thinly sliced
150ml (¼ pt) dry cider
2 bayleaves
parsley or watercress for garnish

Preheat the oven to 180°C (350°F)/Gas 4.

Fillet the herrings and cut them into 3cm (1 in) squares. Slice the celery. Peel, quarter, core and slice the apples. Dice the bacon. Melt the dripping in a flameproof casserole on a low heat. Stir in the celery, bacon and onion and cook them until the onion is soft. Stir in the apples and mix in the cider and mustard. Tuck in the bayleaves, cover and put the casserole into the oven for 40 minutes. Mix in the herrings, cover again, and put back for a further 20 minutes.

Serve garnished with parsley or watercress, accompanied by a green salad and potatoes baked in their jackets.

Celery is often used to flavour a blanquette of veal. Here, they go together to make a mild curry. Serve it with brown rice fried with celery to bring all the flavours of the meal together.

Mild Veal Curry with Celery-Fried Brown Rice

900g (2 lb) pie veal, cut from the leg if possible
24 button onions
350g (12 oz) celery
25g (1 oz) butter
10ml (2 teaspoons) curry powder

10ml (2 teaspoons) turmeric
grated rind and juice 1 lemon
200ml (7 fl oz) stock
2 bayleaves

Cut the veal into 2cm (¾ in) dice. Peel the onions. Chop the celery into 2cm (¾ in) pieces. Melt the butter in a large frying pan or sauté pan on a high heat. Put in the veal and brown it. Remove it and set it aside. Lower the heat and cool the casserole a little. Put in the onions and cook them, stirring around occasionally, until they begin to look transparent. Stir in the curry powder and turmeric and cook them for half a minute more. Stir in the stock and lemon juice and bring them to the boil. Replace the veal, add the lemon rind, and tuck in the bay leaves. Cover the pan and set it on a very low heat for 40 minutes, checking once or twice to make sure the liquid isn't evaporating too fast. If this should happen, draw the pan aside and add more stock by the tablespoon (15ml).

For the Rice

350g (12 oz) long grain brown rice	1 medium onion, thinly sliced
	1 clove garlic, finely chopped
60ml (4 tablespoons) olive oil	30ml (2 tablespoons) chopped
4 sticks celery, thinly sliced	celery leaves

Simmer the rice in lightly salted water for 45 minutes. Drain it and refresh with cold water. Drain again. Heat the oil in a large frying pan on a low heat. Put in the celery, onion and garlic and cook them until the onion is golden. Raise the heat to moderate, fork in the rice and fry it for two minutes, moving it around all the time.

Put it into a warmed serving dish and scatter the chopped leaves over the top.

No section on celery would be complete without a soup, so here is a warming one for winter, flavoured with two different mustards.

Celery and Mustard Soup

225g (8 oz) chopped celery	10ml (2 teaspoons) Dijon mustard
225g (8 oz) chopped onion	
850ml (1½ pt) stock	5ml (1 teaspoon) made English mustard
1 bayleaf	
freshly ground black pepper	275ml (½ pt) milk
pinch sea salt	30ml (2 tablespoons) chopped
25g (1 oz) butter	celery leaves
15ml (1 tablespoon) wholemeal flour	

Put the celery, onion, stock, and bayleaf into a saucepan and season. Bring them to the boil, cover, and simmer for 15 minutes. Remove the bayleaf and work the rest in a blender until it is smooth. Melt the butter in a saucepan on a low heat. Stir in the flour and let it bubble. Take the pan from the heat and stir in the two mustards. Stir in the milk. Put the pan on the heat and keep stirring until you have a thick sauce. Mix in the blended celery and stock. Reheat to serve.

Put the soup into small bowls and scatter the chopped celery leaves over the top.

Green Peppers

One of the latest additions to our salad bowl are the bitter-sweet green peppers or capsicums. They were originally a South American vegetable, discovered by the Spanish in Mexico soon after the arrival of Cortez in 1519. They were taken to Europe with tomatoes and were readily accepted in the hotter countries of the south. By the end of the century, some varieties had reached Hungary and Poland, but they didn't travel westwards in any great quantities until the middle of the twentieth century.

Peppers were known in Mrs Beeton's time, however, as she gives one recipe for Pickled Capsicums, which she flavours with the typically English spices of mace and nutmeg. They were probably grown then as a garden curiosity.

Peppers, like tomatoes, are essentially hot-country vegetables and until glasshouse growing was standard practice, the British weather made large scale cultivation impossible. It is only since the late 1960s that they have been a commercial crop.

They take a long time to grow and need a lot of sunlight, and occupy

225

space in the glasshouses from March to autumn. They are, however, quite an intensive crop. The plants grow fairly close together and the fruits can be picked regularly from July to the end of September. Most green peppers are grown from seed which is planted in trays in March and kept at a temperature of 80°F. When they are a few inches high, they are picked out into 8cm (3 in) peat blocks and planted in rows in the glasshouses about 30cm (10 in) apart. No pruning or trimming of side-shoots is necessary with green peppers as every shoot that grows will eventually produce fruit. They have to be watered every day, either by hand or with a mechanical watering system so each plant receives around two pints.

Once peppers are established for the season, they are a fairly easy crop; but they still have to be watered, string has to be put up and the spaces between the rows kept free from weeds and in some cases covered with straw. On the farm I visited, they are looked over every day and the ripe peppers are picked regularly. The plants reward all this care and attention by producing a healthy, shining and prolific crop. They would carry on later than the end of September, but then they begin to run out of daylight and eventually stop producing fruit; so the plants have to be grubbed up and later new ones will be raised for the following year.

Like all salad vegetables, green peppers can be served raw or cooked and they have the added advantage of having large, hollow centres which can be stuffed with all kinds of fillings.

They have a small, inedible core at the stalk end which needs to be cut away, and it is easier, if you are going to chop them up, to always cut this out first. Just insert the point of a knife all the way round the stem and then pull it out. Then cut the pepper in half lengthways and remove the white pith and the seeds and it is all ready to be sliced or chopped, to be used raw in salads or to be put into cooked dishes.

Sometimes, if you are stuffing peppers, they have to blanched first, usually for five minutes in gently simmering water. Do this before taking out the core so they keep their shape.

Other recipes call for them to be skinned. You do this by charring them under a high grill. Don't be put off by the burnt offering that emerges, but set to with a piece of kitchen paper or a soft cloth (aided by your fingers) and gently rub the blackened skin away. You will end with a complete, but very floppy pepper, with a fairly strong flavour. Treated like this, peppers can be sliced and put into salads or quiches, or mixed at the last minute into goulashes and stews.

All through the winter, green peppers are expensive as they are imported from various parts of the world, so it isn't wise to use them in great quantities until the English-grown ones arrive in July. Chopped up raw they go with lettuce, cucumber or radishes, and charred and peeled they mix with tomatoes and sliced raw mushrooms, and cooked vegetables such as carrots and cauliflower.

Here is a recipe for a pepper salad with raw carrots. The dressing is based on Roman flavours. Use the smallest, sweetest carrots for the best effect.

Green Pepper and Carrot Salad

4 medium sized green peppers, chopped
350g (12 oz) new carrots, sliced paper thin
50g (2 oz) raisins, finely chopped
60ml (4 tablespoons) olive oil
30ml (2 tablespoons) white wine vinegar

10ml (2 teaspoons) clear honey
1 clove garlic, crushed with a pinch of sea salt
freshly ground black pepper
30ml (2 tablespoons) chopped lovage picked from the smallest leaves

Put the peppers, carrots and raisins in a salad bowl. Beat the oil, vinegar and honey together and add the garlic, quite a lot of pepper and the lovage. Mix them into the salad and let it stand for 15 minutes before serving.

This recipe is a little unseasonal as oranges aren't really at their best during late summer, but it nevertheless makes a really tasty first course. It uses Tabasco sauce, which is made from another variety of the pepper family. Use a good quality salami from a Delicatessen, such as a dark German one.

Hot Green Pepper, Orange and Salami Salad

2 medium sized green peppers
2 large oranges
175g (6 oz) spicy salami
30ml (2 tablespoons) white wine vinegar
15ml (1 tablespoon) tomato purée

few drops Tabasco sauce (up to 5ml (1 teaspoon) to taste)
60ml (4 tablespoons) olive oil
1 clove garlic, finely chopped
shredded lettuce for serving

Core and slice the peppers. Cut away all the peel and pith from the oranges, slice them and cut each slice into quarters. Chop the salami. Mix the vinegar, tomato purée and Tabasco sauce together. Heat the oil in a heavy frying pan on a moderate heat. Put in the garlic and let it brown. Add the peppers and stir them around for half a minute. Put in the oranges and salami and let them just heat through. Pour in the vinegar mixture and let it bubble. Spoon all the salad onto a bed of shredded lettuce.

In the following recipe the peppers are blanched so they will be just cooked through and still hot when you serve them. This one is for a first course.

Green Peppers Stuffed with Cheese and Tomato

2 medium sized green peppers
30ml (2 tablespoons) olive oil
1 medium onion, thinly sliced
1 large clove garlic, finely
  chopped
100g (4 oz) curd cheese
8 firm tomatoes, scalded,
  skinned, seeded and roughly
  chopped

15ml (1 tablespoon) chopped
  parsley
15ml (1 tablespoon) chopped
  marjoram

Blanch the peppers whole in gently simmering water for ten minutes. Drain them well. Cut them in half and remove the core and seeds. Prepare the filling while the peppers are simmering so they will both be ready at the same time. Heat the oil in a frying pan on a moderate heat. Put in the onion and garlic and cook them until they are golden. Stir in the cheese, tomatoes and herbs and let them all heat through without letting the cheese get stringy or the tomatoes mushy. Pile the mixture quickly into the prepared pepper halves.

Both paprika and cayenne pepper, like Tabasco sauce, are derived from different varieties of pepper plant. Put them all together with lamb.

Peppered Lamb

675-900g (1½-2 lb) lean boneless
  lamb, cut from the shoulder
4 small green peppers (or 2 large
  ones)
60ml (4 tablespoons) lamb fat or
  25g (1 oz) butter

1 large onion, finely chopped
1 clove garlic, finely chopped
1ml (¼ teaspoon) cayenne
  pepper
10ml (2 teaspoons) paprika
juice 2 lemons

Cut the lamb into 2cm (¾ in) dice. Seed and dice the peppers. Heat the fat in a heavy frying pan or sauté pan on a high heat. Put in the lamb and brown it, moving it around for most of the time. Remove it and set it aside. Lower the heat and put in the onion, garlic, cayenne and paprika. Cook them until the onion is soft. Stir in the lamb and lemon juice. Cover, and cook on the lowest heat possible for 15 minutes. Add the peppers to the pan and continue cooking for a further 20 minutes. Serve the dish with wholemeal pasta.

Green peppers often feature in Chinese cooking, and one of their favourite spices is ginger. Put them together to make a savoury dry-flavoured beef dish.

Topside with Ginger and Green Peppers

4 slices topside about 1.5cm
  (½ in) thick and weighing
  around 175g (6 oz) each
1 large clove garlic
5ml (1 teaspoon) ground ginger

2 large green peppers
30ml (2 tablespoons) olive oil
1 medium onion, thinly sliced
150ml (¼ pt) dry red wine

Crush the garlic with the ginger. Core and slice the peppers. Heat the oil in a large, heavy frying pan or sauté pan on a high heat. Put in the slices of beef and brown them well on both sides. Remove them and set them aside. Lower the heat and cool the pan a little. Put in the onion and cook it until it is soft. Mix in the green peppers and pour in the wine. Bring it to the boil and stir in the garlic and ginger. Replace the beef, cover the pan, and set it on a very low heat for 40 minutes.

Kedgeree was a Victorian English breakfast dish of smoked fish, rice, raisins and peanuts. Omit the rice and add green peppers for a dinner dish.

Green Pepper Kedgeree

675g (1½ lb) smoked cod fillet
1 bayleaf
bouquet garni
6 black peppercorns
1 slice onion
60ml (4 tablespoons) olive oil
1 medium onion, thinly sliced
1 clove garlic, finely chopped

2 small green peppers, sliced
50g (2 oz) peanuts (not salted)
50g (2 oz) raisins
2.5ml (¼ teaspoon) ground mace
30ml (2 tablespoons) chopped
  parsley
grated rind and juice ½ lemon

Put the fish into a shallow pan with the bayleaf, peppercorns, and onion slice. Cover it with water. Cover the pan, bring them to the boil and simmer for five minutes. Lift out the fish and drain it well. Flake it and remove any bones. Heat the oil in a frying pan on a low heat. Put in the onion and garlic, cover them and cook them gently for seven minutes. Mix in the peppers, nuts and raisins, cover again and cook for ten minutes. Fork in the fish and add the mace, parsley and lemon rind and juice. Raise the heat to moderate and heat everything through, mixing everything together well.

Serve the kedgeree with buttered brown rice.

This soup is also given an Italian flavour with the use of marjoram.

Green Pepper Soup

2 large green peppers
25g (1 oz) butter
1 large onion, finely chopped
15ml (1 tablespoon) wholemeal
  flour

750ml (1¼ pt) stock
15ml (1 tablespoon) chopped
  marjoram
150ml (¼ pt) dry sherry

Finely chop the peppers. Melt the butter in a saucepan on a low heat. Stir in the onion and cook it until it is soft. Stir in the flour and then the stock. Bring them to the boil, stirring, and put in the peppers and marjoram. Simmer for 15 minutes and pour in the sherry. Reheat to serve.

Orchard Fruits

There have been orchards in Britain since Roman times and before then both pears and plums were growing here wild. The Romans cultivated these two fruits and brought with them sweet apples, to replace our sour wild crab-apples, and cherries. It is said that many of the wild cherry trees that still survive alongside our straight Roman roads are descendants of those that were unwittingly set by the Roman legions marching along, eating cherries to refresh themselves and spitting out the pips.

Until the arrival of the Normans, most of the bigger orchards were centred around the monasteries, but under the new feudal system fruit trees were planted on nearly every estate. Even so, a lot of fruit was still imported until Henry VIII's gardener, Richard Harrys actually imported the trees and developed many new varieties in 105 acres of Kentish orchards. Since then, Kent has been one of the main fruit-growing counties, along with Herefordshire, Worcestershire, Gloucestershire, Somerset, Hampshire, Sussex, Essex, Norfolk and Suffolk.

Work goes on in the orchards all the year round. Soon after Christmas, the pruning begins, to keep the trees down to size and to remove any dead or broken branches. Every tree is looked over and the job is done by hand. As the weather gets warmer, it is time for the skilled and time-consuming job of grafting. This is a process used by the Romans which is still the best way of changing your variety of apple or pear without grubbing up all the trees and planting new ones. All the branches of the tree to be changed are cut back and twigs of the new variety grafted on. There are many ways of cutting the branch and the new twig and fitting them together and probably every fruit farmer gives it his own individual touch. When they are fixed, the joints are bound with sticky tape and sealed with grafting wax. The basic method has been the same for centuries and the joints have been sealed with hazel bark and clay, and sometimes even clay and cow-dung. Within three years after grafting the crop of new fruit will be as large as that of the old before the type was changed.

After grafting is over, just before the blossom appears, spraying begins with a non-poisonous insecticide and this is carried on at regular intervals, missing out the period of pollination during blossom-time, all through the spring and summer until about three weeks before picking.

After picking, all the fruit is weighed and recorded at a central point, and some is sent out to local shops and wholesale markets straight away, while some is sold at the farm gate. Cherries and plums are dealt with in this way as they do not store and are best sold as soon as they are picked.

Some of the apples and pears are also sent quickly to market, but much of the crop now goes off to packhouses to be sorted and graded and sent out on a controlled basis to ensure the markets are not flooded with fruit one day and suffering from a shortage the next. Many fruit farmers now belong to co-operatives under whose name the fruit is graded, packed and marketed. Their central offices are more like the stock exchange than markets, with packhouses phoning in every day to declare their stock of fruit and messages coming in from the markets as to demand. All the sets of information are correlated and messages go back to the packhouses to tell them where to send their fruit. In this way, every housewife all over the country is able to choose from a large selection of fresh fruit from all the orchard counties.

I love fruit as fresh as possible — cherries bought from the farm shop on a warm summer afternoon, or Conference pears and Russet apples straight from the tree, still cold from the early autumn mists. But fruit never keeps very well without some form of preserving. At one time it was dried or bottled and never tasted quite the same when it was re-cooked; but apples and pears straight from the cold store are as near to autumn freshness as they possibly could be.

I always try, if I can, to buy British fruit and vegetables because I think that our farmers should be supported as much as possible and our fruit, certainly, always seems to have so much more flavour. We have so many different kinds to choose from that vary in colour, texture and sharpness.

All orchard fruits can be eaten raw, cooked as a sweet, or cooked in savoury ways with meat or fish. Most of them can be put into salads or eaten with cheese; and apples can add flavour to vegetable dishes.

Apples

The apple must be our most popular and our most universally used fruit, and is the only one that is still put quite readily by everybody into meat dishes, that is made into savoury sauces and mixed into salads.

232

It seems we have always been fond of apples. Wild crab apples were growing in Britain in pre-historic times and remains of the seeds have been found in ancient cooking pots. Then came the Romans, bringing with them their dessert apples, smaller than most we know today, but sweeter than the wild ones. Orchards were planted around the country villas and many different varieties were developed and propagated including sweet juicy ones for eating as a dessert soon after they were picked, and those that could be stored easily for winter use in airy lofts, or sliced into two or three pieces and dried in the sun.

When the Romans left, apple growing was mostly confined to the monasteries until the Normans established a relative peace in the land and more time was available for long-term fruit growing on country estates. The first apple actually to be mentioned in any written record was the Pearmain. Around the year 1200, between 105 and 200 Pearmains were paid to the crown as part of the annual payment for the Lordship of Runham in Norfolk. Both eating and cooking apples were grown then, and they were preferred after they had been kept for a time and had become soft and sweet.

The most popular way of cooking apples in Medieval Britain was to make them into fritters. These were sometimes apple slices, coated in batter and fried and then sprinkled with spices and honey, or occasionally sugar; or sometimes they were made of minced or chopped apples, mixed with dried fruit, spices again and bound with eggs before being made into small cakes and fried. Another Medieval dish was 'appelmus', 'apple moys' or 'appelmoise' (there are probably many more variations!) which was made on a base of cooked and sieved apples. This started off as a sweet-come-savoury kind of purée that was served with meat or fish. On fish days or fasting days which were every Friday and every day of Lent it was made with a substitute milk of ground almonds, olive oil, sugar and saffron, but on days when animal products were allowed with 'goud fat broth of bef and white grese, sugur and safron'. Later, in the seventeenth century appelmoise was still made, but it was then only a sweet dish, made with eggs, butter, sugar and spices.

Other savoury dishes using apples were 'rapeye', which was a Lenten sauce for fish made with all kinds of herbs, and apple soup of apples and mutton broth, for which recipes were still being written in the eighteenth century, very similar, but not so heavily spiced.

Raw apples were occasionally eaten with cheese at the end of a meal during later Medieval times, but for many years people were suspicious of raw fruit and so most meals ended with a roasted apple, strewn with sugar and fennel seed or aniseed.

Fruit tarts were popular in Tudor and Stuart times, which were often filled with a purée of cooked fruit, sweetened with sugar, spiced with cinnamon and ginger, and mixed perhaps with a little red wine. Taffety Tarts were made from sliced apples, candied peel, spices and dried fruits in the seventeenth century, and later, in the eighteenth century apples, lemon juice and shredded fresh lemon peel were common tart ingredients.

Over the years there have been many different ways of candying and preserving apples to be served as sweetmeats, eaten as a dessert, or offered to callers in the same way that we hand round the biscuits. Apples have been made into jelly for serving with meat, and have been put into preserves or marmalades, either alone or added, as a stiffener, to the orange or lemon ones.

Apples are a hardy fruit, but even so, they were concentrated mainly in the Midlands and south of England. An orchard was planted in Yorkshire in 1618, but in Lancashire, the North West and Scotland fruit was hardly known among the ordinary people until the eighteenth century. Then, the newly-built canals allowed apples and plums to be carried up from the South, and from then on fruit pies and tarts were a common sweet all over the country.

In apple counties, apples and pork have always been served together. The pigs rooted around in the orchards eating the windfalls making their meat rich and succulent, needing for a contrast, when it arrived at the table, the sharpness of apple sauce. There were pork and apple puddings and pork and apple pies. In winter when there was no fresh meat, bacon was used instead, and when this was scarce as well you could have apple and onion pie with cheese just underneath the crust. In the West Country the cheese was replaced with a dollop of clotted cream.

In talking of apples, we must never forget cider, the working man's drink in all apple counties. Farm cider is still made today and it really is the best for cooking and for drinking. In many cases it is sweetened but the best is made simply of fermented apple juice and drawn from the barrel unfiltered, unpasteurized and not carbonated.

Apple wine is not made commercially in such vast quantities as cider, but it is another good way of putting windfalls to good use. Home-brewed apple wine is pale, dry and clear, ideal for serving chilled on a summer afternoon, slightly richer and stronger than ordinary cider but not thick and sweet like the vintage.

If I am going to serve fruit as a sweet, I like it plain and simple, and only usually serve sweet dishes on special occasions. However, I use fruit a lot in salads and savouries, and probably apples end up in these dishes most frequently.

Salad hors d'oevres are perfect for hot summer days in the middle of August when the first, tart green apples are ready for picking. There is no need to peel apples for salads as you don't actually have to sink your

234

teeth into the outer skin. Sliced raw apple looks attractive if it is bordered by a deep green or crimson line, and what's more, just underneath that attractive line is where much of the goodness lies. Peel quarter, and core the apples. Slice them or chop them and mix them with diced cheese, or crispy grilled bacon, and mayonnaise, or a French dressing to which you have added some grated cheese.

Or hollow them out and stuff them.

Stuffed New Apple Salad

4 new George Cave apples (or any other crisp, new early apple)
juice 1 lemon
100g (4 oz) spicy salami (a good-quality foreign one)

60ml (4 tablespoons) freshly made mayonnaise
10 chopped sage leaves

Cut the tops off the apples and brush their undersides immediately with lemon juice. Hollow out the middles, leaving shells 0.25-0.75cm (⅛-¼ in) thick. Discard all the pieces of core and chop the rest. Brush the insides of the shell with lemon juice. Chop the salami into small squares and put it into a bowl with the chopped apple. Mix in the mayonnaise and fill the apple shells with this salad. Set the caps back on at a jaunty angle.

Sharp apples and sharp grapefruit are a good combination. Heap them up to look attractive, and stuff them with curd cheese.

Grapefruit and Apple Mounds

2 grapefruit
2 large crisp new apples
100g (4 oz) curd cheese

30ml (2 tablespoons) chopped walnuts
4 walnut halves

Core the apples but do not peel them. Cut each one into six rounds. Peel the grapefruit, removing all the pith from the outside. Cut each one into six rounds and take all the pith from the middles leaving a small hole. Use four small plates. Put one of the largest grapefruit slices on each. Then one of the largest apple slices and pile them up ending with the smallest apple slice. Mix the cheese and chopped walnuts together and stuff them down the centre holes. Top with the walnut halves.

New, sharp eating apples can make simple but attractive garnishes for roast pork, grilled pork chops and sausages, and also for plainly cooked herrings and mackerel. Core them, leave the skins on and cut them into rounds. Fry them in butter on a moderate heat until they are

235

golden. As they are cooking, sprinkle over a little cinnamon, or add some onion rings to the pan as well.

The first cooking apples are usually picked at the beginning of September. Grenadiers are usually the first, and later come Bramleys, the best of all, which in the cold stores will last until the following June. As they get older and more mellow, they are better than dessert apples for salads. For eating them raw, there is no need to peel them, but it is best to do so for most cooked dishes as the skin will not cook down and soften with the rest of the apple.

Baked apples are a lovely, warming winter sweet. You can fill them with dried fruits or a well of honey; or how about trying cheese? This recipe will do either as a first course or as a sweet-come-cheese course at the end of the meal.

Baked Apples and Stilton

4 medium-sized Bramleys   little butter for greasing dish
100g (4 oz) Stilton cheese

Preheat the oven to 190°C (375°F)/Gas 5.

Peel and core the apples. Either chop the Stilton very small, grate it or cream it depending on how soft and ripe it is. Set the apples in a lightly buttered oven-proof dish and press the Stilton into the centres. Bake the apples for 20 minutes. They will be firm but heated completely through and the Stilton will be melty on the outside and soft in the centre.

Apples are superb with herrings and mackerel. This recipe will make a first course for 4.

Mackerel with Apple Sauce

2 small or 1 really large   1 medium sized Bramley apple
  mackerel   5ml (1 teaspoon) soft brown
5ml (1 teaspoon) mustard   sugar
  powder   60ml (4 tablespoons) dry cider
1 small onion, sliced thinly into
  rings

For finishing the sauce:

10ml (2 teaspoons) grated
  horseradish

For garnish:

8 leafy sprigs watercress

236

Preheat the oven to 180°C (350°F)/Gas 4.

Fillet the mackerel. Leave the fillets whole if you are using small fish or cut the large ones in half crossways. Lay them in a flat oven-proof dish. Rub the mustard into the cut surface of the fish. Scatter the onion rings over the top. Peel and core the apple and cut it into very thin slices. Lay these over the onion and sprinkle over the sugar. Pour in the cider. Cover the dish with foil and put it into the oven for 25 minutes. Let everything cool completely in the dish, still covered. Gently remove all the pieces of onion and apple from the mackerel and lay each fillet on a small plate. Set aside the onion rings and rub the apple and all the liquid in the dish through a sieve. Mix in the horseradish. Spoon the sauce over the mackerel and lay three onion rings on top of each piece in descending size from head to tail. Lay a watercress sprig on either side of the fish, leafy end towards the head end, so you have a fan-shape on the plate, dark green on the outside and pale in the centre.

Apples are served with pork, and dried fruits put into curries. Here they are all put together.

Curry-Brushed Pork Chops with Apples and Raisins

4 loin pork chops
1 large or 2 small cloves garlic,
  crushed with a pinch of sea-
  salt
10ml (2 teaspoons) curry powder
30ml (2 tablespoons) olive oil

60ml (4 tablespoons) finely
  chopped onion
2 small Bramleys
30ml (2 tablespoons) raisins

Mix the garlic, curry powder and olive oil together. Peel and core the apples and cut them into 0.75cm (¼ in) slices. Preheat the grill to high. Brush one side of the chops with half the curry mixture. Put the chops, brushed side down, on the heated grill rack. Brush the upper surface. Grill them close to the heat, without turning until the upper side is golden brown. Turn them over and scatter over the chopped onion. Put the pan back under the high grill, still close to the heat until the onions are brown. Turn them about on top of the chops and grill them for one minute more so they are well-browned. Lay either two or three apple rings on each chop (depending on their size). Fill the centre of each ring with raisins. Put the pan back under the grill until the apples are just browning.

Serve the chops with buttered brown rice.

Patés are often given an extra tang with brandy or whisky. You can't beat spirits, but if you make patés fairly frequently it can become expensive. Cooking apples can make a good substitute.

Beef and Chicken Liver Paté with Apple

100g (4 oz) chicken livers
50g (2 oz) lean bacon
25g (1 oz) butter
1 medium onion, finely chopped
1 clove garlic, finely chopped
225g (8 oz) best quality minced
   beef

25g (1 oz) grated cooking apple,
   the harder and sharper the
   better
6 chopped sage leaves
freshly ground black pepper

Chop the chicken liver finely, removing any stringy pieces. Chop the bacon. Melt the butter in a heavy frying pan on a low heat. Put in the onion and garlic and cook them until the onion is soft. Stir in the livers, bacon and beef and stew the whole lot gently together for 15 minutes. Cool them slightly and put them through the fine blade of the mincer. Beat them well and beat in the apple, sage and pepper. Pile the mixture into a small earthenware terrine or dish. Cover, and chill until firm.

Serve it with brown toast for lunch.

Apples and eggs might seem unusual, but with bacon they make a tasty omelette. You can omit the chicken liver here if you like. It isn't at all essential but it is rather a good way of using up the one liver that comes with a fresh chicken. The omelette can serve two as a main course or four as a first course; or it can be served alongside cold meats or meat pies or quiches.

Apple Omelette

15g (½ oz) butter
1 small onion, thinly sliced
2 rashers lean bacon, chopped
1 small cooking apple, peeled,
   quartered, cored and sliced
1 chicken liver, chopped very
   small (not essential)

4 eggs
15ml (1 tablespoon) chopped
   parsley
10 chopped sage leaves

Melt the butter in an omelette pan on a low heat. Put in the onion and bacon and cook them until the onion is soft. Raise the heat to moderate and put in the apple and chicken liver. Cook them, stirring around, for 1½ minutes. Mix the sage and parsley into the eggs. Turn the grill to high. Pour the eggs into the pan and cook, tipping the pan and lifting the edges of the omelette to get as much of the egg as possible to the bottom and sides of the pan. When the underside is golden and the top nearly set, put the pan under the high grill so the omelette cooks right through and browns on top.

To take a leaf from the fourteenth century recipe book, here is a turnip and apple soup which has a creamy texture and colour and earthy flavour.

Turnip and Apple Soup

350g (12 oz) white turnips	25g (1 oz) butter
1 large onion	850ml (1½ pt) stock
1 really large Bramley or 2 small ones	bouquet garni

Scrub and trim the turnips, cut them in quarters and slice them thinly. Finely chop the onion. Peel, quarter, core and chop the apples. Melt the butter in a saucepan on a low heat. Stir in the turnips and onion, cover, and let them sweat for ten minutes. Stir in the apple and then the stock. Bring them to the boil, add the bouquet garni and simmer for 15 minutes. Remove the bouquet garni and work the soup in a blender until it is smooth. Reheat to serve.

Pears

Pears have never been as widely available nor as universally used as apples, but they too can be put into both sweet and savoury dishes, and as they are not sharp they can mix with creamy dressings and subtle herbs and the milder flavoured meats.

The Romans first brought cultivated pears to Britain and they made them into what were called 'patinae', small hors d'oevres made of a combination of a savoury such as eggs or brains or some other small delicacy, and a fruit. They preserved pears for the winter by sealing them in earthenware jars and burying them in the ground.

After the Roman occupation, some of their varieties of pears were kept, and later others were developed, mainly in monastery orchards, from wild pears. Pears were not put into many savoury dishes, but they were an essential inclusion in a pie that was baked, in Medieval times, to mark the mid-point of Lent, probably to cheer people up in the long, seemingly interminable fish-eating days. Other ingredients were figs, raisins, apples, spices, wine, sugar and boiled fish. They were sealed in a raised pastry case which was decorated on the outside with dates.

One of the most popular ways of serving pears since the fourteenth century, has been to cook them in a sweet syrup with wine and spices and colour them red. A dish such as this was one of the first for which a fork was used, and they seem to have been a great favourite of kings. Pears in syrup were served at the wedding feast of Henry IV and too many pears and too much ale are said to have been partly responsible for the death of King John.

Pears were also put into the Elizabethan fruit tarts, cooked and pulped first in the same way as apples, and mixed with red wine and spices. In the eighteenth century, they were made into thick, solid marmelades, and were sometimes candied or dried for the winter.

Pears were never grown on such a large scale as apples, and so the drink made from them, perry, was never made in such quantities as cider. Occasionally, cider was made with a mixture of apples and pears and in the fourteenth century a cheap version called 'piriwit' was mixed with the cheapest kind of ale and served to poor labourers. Warden pears were grown especially for perry in Henry VIII's reign, but very little was made commercially except in some areas of Worcester and Herefordshire where it is still made today. It is soft, pale and delicate in colour and flavour and it very often re-ferments in the bottle to produce a 'champagne'. In its counties of origin it was sometimes called 'merrylegs' and what an apt description of its effects this is!

The best pears for salads and savoury dishes are Conference, as they are the firmest and not quite as sweet and pungent in flavour as the others. Although the Lenten pie seemed a strange mixture at first, pears do mix with the milder fishy flavours.

Here is a simple salad flavoured with anchovies for a light and refreshing first course.

Pear and Anchovy Salad

4 firm Conference pears
8 flat anchovy fillets
1 carton (5 fl oz) natural yoghurt
30ml (2 tablespoons) cider
  vinegar
2 boxes mustard and cress

Peel, quarter, core and chop the pears. Pound four of the anchovy fillets to a paste and mix them with the yoghurt and vinegar. Mix the pears and cress into the dressing. Put the salad into four small bowls. Cut the remaining anchovy fillets in half lengthways and make crosses with them on top of the salads.

Make pears and prawns into a light and attractive first course for a special dinner party.

Prawn and Pear Salad

4 firm Conference pears
juice 1 lemon
575ml (1 pt) prawns or 175g
  (6 oz) shelled prawns
60ml (4 tablespoons) freshly
  made mayonnaise
15ml (1 tablespoon) tarragon
  mustard

Peel the pears and brush the outsides with lemon juice to stop them turning brown. Cut each one in half lengthways and scoop out and discard the cores. Scoop out the rest of the pear with a teaspoon, leaving shells 0.25cm (⅛ in) thick. Brush the insides with lemon juice. Chop the scooped-out pieces. Mix the mayonnaise and mustard together for the dressing and mix in the chopped pear immediately. Shell the prawns and mix them into the dressing with the pear. Once you have got this far, you can safely leave everything for several hours if needs be if you like to prepare things in advance.

To serve, put the salad inside the pear shells.

This hot salad can be served as a first course or as an accompaniment to cold meats, particularly pork, ham or brawn.

Hot Pear and Bacon Salad

4 fairly small, firm, Conference pears
175g (6 oz) streaky bacon
1 large onion, thinly sliced
10 chopped sage leaves

pinch ground allspice (or 6 crushed allspice berries)
60ml (4 tablespoons) cider vinegar

Dice the bacon and put it into a frying pan with no fat. Set it on a low heat. When the fat begins to run, put in the onion and cook it until it is just beginning to soften. Meanwhile, peel, quarter and core the pears. Cut each quarter in half crossways and the bottom half lengthways as well to give even-sized pieces. Put the pears, sage and allspice into the pan and pour in the vinegar. Let it boil for half a minute and serve the salad as soon as possible.

Pickled pears have often been served with cold meats, but here the pork and the pears are cooked together with the spices.

Pickled Pork and Pears

900g (2 lb) lean end of the belly of pork
4 small, firm Conference pears
30ml (2 tablespoons) pork fat or 15g (½ oz) butter
30ml (2 tablespoons) white wine vinegar

6 allspice berries (crushed) (or pinch ground allspice)
6 black peppercorns, crushed
little freshly grated nutmeg
2.5ml (½ teaspoon) ground cinnamon
150ml (¼ pt) stock

Bone and thinly slice the pork. Peel, quarter and core the pears and cut each quarter into two crossways. Heat the fat or dripping in a large frying pan on a high heat. Put in the slices of pork and brown them on

241

both sides. Remove them and set them aside. Pour in the stock and vinegar and bring them to the boil, stirring in any residue in the bottom of the pan. Add the spices. Replace the pork and put in the pears. Cover tightly and simmer for 25 minutes.

Chicken goes with tarragon and so do pears, so put them all together.

Chicken, Pears and Tarragon

One 1.5kg (3-3½ lb) roasting chicken
30ml (2 tablespoons) chicken fat or 15g (½ oz) butter
150ml (¼ pt) stock
30ml (2 tablespoons) tarragon vinegar

10ml (2 teaspoons) chopped tarragon or 5ml (1 teaspoon) dried (through most of the pear season there will be no fresh)
4 small, firm Conference pears

Joint the chicken. Heat the fat or butter in a sauté pan or large frying pan on a moderate heat. Put in the chicken pieces, skin-side down first and cook them until they are golden on both sides. Remove them and set them aside. Pour off all but a thin film of fat from the pan and set it back on the heat. Pour in the stock and vinegar and bring them to the boil. Replace the chicken, cover the pan, and set it on a low heat for 15 minutes. Peel, quarter, and core the pears. (Don't do this before or they will turn brown.) Put the pear quarters into the pan with the chicken and cook for a further 20 minutes. Keep the lid on tightly, but turn the chicken and let the pears get to the bottom of the pan several times. The liquid will reduce and give just enough thick glaze to provide around 15ml (1 tablespoon) for each joint.

Plums

Plums are fruit with a short season and as they do not keep or travel well many of them are sold as close to the home orchards as possible.

They were grown by the Romans and planted in Medieval gardens and at that time were usually served as an appetizer at the beginning of the meal.

In Elizabethan times they were made into sweet compotes and marmalades, and sometimes dried for winter sweets. In the eighteenth century they were preserved by drying, and also in syrup, and they were made into a sugary paste which was formed into cakes and dried and served like biscuits. A few plum cakes did actually contain plums as well as dried fruits, and at Nympsfield in Gloucester on St. Margaret's day they were made into a dumpling called Hegpeg Dump.

Jams and preserves have often been made from plums and also a sauce for steamed or baked puddings.

Plum wines have been made since the seventeenth century and to the end of the nineteenth one made from the dark ones was often fortified with a little brandy and sold as a crafty substitute for port.

The plum crop seems to be getting smaller each year, and most of those we buy now are usually made into tarts or jams and a few are eaten raw; but if you have plums to spare, or don't often make sweet dishes, try cooking them in the following ways.

The very first plums to arrive are the rarest of all. They are what are known as cherry plums, an old variety, which are tiny, round and bright red — in appearance like a cross between a cherry and a plum. Their flesh is yellow and sweet like a dessert plum and their skin slightly sharp. You may need more in weight than the larger plums as being tiny, there are more of them, and therefore more stones. They are excellent raw in fruit salads and in savoury salads and cooked dishes as well.

These first two recipes are made with cherry plums, but if you can't obtain them, use a different variety. In this mincemeat dish the best substitute is one of the fairly dark sharper ones, so they can contrast with the mellow flavour of the allspice.

Quick Mincemeat and Plums

350g (12 oz) cherry plums or dark, tart plums
900g (2 lb) best quality minced beef
2 cloves garlic, finely chopped
60ml (4 tablespoons) chopped parsley

150ml (¼ pt) dry white wine
12 crushed allspice berries (or 2.5ml (½ teaspoon) ground allspice)

Cut the cherry plums in half and stone them. If you are using the dark plums, quarter them lengthways as they are larger. Heat a large, heavy frying pan or sauté pan on a high heat with no fat. Put in the mincemeat and move it around until it browns and is well broken up and the fat has begun to run. Add the garlic and parsley and continue cooking and stirring for two minutes. Mix in the wine and allspice, lower the heat and simmer, uncovered for two minutes more. Mix in the prepared plums and continue to cook for half a minute. Serve the beef with tiny potatoes, boiled in their skins and tossed with butter and parsley.

The best substitute for cherry plums in this salad would be one of the dessert varieties. Victorias would be the first choice. It's a very attractive dish, with the chicken golden brown and encrusted with the ground ginger, with the bright skins of the plums and the green salad underneath.

Chicken, Plum and Ginger Salad

1.5kg (3-3½ lb) roasting chicken
1 sprig mint
1 sprig parsley
1 bayleaf
25g (1 oz) softened butter
10ml (2 teaspoons) ground
   ginger
150ml (¼ pt) dry white wine
1 Density or Webbs lettuce

8 medium sized salad onions,
   chopped
30ml (2 tablespoons) chopped
   mint
350g (12 oz) cherry plums or
   Victoria or any dessert plums
4 pieces stem ginger in syrup
15ml (1 tablespoon) tarragon
   vinegar

Preheat the oven to 180°C (350°F)/Gas 4.

Put the mint and parsley sprigs and the bayleaf inside the chicken and truss it. Work the butter and ground ginger together in a plate with a fork as though you were making kneaded butter. Put the chicken in a roasting tin and spread over all the butter mixture. Cover it completely with foil and put it into the oven for 1¼ hours. Raise the heat to 200°C (400°F)/Gas 6. Remove the foil and pour the wine into the tin. Put it back into the oven for 15 minutes. Take out the chicken and let it cool completely. Pour off all the juices from the pan and let them cool. Tear the lettuce into small pieces and put it into a bowl with the onions and mint. Stone and halve the cherry plums, or slice the larger plums and mix them into the lettuce. Skim the fat from the cooking juices and if they have set to a jelly put their container into a saucepan of water and set it on a low heat until they melt. Take them away from the heat. Finely chop the ginger and mix it into the pan juices with the tarragon vinegar.

Dress the salad with this mixture and arrange it on a large serving plate. Joint the chicken and put the joints on top of the salad.

Lamb always goes well with a fruit sauce. Pot-roast a shoulder of lamb with herbs and dark, tart cooking plums. You could also use damsons instead.

Pot-Roasted Lamb with Plums

1 piece shoulder of lamb
3 sprigs each lemon thyme and
   marjoram
15g (½ oz) butter

1 small onion, thinly sliced
275ml (½ pt) stock
225g (8 oz) small, dark cooking
   plums, halved and stoned

244

Preheat the oven to 180°C (350°F)/Gas 4.

Remove the bones from the lamb. Chop two sprigs each of the herbs and scatter them over the cut surface of the meat. Roll up the joint and tie it with strong thread or fine cotton string. Melt the butter in a flameproof casserole on a high heat. Put in the lamb and brown it all over. Remove it and set it aside. Lower the heat, put in the onion and cook it until it is soft. Stir in the stock and plums and bring them to the boil. Replace the lamb and put in the remaining herbs. Cover the casserole and put it into the oven for 1¼ hours. Lift out the lamb and keep it warm. Strain the sauce through a sieve, pressing down hard to get as much pulp from the plums as possible. Reheat the sauce while you carve the lamb. Serve them both separately.

In this recipe, the pork and the same, tart plums are cooked separately, and the juices from both combined at the end to make a fruity sauce.

Pot-Roasted Pork with Plum Sauce

1kg (2-2½ lb) loin pork joint or lean end of the belly	1 small onion, cut in half but not peeled
15ml (1 tablespoon) chopped marjoram	1 small stick celery
10 chopped sage leaves	6 small, dark tart plums
30ml (2 tablespoons) pork fat or 15g (½ oz) butter	150ml (¼ pt) dry cider
	5cm (1½ in) piece cinnamon stick
150ml (¼ pt) stock	kneaded butter made from 7.5ml (½ tablespoon) each butter and flour
bouquet of sage and marjoram	
1 small carrot	

Preheat the oven to 180°C (350°F)/Gas 4.

Remove the rind and bones from the pork. Scatter the chopped herbs over the cut surface. Roll up the meat and tie it with strong thread or fine cotton string. Heat the fat in a flameproof casserole on a high heat. Put in the pork and brown it all over. Remove it and set it aside. Pour off all but a thin film of fat from the pan. Set it back on the heat, pour in the stock and bring it to the boil. Replace the pork and surround it with the bouquet garni, carrot, onion and celery. Cover the casserole and put it into the oven for 1¼ hours. Stone and slice the plums and put them into a saucepan with the cider and cinnamon. Bring them to the boil, cover, and simmer for 15 minutes. Remove the cinnamon and rub the sauce through a sieve. When the pork is cooked, take it from the casserole and keep it warm. Strain the juices in the casserole into the plum sauce and put them into a saucepan. Set them on a moderate heat and bring them to the boil. Whisk in as much kneaded butter as necessary. Let the sauce simmer gently while you carve the pork and arrange it on a warm serving dish. Serve the pork and the sauce separately.

The big, sweet, juicy Victoria plums are by far the best for eating raw, either alone or in fresh fruit salads. Here they are put with pork chops and anchovies in a very similar way to dried prunes.

Pork Chops and Plums

4 loin pork chops
5ml (1 teaspoon) ground allspice
15g (½ oz) pork dripping or
  butter
1 medium onion, thinly sliced
150ml (¼ pt) dry red wine

4 flat anchovy fillets, pounded to
  a paste
225g (½ lb) Victoria or other
  dessert plums (stoned and
  sliced)

Rub the allspice into the surface of the chops. Melt the dripping or butter in a heavy frying pan on a moderate heat. Put in the chops and brown them on both sides. Remove them and set them aside. Lower the heat, put in the onion and cook it until it is soft. Pour in the wine and bring it to the boil. Stir in the anchovies, replace the chops and put in the plums. Cover the pan and set it on a low heat for 25 minutes.

Cherries

For a few weeks in July cherry trees look absolutely weighed down, their branches heavy with bright red or black fruits. Fresh cherries do not keep very long and so ways have had to be found for eating the abundant crop quickly or of preserving them for autumn and winter use.

In Medieval times cherry-feasts and cherry-fairs were held in the orchards and 'cherryes on the ryse' (on the twig) were cried in the streets of London. Over-eating at these times often had its disastrous consequences which people associated with eating any quantity of raw fruit rather than over-indulging, and later cherries were cooked and pulped and made into sweet pottages that were thickened with breadcrumbs and cereal flour.

A purée of cooked cherries was sometimes put into the Elizabethan fruit tarts, sometimes alone, and sometimes mixed with dried fruits and candied orange and lemon peel.

The eighteenth century was the great age of preserving all kinds of fruit, and cherries were dried, preserved in syrup, and made into jams and cherry-cheese. Hannah Glass has a recipe to preserve 'cherries with the leaves and stalks green' and she adds 'they look very pretty at candlelight in a dessert.'

Cherries are not exceptionally good travellers and so they were mainly used in the counties in which they were grown, and in Kent, Herefordshire and Worcestershire there were cherry pies, cherry puddings and cherry batters which were never as popular elsewhere.

By far and away the best way to deal with a large cherry crop was to make some form of delicious alcoholic beverage. Country wines became popular in the seventeenth century, and cherries made one that was rich, red and heavy. It could be made with any type of cherry, but Morellos were best of all. Cherry ale was made by fermenting cherries in a crock with strong beer, and cherry brandy by steeping pricked cherries with sugar in French brandy. After several months you had a rich liqueur and some alcoholic cherries to put into puddings and tarts. Another drink was called 'cherry bounce' and among its ingredients were 12 pounds of cherries, a quart of brandy and a quart of rum! Not quite the economical brew that home wine-makers are looking for now, but if you are lucky enough to get enough cherries they can still be made into an excellent wine.

Fewer and fewer cherries are being grown now and what there are can be quite expensive, so buy a few and make the most of them.

Cherries, like apples and pears, can make refreshing first course salads. If you like, with this one, you can omit the cheese and serve the cherries and grapefruit alone.

Cherry and Grapefruit Salad

225g (½ lb) sharp yellow and red cherries
2 grapefruit
30ml (2 tablespoons) olive oil
15ml (1 tablespoon) white wine vinegar
30ml (2 tablespoons) chopped mint
100g (4 oz) curd cheese
freshly ground black pepper
1 clove garlic crushed with a pinch of sea salt

Stone the cherries. Cut each grapefruit in half and cut them into segments as you would if you were serving them plain. Put them into a bowl with all but four of the cherries and the mint. Combine the oil and vinegar and mix them into the fruit. Work the black pepper and garlic into the cheese. Pile the salad back into the grapefruit shells. Put a blob of cheese on top of each one and top each with one of the reserved cherries.

Put expensive cherries with a fairly cheap ingredient. Shrimps are at their largest at cherry time and always go well with fruit.

Cherry and Shrimp Salad

225g (½ lb) red cherries
850ml (1½ pt) shrimps
30ml (2 tablespoons) chopped
    fennel
60ml (4 tablespoons) olive oil

juice 1 lemon
2.5ml (½ teaspoon) Tabasco
    sauce
lettuce leaves for serving

Stone and quarter the cherries. Shell the shrimps. Put them into a bowl with the fennel. Mix the oil, lemon and Tabasco sauce together. Arrange three large lettuce leaves on each of four small plates and pile the salad on top.

N.B. If you are preparing the dish in advance, coat the cherries with a little of the lemon juice and keep them in the 'fridge, otherwise they will quickly go brown. Mix in the shrimps at the last minute.

This salad is one for a summer lunch. Mint is an unusual herb for ham but with the cider vinegar the flavours blend very well.

Cherry, Ham and Cheese Salad

350g (12 oz) lean ham (home
    cooked or cut from the bone),
    diced
45ml (3 tablespoons) cider
    vinegar

30ml (2 tablespoons) chopped
    mint
225g (½ lb) red cherries
450g (1 lb) cottage cheese
lettuce leaves for serving

Put the ham into a bowl with the vinegar and mint and let it stand for 15 minutes. Stone the cherries and put them with the ham. Mix in the cheese. Line a salad bowl with lettuce leaves so the wide tops of the leaves come to the top of the sides. Pile the salad inside.

Lamb always goes well with red fruits and mint is the perfect flavourer.

Lamb Chops and Black Cherries

8 lamb chops
freshly ground black pepper

1 medium onion, finely chopped
350g (¾ lb) black cherries

For the sauce:

1 small onion, thinly sliced
6 allspice berries
6 juniper berries
6 black peppercorns
1 sprig mint
150ml (¼ pt) red wine

150ml (¼ pt) stock
15ml (1 tablespoon) red wine
    vinegar
15ml (1 tablespoon) chopped
    mint

248

Grate plenty of black pepper over the chops and let them stand while you prepare the sauce. Stone 225g (½ lb) of the cherries and put them into a saucepan with all the ingredients for the sauce, except the vinegar and chopped mint. Put them on a low heat and bring them to the boil. Cover, and simmer them for 30 minutes. Rub the sauce through a sieve and stir in the vinegar and chopped mint. Stone and quarter the remaining cherries and add these to the sauce. Preheat the grill to high, put the chops as close to the heat as possible and cook them until they are brown on both sides and almost cooked through. Pour off all the fat that will have collected in the pan. Remove the rack and put the chops in the bottom. Scatter over the chopped onion and put the pan back under the grill until the onion begins to brown. Pour over the sauce and turn the chops in it. Grill them for one minute more on each side. Put the chops in a warm serving dish and pour the sauce over the top.

Cold sliced breast of lamb is ideal for summer meals. Garnish it with a cherry salad to make a party dish.

Spiced Breast of Lamb with Cherries

2 pieces breast of lamb

For boiling:

*1 onion, cut in half but not
    peeled
1 carrot
1 stick celery plus a few leaves
10cm (3 in) piece cinnamon
    stick
10 cloves
10 black peppercorns*

*10 allspice berries
1 blade mace
bouquet garni which includes
    rosemary
2 bayleaves
30ml (2 tablespoons) wine
    vinegar
water to cover*

For the glaze:

*4 juniper berries
4 allspice berries
6 black peppercorns
45ml (3 tablespoons) redcurrant
    jelly*

*30ml (2 tablespoons) red wine
    vinegar*

For roasting:

*30ml (2 tablespoons) chopped
    mint
30ml (2 tablespoons) finely
    chopped onion*

*125g (¼ lb) red cherries (stoned
    and chopped)*

few cherries for decoration

249

For the salad:

350g (¾ lb) red cherries
30ml (2 tablespoons) chopped
  mint

30ml (2 tablespoons) olive oil
15ml (1 tablespoon) red wine
  vinegar

Put all the boiling ingredients into a large saucepan with enough water to cover the lamb. Bring them to the boil and simmer for ten minutes. Put in the lamb and simmer for 1¼ hours. Let the pieces cool in the liquid until they are just cool enough to handle. Lift them out, one at a time, and remove all the bones, skin, and as much fat as possible. Lay them down, slightly overlapping and press them overnight with a heavy weight.

Preheat the oven to 190°C (375°F)/Gas 5.

To make the glaze, crush the spices together and put them into a small saucepan with the redcurrant jelly and vinegar. Set them on a low heat and let the jelly dissolve without boiling. Brush the inner surface of the lamb with the glaze. Scatter over the chopped mint, onion and cherries. Carefully roll the two pieces of lamb together and tie them lengthways and crossways with fine cotton string. Set them in a roasting tin and put them into the oven for 40 minutes. Brush the outside of the lamb with the glaze and return it to the oven for a further five minutes. Take the lamb from the oven and let it stand, still tied, until it is completely cool. Untie it and set it on a serving dish. Stone and slice three cherries crossways (so you have small rings) and arrange them in a pattern on the lamb. Melt the glaze again and brush it over the lamb and cherries. Let the glaze set. Stone the remaining cherries and put them in a bowl with the mint. Mix the oil and vinegar together and stir them into the bowl. Arrange the cherry salad down either side of the lamb.

Soft Fruits

At one time the only soft fruits we had were wild ones. Raspberries and currants are scarce enough now, and even buying them I feel as though I have achieved a rare prize, but imagine what a treat it must have been to gather a few sweet handfuls from woodland or forest at a time when there were no other fruits around. But rewarding as it must have been, this foraging was a time-consuming and unreliable occupation and very soon the small wild plants were brought into cottage gardens and cultivated, some of them, regrettably, losing a certain amount of sweetness and strength of flavour. By the late sixteenth century they were all well-established and growing together. Thomas Tusser wrote in 1590: 'The gooseberry, raspberry, and roses, all three,
        With strawberries under them, trimly agree.'
From early June to the end of July, punnets of soft fruits grace greengrocers shelves and market stalls like boxes of brightly coloured jewels. Very early strawberries sometimes appear first in the middle of May, but of the main crops the small, tart, bright green gooseberries are the first arrivals, followed by the soft, large, mellow-flavoured ones with slight pink blushes. In late June come the scarlet strawberries, which are quickly followed by crimson raspberries and shiny, deeply coloured red and black currants. Their season is relatively short and they certainly don't store like apples and pears, so in a few weeks we must use our wealth of precious fruit to its best advantage; in fresh fruit salads, fruit fools and summer puddings and, if we have enough, in savoury dishes and salads as well.

Gooseberries make unusual sauces for meat and fish, and red-currants have for many years been used as a garnish for salads and have been made into redcurrant jelly to serve with lamb and game. Strawberries are plentiful enough to be used in savoury salads, but raspberries can be a little scarce, so choose to make sweets with these first and savoury dishes when you have some to spare. I have omitted blackcurrant recipes here altogether as any that I usually buy I make into sweets or Vitamin-C-rich cordials. There are never enough for savouries as well.

Soft fruits are fairly costly crops to grow, pick and pack, but lately

251

the 'Pick-Your-Own' idea has made many of them a more viable proposition and has increased or at least preserved, their availability. The system seems to be good for everybody. The farmer sells his fruit without having to worry about paying pickers or buying trays and punnets, and his customers get the pleasure of sharing in a small part of the harvest.

Gooseberries

Gooseberries were growing wild in Britain in Anglo-Saxon times when they were probably known as 'thefe-thorns'. Other names for them have included 'carberry', 'feaberry' and 'feabas'. The first record of them as a garden fruit was in the thirteenth century when they were planted in the royal garden at Westminster, and by the sixteenth century they were common in most gardens. During the reign of Elizabeth I, gooseberries were often put into tarts and pies with fish and chicken. These had a little sugar or honey added, but none of the usual dried fruits, and one recipe for a gooseberry and chicken pie is called 'To bake chickens without fruit'.

Chicken and gooseberries and later mackerel and gooseberries seem to have been the most popular combinations from the sixteenth to the eighteenth centuries. Chickens were baked with fresh or pickled gooseberries, or served with a sauce of gooseberries and sorrel. Baked mackerel was served with a gooseberry sauce.

Where some fruits such as raspberries and cherries have been used to flavour vinegar, gooseberries actually made a vinegar. I have an eighteenth century recipe which instructs you to boil the fruit with sugar and then ferment it with brown toast spread with yeast, bottle it and leave it for a year. Mrs Beeton makes it with gooseberries, water and 'foot sugar', which is what we now call Barbados sugar. She says that it is 'greatly superior to much that is sold under the name of the best white vinegar'.

In all this talk of savoury dishes and vinegars, we must not forget the sweets for which gooseberries were so often used. Gooseberry tarts were always popular. In the sixteenth and seventeenth centuries the gooseberries were puréed and highly spiced and later they were simply sugared. In Nottinghamshire, little raised pies were made with gooseberries in the same manner as pork pies, a possible carry-over from the earlier gooseberry and meat ones. Mixtures of gooseberries and eggs were made into gooseberry custard and gooseberry tansy which was rather like a sweet omelette; and in the seventeenth century,

252

gooseberry purée was beaten for hours with egg whites and then made into little sugary cakes by cooking blobs of the mixture for a long time in a slow oven. There were also gooseberry creams and gooseberry fools, puddings, jellies and trifles.

Gooseberry bushes are hardy and will grow well on any kind of soil. Once they are established they will produce quantities of fruit every year and a row of even six will supply more than enough for any family. you can imagine, then, that in many country homes all sorts of ways were found for preserving them. They were dried in a sugar syrup, or bottled, or made into jams and jellies, and of course made into country wine.

Nowadays, gooseberries are grown on market gardens and in small areas on farms. The bushes can be reared from cuttings or bought more expensively when they are older and more mature. They start fruiting in their first year, but really take three or even four years to grow into a good-sized bush with a harvestable crop. Gooseberry bushes, like fruit trees, have to be pruned to make them grow to the right shape and to make picking as easy as possible. Even so, the height of the bushes makes them awkward to prune and also to pick. Usually, the pickers sit down to their task and pick the gooseberries into ten pound trays.

As they fruit so well, gooseberries are generally cheaper than strawberries or raspberries and so we need have no qualms of conscience when we put them into savoury dishes as well as into tarts and custards.

Topping and tailing them to get them ready for cooking is a fiddly occupation and I often get round this by cooking them all first and then rubbing them through a sieve to produce a gooseberry purée. The time involved then comes at the other end of cooking, but somehow it is a much more satisfying way of doing things.

To make a purée from 450g (1 lb) of gooseberries, put them into a saucepan with 90ml (6 tablespoons) water, cover them, and set them on a low heat for 15 minutes, beating them occasionally with a wooden spoon to make them pulpy. Then cool them and rub them through a sieve. Sweeten the purée with honey or brown sugar according to the recipe you are going to make. For a savoury dish you may need only 5ml (1 teaspoon) but for a custard or mousse you will need much more. If you can find any elder bushes in flower cook a white sprig with your gooseberries for a pungent addition to the flavour. You can also use white wine instead of water and flavour the purée with a small piece of cinnamon.

A sweet purée of gooseberries can be put into tiny tarts or into a large flan case and topped with beaten egg whites like a lemon-meringue pie. Mix it with whipped cream for a gooseberry fool or with beaten eggs and milk for a fruit custard. For a simple jelly, soak half an ounce of gelatine in 60ml (4 tablespoons) of water and stir it into the warm purée until it melts.

You can make use of the sharpness of unsweetened gooseberries in exactly the same way as lemon juice. Instead of making a sauce for mackerel with gooseberries, combine them to make a meaty and succulent terrine. Serve it for lunch on a warm summer day, or as a first course for dinner, garnished with a sprig of elder flowers. For lunch time, serve it with a green salad dressed very simply with oil and vinegar and flavoured with fennel. Radishes will add to the picture.

Mackerel and Gooseberry Terrine

2 medium to large mackerel
weighing together about 1kg
(2¼ lb) before cleaning and
filleting
30ml (2 tablespoons) dry cider

30ml (2 tablespoons) chopped
fennel
100g (¼ lb) green gooseberries
15ml (1 tablespoon) chopped
chives

Preheat the oven to 160°C (325°F)/Gas 3.

Fillet the mackerel and cut half of one fillet into small strips. Put it into a bowl with the cider and half the fennel. Top and tail all the gooseberries and thinly slice four of them. Put these with the mackerel strips and cider. Put all the rest of the mackerel and gooseberries through the fine blade of the mincer. Mix in the remaining fennel and the chives. Put a third of the mixture into a 450g (1 lb) terrine or loaf tin. Arrange half of the mackerel pieces, sliced gooseberries and fennel on top. Put in another third of the minced mixture, the remaining pieces and fennel and top with the final amount of minced mixture. Cover the terrine and put it into the oven for 1¼ hours. Leave it until it is quite cold before turning out.

Herrings are another oily fish that need sharp flavours for contrast. Make some roll-mops for a cold meal that keeps well for a day or more in the 'fridge. For a first course, halve the amounts for four people.

Gooseberry Rollmops

4 medium sized herrings
10ml (2 teaspoons) dill seeds
1 medium onion, finely chopped
175g (6 oz) green gooseberries,
thinly sliced

60ml (4 tablespoons) white wine
vinegar
30ml (2 tablespoons) water
8 cocktail sticks

Preheat the oven to 180°C (350°F)/Gas 4.

Fillet the herrings and lay them out flat. Scatter the dill, onion and gooseberries equally over each fillet. Fold them up into parcels with

254

the tail and head meeting in the middle and secure them with cocktail sticks. Some of the gooseberries and onion may fall out when you do this, but poke them back in when the sticks are in place. Lay the rolls, fairly tightly packed in an ovenproof dish. Pour in the vinegar and water. Cover with foil and bake them for 20 minutes. Leave the foil over them and let the herrings get quite cold before serving.

If you are going to keep them overnight, leave them, undisturbed, in the 'fridge.

Gooseberries cooked in with the meat could make the dish very sharp, but here this is counteracted by the slight sweetness of cinnamon. The final result is a rich brown dish of lamb in which the gooseberries cook down to make a thick sauce.

Cinnamon-Lamb and Gooseberries

675-900g (1½-2 lb) lean boneless lamb cut from the shoulder
60ml (4 tablespoons) lamb fat or 25g (1 oz) butter
1 large onion, thinly sliced

150ml (¼ pt) dry white wine
225g (½ lb) green gooseberries, chopped
10ml (2 teaspoons) ground cinnamon

Cut the lamb into 2cm (¾ in) dice. Heat the fat or butter in a large frying pan or sauté pan on a high heat. Put in the lamb and brown it well, moving it around all the time to drive away any moisture. Remove it and set it aside. Lower the heat and cool the pan a little. Put in the onion and cook it until it is soft. Pour in the wine and bring it to the boil. Mix in the lamb, gooseberries and cinnamon. Cover the pan and set it on the lowest heat possible for half an hour. Serve it with buttered brown rice.

At gooseberry time there are many warm days when you feel like a cold meal. Serve this attractive one at a dinner party or special lunch. The slices of pork have a golden edge with green gooseberries in the middle, and the soft green of the spiced gooseberries makes a perfect garnish.

Cold Pork with Spiced Gooseberries

piece lean end of the belly of pork, weighing before boning 1-1.35kg (2½-3 lb)
20ml (4 teaspoons) clear honey
8 allspice berries
1ml (¼ teaspoon) freshly ground black pepper

1 clove garlic, finely chopped
pinch fine sea salt
450g (1 lb) green gooseberries, topped and tailed

For spicing:

150ml (¼ pt) dry cider   6cm (2 in) piece cinnamon stick
150ml (¼ pt) cider vinegar   4 cloves
5ml (1 teaspoon) allspice berries   15ml (1 tablespoon) clear honey

Preheat the oven to 180°C (350°F)/Gas 4.

Remove the rind and bones from the pork. Spread 10ml (2 teaspoons) of the honey over the underside. Crush the allspice berries, pepper, garlic and salt together with a pestle and mortar. Spread them over the honey. Thinly slice 50g (2 oz) of the gooseberries and scatter these over the top. Roll up the joint and tie it with strong thread or fine cotton string. Put it in a roasting tin and put it into the oven for one hour. Spread over the remaining 10ml (2 teaspoons) of honey and cook it for a further 30 minutes. Take the pork from the tin and let it cool completely before removing the string and carving. To make the spiced gooseberries, put the cider, vinegar and spices into a saucepan and bring them to the boil. Cover them and simmer for ten minutes. Strain the liquid, return it to the saucepan and stir in the honey. Set the pan on a low heat and when the honey has dissolved, add the remaining gooseberries. Simmer them gently for ten minutes so they are just tender but still whole. Keep a careful watch on them towards the end of cooking time as they can suddenly overcook without warning. Let the gooseberries get quite cool in the liquid.

Carve the pork and arrange it down the centre of a serving dish. Put three quarters of the spiced gooseberries on the dish, on either side of the pork. Hand the remaining gooseberries and spiced liquid separately in a sauce boat, so everyone can pour as much or as little over their pork as they wish.

You find all sorts of things under gooseberry bushes — or so I'm told! But I never expected to find a bag of fish. I went one day to see some gooseberry pickers and arrived at the same time as one of the farm workers who had been on a fishing trip and had a big box full of plaice and Dover sole. You can't miss an opportunity like that! I bought some sole, some gooseberries and picked an elderflower on the way home.

The result was plainly grilled Dover sole and this sharp but creamy sauce. You can also serve it with plaice, haddock or skate.

Gooseberry Sauce for White Fish

225g (½ lb) green gooseberries   1 egg yolk
1 sprig elderflower   30ml (2 tablespoons) chopped
150ml (¼ pt) dry white wine   fennel

Put the gooseberries, elder sprig and wine into a saucepan. Cover them, bring them to the boil and simmer for 15 minutes. Cool them slightly and rub them through a sieve. Return to the purée to the rinsed-out pan and stir in the egg yolk and fennel. Set the pan on a low heat and stir until the sauce thickens without letting it boil.

Serve it hot in a sauce boat.

Strawberries

'Doubtless God could have made a better berry, but doubtless God never did.' So said William Butler of strawberries in the sixteenth century.

Tiny, sweet wild strawberries were growing in Britain before the Romans arrived, and in Medieval times they were transplanted into gardens so that a small crop at least could always be relied on. When it was large and there was fruit to spare, strawberries were taken to the towns and hawked in the streets.

Many must have been eaten raw, for who could resist these tiny delicacies, but there was a mistrust of raw fruit nevertheless, and in the houses of the rich they were put into sweet, thick pottages to be served at the end of the meal. One fifteenth century recipe recommends that they be soaked in red wine, rubbed through a cloth and then simmered with almond milk and rice flour, raisins, saffron, pepper, 'Sugre grete plente', ginger and cinnamon. The result was sharpened with vinegar and coloured red, and the resulting indistinguishable concoction served garnished with pomegranate sauce. Did they know whether they were eating strawberries or red porridge?

A hundred years later, simplicity was appreciated and Boorde wrote in 1542 that 'Rawe crayme undecocted, eaten with strawberys is a rurall mennes benket.' Throughout the sixteenth century, strawberry plants were still brought in from the wild, but although they were sweet, they were very small. In order to obtain bigger ones, they were crossed with a slightly larger, musky-flavoured variety that was being grown on the continent. At the beginning of the seventeenth century another cross was made, this time with a strawberry with a better flavour from Virginia, but like the original ones, it was small. Then in the eighteenth century a French naval officer discovered a large but colourless and flavourless variety near Quito in Equador which became known as the Chilean strawberry. He managed to keep two plants alive on the journey home, and the ones we grow today are descendants of both this and the Virginian kind.

The old tradition of highly spicing and flavouring fruits was still carried on in the strawberry tarts of the sixteenth and seventeenth centuries, but at least the strawberries were left whole and not pulped like apples or pears. In the eighteenth century, they were simply sweetened with sugar, and nothing else was added.

Strawberries were made into the stiff jellies and sugary sweetmeats that were favourites in Tudor times, and later into jams, jellies and fruit compotes. Eliza Acton has a recipe for a strawberry vinegar. She steeps them in wine vinegar, strains the resulting liquid and sweetens it; and serves it not as a salad dressing or pickle, but as a health-giving summer drink or a sauce for sweet puddings.

Delicious and sweet as they are, strawberries tend to lose their colour and flavour when they are made into wine, and if they are steeped in brandy in the same way as cherries, they become overpowered by the spirit. Some of the best looking recipes I have found, though never tried, have been for soaking strawberries in Canary wine, straining, sweetening, and bottling straight away.

It takes at least a year for a strawberry plant to produce its first fruit, so once the land has been chosen and planted, the farmer has a long wait before he can reap any returns. New strawberry land is always the most productive and the best strawberries always come in the first year. The plants usually only last for four seasons and on the bigger farms the fields are dug up and replanted in rotation.

Plants can be set in the autumn or spring, but the best time for planting is July, so high summer can be really busy for the strawberry grower, gathering in this year's crop and making sure next year's will be just as good. On small plots and market gardens strawberry plants are very often set by hand, but large fields are planted up mechanically in a very similar way to cabbage fields.

If they are set in July, the plants will produce their first fruit the following year, but the later-sown ones have their flowers picked off in the first summer so all the growth can be concentrated in the plant.

Boorde's 'rural mennes banket' is still the best way of serving strawberries. Put them in a dish and pour over some double cream. For a change, whip the cream and flavour it with brandy or vintage cider; or use natural yoghurt for a summer breakfast. If your strawberries are squashy, rub them through a sieve and you have a simple fruit sauce. Sweeten it with honey if you think it necessary, and pour it over junkets, home-made custards or ice-cream; or over other fruits such as slices of ripe melon or stoned and halved peaches.

Served in savoury ways, strawberries go well with cheese. Serve them as a first course in a light, garlic-y French dressing with a blob of curd cheese on the top, or omit the garlic from the dressing and mix it into the cheese along with some fresh mint. You can also mix sliced strawberries into the curd cheese along with the garlic, adding a little lemon juice as well. Strawberries and cheese on toast make a surprisingly good snack. Toast one side of some slices of brown bread and butter the other side. Lay on strawberry halves, cut side down and then some thin slices of Cheddar cheese. Put them under the grill until the cheese has melted.

This salad with Demi Sel Cheese can be served as a first course or at the end of the meal as a sweet-come-cheese course.

Strawberries and Demi-Sel Cheese

450g (1 lb) strawberries   1 clove garlic, crushed with a
125g (4 oz) Demi Sel cheese   pinch of sea salt
1 carton (5 fl oz) natural yoghurt   freshly ground black pepper

Chop half the strawberries and cut the rest in half. Work the yoghurt into the cheese and beat in the garlic and pepper. Mix the chopped strawberries into the cheese mixture and then divide it between four small serving bowls. Put the strawberry halves on top.

Mild-flavoured cottage cheese is a good one for mixing with fruits to make salads. This one makes a lunch dish for four. You can change the bacon to lean diced ham or for a first course omit it altogether.

Strawberry, Cheese and Bacon Salad

450g (1 lb) strawberries   30ml (2 tablespoons) tarragon
225g (8 oz) green streaky bacon   vinegar
450g (1 lb) cottage cheese   lettuce leaves for serving

Cut all the strawberries in half. Grill the bacon until it is cooked through but not crisp. Cool it and cut it into small pieces. Put the cheese into a bowl and mix in the vinegar. Fold in the strawberries and bacon. Line a salad bowl with lettuce leaves and pile the salad inside.

Cucumber and yoghurt are ideal summer refreshers. Put them with strawberries for another first course.

Strawberry and Cucumber Salad

1 carton (5 fl oz) natural yoghurt   225g (8 oz) strawberries
1 large cucumber
1 clove garlic, crushed with a
   pinch of sea salt

Put the yoghurt into a bowl. Cut 12 thin slices from the cucumber and grate the rest into the yoghurt. Mix in the garlic and pepper. Reserve eight small strawberries and quarter the rest. Mix the quartered ones into the yoghurt and cucumber. Put the salad into four small bowls and garnish with the slices of cucumber and the remaining strawberries cut in half.

Broad beans come along at the same time as strawberries and with tarragon they go together surprisingly well to make another unusual first course.

Strawberry and Broad Bean Salad

900g (2 lb) broad beans, weighed in their shells
60ml (4 tablespoons) olive oil
30ml (2 tablespoons) tarragon vinegar
225g (8 oz) strawberries
30ml (2 tablespoons) chopped tarragon
100g (4 oz) curd cheese

Shell the beans and put them into a saucepan with the oil. Set them on a low heat for 15 minutes, stirring occasionally. Stir in the vinegar and turn them out into a bowl to cool completely. Quarter the strawberries and mix them into the beans with the tarragon. Divide the salad between four small bowls and top each with a blob of curd cheese.

This main-course salad is best served very slightly chilled. It is savoury and pungent but not at all sweet and uses the old fashioned spices that always go so well with pork.

Pork Chop and Strawberry Salad

4 pork chops (loin)
12 allspice berries
1 large or 2 small cloves garlic, chopped
2.5ml (¼ teaspoon) fine sea salt
2.5ml (¼ teaspoon) ground cinnamon
120ml (8 tablespoons) dry white wine
30ml (2 tablespoons) white wine vinegar
350g (12 oz) strawberries

Preheat the oven to 180°C (350°F)/Gas 4.

Crush the allspice berries, garlic, salt and cinnamon together and rub them into the surface of the pork. Lay the chops in a flat oven-proof dish and pour in the wine and vinegar. Cover them with foil and put them into the oven for 45 minutes. Remove them from the oven and let them cool as they are, still covered. Take the chops from the dish and put them in a cool place or in the 'fridge. Quarter the strawberries and put them in a bowl. Pour over the cooking juices and put them into the 'fridge for four hours. Skim away any fat that has collected on the surface. By this time the juices should be very slightly jellied so this should be easy.

Serve the chops with the strawberries and shimmery juices spooned over them.

260

Raspberries

Not so much has been written in praise of raspberries as there has of strawberries, but there are many who prefer this deeper-coloured, softer, and at times slightly sharper-flavoured berry.

Cultivated raspberries were first grown in Britain in the middle of the sixteenth century, and throughout the next two hundred and more years, raspberry canes were a common inclusion in nearly every cottage garden.

Raspberries have always been eaten raw with cream, and one of the most popular ways of serving them was to bruise them into whipped cream to give a pale pink fluff, flecked with deep red. In Tudor and Stuart times raspberries were puréed and mixed with sugar syrup to make a stiff jelly, to be eaten not as a dessert but as a sweetmeat which, carefully boxed, would keep for a year.

Because there has always been a crop to gather just outside the kitchen door, raspberries have been made into numerous tarts, jams, preserves and vinegars, and have been one of the most popular fruits for wine, as unlike strawberries, they make one that has a distinctive flavour and rich colour. In the late seventeenth century, the juice of the fruits was combined with sugar and mixed with either white wine or the sherry-like sack, but later, as French wines became more expensive, raspberries were used alone to make a true country wine.

Only if you grow or in some cases, pick, your own could you find enough raspberries to make into wine now, and even if you picked them yourself the price would be high for raspberries are an expensive crop to grow on a large scale. The canes are all planted by hand in the winter and then there is a wait of two and a half years before you have any fruit that is worth picking. The season is a very short one, so even after waiting, the land remains unproductive for most of the year. All the returns have to be gained in a few short weeks. They are very small and fiddly to pick, and to fill a punnet takes twice or even three times as long as it would to fill one with strawberries. Perhaps we should all start to grow raspberries up the garden fence — then we might have enough for all those wines and jams again!

Raspberries as a sweet are best served very simply with cream or yoghurt and the old method of bruising them as you mix in the cream is well worth trying. Try moistening them, too, with a little sherry or vintage cider and leaving them to steep for a while in the sun. If they need sweetening, use honey instead of sugar and instead of mixing it into the raspberries, beat it first into your cream. Use sour cream instead for a change or some rich, sweet cream cheese such as the Somerset cheese.

If you are new to using fruits in savoury ways, it is perhaps a good idea first, to mix just a little into a side-salad to see how you like the combination of meat and fruit.

This one has a very Elizabethan flavour as it has a good selection of herbs, a slight touch of onion and no garlic. The tarragon vinegar and the raspberries together provide a sweet-come-sharp flavour. The salad looks attractive with bright crimson raspberries amongst the green. Serve it with chicken, pork or lamb.

Green Salad with Raspberries

1 small lettuce
1 small cucumber
225g (½ lb) raspberries
15ml (1 tablespoon) chopped
* tarragon*
15ml (1 tablespoon) chopped
* mint*
10 chopped sage leaves

green parts of 4 salad onions,
* chopped*
60ml (4 tablespoons) olive oil
30ml (2 tablespoons) tarragon
* vinegar*
freshly ground black pepper
pinch fine sea salt

Tear the lettuce into small pieces. Cut the cucumber into quarters lengthways and slice it thinly. Put them both into a salad bowl with the raspberries, herbs and chopped onions. Blend the oil, vinegar and seasonings together and stir them into the salad.

Cucumber is used again here to give a fresh taste to a low caloried summer first course. It is very attractive, the cucumber skin making the cheese mixture a delicate pale green. Cottage cheeses tend to vary in texture — use one of the softer, creamier ones.

Raspberry, Cucumber and Cheese Salad

½ medium sized cucumber
225g (½ lb) cottage cheese
grated rind 1 lemon
15ml (1 tablespoon) chopped
* mint*
30ml (2 tablespoons) chopped
* chives*

1 clove garlic, crushed with a
* pinch of sea salt*
freshly ground black pepper
225g (½ lb) raspberries

Wipe the cucumber but do not peel it. Grate it and put it into a sieve over a bowl for 15 minutes to drain. Mix it into the cheese with the lemon rind, mint, garlic, chives and black pepper. Fold in the raspberries last of all and chill.

Serve the salad in earthenware bowls.

262

If you find your raspberries rather expensive, use a cheap cut of pork to make another fruity first course.

Pork and Raspberry Salad

4 lean belly of pork rashers
60ml (4 tablespoons) dry red
wine
30ml (2 tablespoons) red wine
vinegar

1 small onion, finely chopped
bouquet of sage
100g (¼ lb) raspberries
10 chopped sage leaves
lettuce leaves for serving

Preheat the oven to 200°C (400°F)/Gas 6.

Cut the rinds from the rashers. Curl each one into a flat circle and lay them on a flat ovenproof dish. Pour over the wine and vinegar. Scatter over the onion and tuck in the bouquet of sage. Cover with foil and put them into the oven for 45 minutes. Cool everything slightly and lift the pork onto a plate, leaving the onion pieces behind. Discard the bouquet of sage. Put the raspberries into a bowl and fold in the juices and the onion from the dish. Cool everything completely and chill them very slightly.

Put some crisp lettuce leaves onto four small plates and put a curl of pork on each one. Spoon the raspberries and the juices (which should be very slightly jellied) over the pork.

This chicken salad makes a good light lunch. If you are cooking the chicken specially then poach it, so it will be nice and moist. Cooking the onion first softens it in both taste and texture, and gently flavours the oil, which brings all the sweet and savoury parts of the salad together.

Chicken and Raspberry Salad

1 small cooked chicken 1.125-
1.4kg (2½-3 lb) before cooking
60ml (4 tablespoons) olive oil
1 large onion, thinly sliced
1 clove garlic, finely chopped
30ml (2 tablespoons) white wine
vinegar

5ml (1 teaspoon) ground
cinnamon
30ml (2 tablespoons) chopped
fennel
225g (8 oz) raspberries
1 small lettuce for serving

Dice the chicken. Put the oil into a saucepan with the onion and garlic. Cover them and set them on a low heat for ten minutes. Pour in the vinegar and let it bubble. Take the pan from the heat and mix in the chicken, cinnamon and fennel. Turn the mixture into a bowl to cool. Mix in the raspberries taking care, if they are ripe, not to break them up. Chill the salad slightly. Line a salad bowl attractively with whole lettuce leaves so the rounded edges just come to the top of the bowl.

263

Pile the salad inside. There should be just enough dressing to coat the lettuce as well.

Serve it with a salad of brown rice.

Raspberries might seem a surprising accompaniment for beef, but this dish really works and the flavours go perfectly. As with most fruit meals, the appearance is good too with deep red raspberries in a rich brown jelly, acting as a kind of sweet pickle.

Cold Braised Brisket and Raspberries

1 joint rolled brisket of beef weighing around 1.125kg (2½ lb)
60ml (4 tablespoons) red wine vinegar

120ml (8 tablespoons) stock
10ml (2 teaspoons) clear honey
freshly ground black pepper
225g (8 oz) raspberries

Preheat the oven to 160°C (325°F)/Gas 3.

Put the beef into a casserole. Mix the vinegar, stock and honey together and pour them over the beef. Season with a generous amount of black pepper. Cover the casserole and put it into the oven for two hours. Lift out the beef and let it cool completely. Pour the casserole juices into a bowl and skim them. When they are just cool, gently fold in the raspberries. Put them into the 'fridge for the juices to jelly very slightly. Carve the beef and arrange it on a serving dish. Spoon the jellied raspberries on and around it.

Currants, Red and Black

Black and red currants are probably now the most scarce of the summer fruits in the shops because so many of them go for processing: the redcurrants for jams and jellies and the blackcurrants for drinks. In 1975 only 10,000 acres of blackcurrants were grown at all and 8,000 of these went off to various factories.

Currants were growing wild in Britain around the tenth century but they were first cultivated as garden plants on the continent. They were certainly in Elizabethan gardens, and sometimes, in confusion with the dried currants and raisins, they were known as 'bastard Corinths' and even just 'raisins'. Another name for them was 'beyond sea gooseberry'. Their bright colours made currants ideal for garnishes, sometimes for fish, and pickled in wine and vinegar for salads.

They were used in the early, spicy fruit tarts and the ones in the eighteenth century that were simply sweetened with sugar or honey.

Redcurrants were candied with a sugar syrup, dried, and cut into small cakes to eat like sweets; and purées of both fruits were mixed with cream to make a fool which was sometimes enriched with ground almonds. Redcurrants have always been the more popular of the two for summer puddings and for making into a jelly to serve with meat or game; and blackcurrants have always made the better jam.

For many years, the Vitamin-C-rich blackcurrant has been made into cordials, while redcurrants were made into a wine so good as to earn it the title of 'English Champagne'. In East Anglia, red mead was made for which the honey was fermented with redcurrant juice instead of water. It must have been like absolute nectar, but how expensive it would be to make now when sometimes we can barely obtain enough currants for a mere 1.4kg (3 lb) of redcurrant jelly.

The main reason for their scarcity is because they are so fiddly and time-consuming to pick by hand. Redcurrants are not quite so bad as they at least come off in clusters, but blackcurrants have to be taken almost one at a time. Picker's wages will inevitably be high in proportion to their output and on top of this the farmer will have to provide punnets and carriage. One can hardly blame him, then, for producing the fruit under contract to cordial-making firms, who provide all the containers and transport for the acres of machine-picked black-currants.

Any blackcurrants I buy during their short season I make into my own cordial or into sorbets or have them for breakfast worked in a blender with yoghurt and honey. Sometimes there is enough for a pie or a cream, but never really for savoury dishes and salads.

Redcurrants, however, I do use in other ways. Homemade redcurrant jelly is always more concentrated and fruity than the shop-bought kinds, so inevitably some are kept for this, so the flavour of the fruit at least can be preserved for the rest of the year, for serving with roast meats or game and mixing into sauces. While the fresh ones are around, I use these instead.

In this first recipe the slightly sharp currants and the sweeter orange juice are all that is needed to make a sauce for lamb chops.

Lamb Chops with Redcurrants and Orange

8 loin lamb chops
freshly ground black pepper
30ml (2 tablespoons) lamb fat or 15g (½ oz) butter
1 small onion, finely chopped
225g (8 oz) redcurrants

grated rind and juice 1 small orange
15ml (1 tablespoon) chopped marjoram
10ml (2 teaspoons) chopped rosemary

Trim the chops of any excess fat and grind over some black pepper. Heat the fat in a large frying pan on a high heat. Put in the chops (you may have to do this four at a time) and brown them on both sides. Remove them and set them aside. Lower the heat, pour off all but 15ml (1 tablespoon) of the fat and cool the pan a little. Put in the onion and cook it until it is soft. Stir in the redcurrants, herbs and orange rind and juice. Let the juice bubble and replace the chops, packing them all in together. Cover the pan and cook on a very low heat for 20 minutes.

With liver, currants make a fairly cheap dish that is quick and easy to prepare but nevertheless looks and tastes expensive. Serve it with brown rice tossed with butter and parsley, and a fresh green salad.

Lamb's Liver and Redcurrants

175g (1½ lb) lamb's liver
40g (1½ oz) butter
1 medium onion, finely chopped
150ml (¼ pt) dry red wine

225g (8 oz) redcurrants
15ml (1 tablespoon) chopped thyme

Cut the liver into small, thin strips. Melt 25g (1 oz) of the butter in a heavy frying pan on a high heat. Put in the strips of liver (in two batches) and brown them quickly. Remove them and set them aside. Lower the heat and cool the pan a little. Melt the remaining butter. Put in the onion and cook it until it is soft. Pour in the wine, raise the heat a little and bring it to the boil, stirring and scraping in any brown pieces from the bottom of the pan. Stir in the redcurrants and thyme and replace the liver. Cover and cook on a very low heat for ten minutes.

Cold dishes are often the order of the day during the currant season, even for dinner parties. This leg of lamb is served with its own kind of redcurrant jelly that is also used for the glaze. The jelly itself is a soft, translucent pink dotted with green mint and full of bright red, whole currants. A very savoury-flavoured potato salad is a good accompaniment.

Cold Leg of Lamb and Redcurrants

bottom end of a leg of lamb
275ml (½ pt) dry red wine
225g (8 oz) redcurrants
6 juniper berries

1 sprig mint
10g (½ oz) gelatine
30ml (2 tablespoons) chopped mint

Preheat the oven to 180°C (350°F)/Gas 4.
    Put the lamb into a large casserole. Pour in the wine and put in half the redcurrants, the juniper berries and the mint sprig. Cover and put

the casserole into the oven for 1½ hours. Lift out the lamb and let it cool completely. Rub all the rest of the contents of the casserole through a sieve. Let the resulting liquid cool and skim it well. Soak the gelatine in 60ml (4 tablespoons) of the liquid. Put it in a small saucepan and melt it on a very low heat without letting it boil. Stir in the rest of the juices and take the pan from the heat. Cool them slightly. Mix in the chopped mint. Brush the lamb with this jelly, letting a lot of the mint stick to it as well. Let the glaze set and brush the lamb again. Stir the remaining redcurrants into the jelly and pour them into a bowl to set completely.

Set the lamb on a serving dish. Break up the jellied currants and spoon them round the lamb. Carve it at the table.

This salad with pork is another attractive one. As the pork cooks the outside goes slightly pink and the redcurrants are rosy in a light brown, shimmery jelly. Don't be afraid to tuck in to it though for the flavour will match the appearance. The currants are just slightly sharp and the pork a good, plain savoury flavour with the sage.

Pickled Pork and Redcurrants

1 piece lean end of the belly of
   pork, weighing with the bones
   around 1.125kg (2½ lb)
pinch sea salt
freshly ground black pepper

8 chopped sage leaves
30ml (2 tablespoons) white wine
   vinegar
60ml (4 tablespoons) stock

For the pickle:

60ml (4 tablespoons) white wine
   vinegar
5ml (1 teaspoon) mustard seed
6 allspice berries

3cm (1 in) piece cinnamon stick
2 sage leaves

225g (8 oz) redcurrants

Preheat the oven to 180°C (350°F)/Gas 4.
   Bone the pork and cut off the rind. Sprinkle the cut surface with the salt, pepper and chopped sage. Roll up the joint and tie it with strong thread. Put it into a casserole and pour in the vinegar and stock. Cover and put into the oven for 1½ hours. Make the pickle as soon as the pork is in the oven. Put the vinegar, mustard seed, allspice, cinnamon and sage leaves into a saucepan and set them on a low heat. Cover them and bring them to the boil. Take the pan from the heat and cool the contents completely. Put the redcurrants into a bowl and strain over the pickle.
N.B. There will only be a very little vinegar — just enough for flavour.
Take the pork from the casserole and let it get cold. When the juices

are only just cool, pour them into the bowl with the redcurrants and vinegar. Put them into the 'fridge to set to a very light jelly.

Carve the pork and arrange it on a serving dish. Skim any fat from the top of the currants. Gently break up the jelly and spoon the currants over the pork.

This fish dish is for a first course, inspired by the sixteenth and seventeenth century redcurrant pickles that were served with white fish. Here, the currants contrast well with the buttery, tarragon-flavoured haddock.

Potted Fish and Redcurrants

350g (¾ lb) fresh haddock
120ml (8 tablespoons) dry white
  wine
bouquet garni, including a sprig
  of tarragon

6 black peppercorns
75g (3 oz) butter
15ml (1 tablespoon) chopped
  tarragon
100g (4 oz) redcurrants

For garnish:

2 sprigs tarragon

2-4 long strings redcurrants

Preheat the oven to 180°C (350°F)/Gas 4.

Cut the haddock into about four pieces. Lay them in a flat, oven-proof dish and pour in the wine. Put in the bouquet garni and peppercorns and cover with foil. Put the fish into the oven for 20 minutes. Take it out, remove all the skin and any bones, and flake it. Melt the butter in a frying pan on a very low heat. Put in the fish and mash it into the butter with a fork. Mix in the tarragon and take the pan from the heat. Gently mix in the redcurrants, taking care not to break them up. Put the mixture into a bowl and press it down lightly. Chill it until it is firm. Run a knife round the edge and turn it out carefully onto a plate. (If any sticks in the bowl, the fish will be quite manageable and you can easily fix it back together again and smooth it over!) Garnish it with the tarragon sprigs and strings of currants.

Rhubarb

Whenever you mention rhubarb, people laugh, probably because of its old associations with purgatives and medicines; but really it is one of the most useful of fruits, the outdoor crop coming along just as cooking apples are beginning to run short and before the gooseberries are ready. I will call it a fruit, as that is how it is normally used, but in fact it is technically a vegetable of which we eat the stem.

Rhubarb as we know it was one of the latest garden fruits to be cultivated in England. Earlier, there were other variations, including Turkey and Barbary rhubarb which were grown in Elizabethan herb gardens as a curiosity and for medical purposes. The kind we grow today arrived from Italy in the seventeenth century. The syrup from the juice was still used at first as a gentle purgative, but gradually its potential as a fruit was discovered, and by the eighteenth century it was being put into pies and fruit fools and creams. Later, it was used for jams and chutneys, and Eliza Acton has a recipe which she calls a 'Compote of Spring Fruit', as though the name rhubarb were still something not to be mentioned!

Rhubarb is an amazingly prolific plant and as such it has often been used to make gallons of country wine; but care has to be taken with it as it can easily turn out to be quite sharp. It is best if it is mixed with something mellower like raisins, which bring out the underlying roundness in the flavour of the fruit.

Two types of rhubarb are grown in this country now, the forced kind and the outdoor. Both are planted between October and December and it usually takes two years before the first crop is ready. Most of the forced rhubarb is grown in Yorkshire and Cheshire. The plants are lifted in the autumn and put into a greenhouse or a special forcing shed, so the stalks will be long enough for picking by January. Outdoor rhubarb is thicker and redder and more robust looking. The stems push their way through the ground around the end of February mounding up the earth around them as they do so, and they are ready for pulling by mid-March. They are simply pulled out of the ground by hand, the piece of light skin at the bottom is pulled off and the huge leaves sliced off with a knife. Then they are put into crates or boxes and either sent directly to shops or markets; or taken to a packhouse, where they are washed, trimmed to equal lengths and wrapped up in polythene to be sent out to supermarket depots — 'pot-ready', to use the term of one packhouse manager!

Rhubarb can be chopped and put raw into pies, layered with sugar and cinnamon, or it can be cooked and sweetened first. In April, there aren't many fresh fruits around and it is surprising what you can do with this one-time medicine to ring the changes. Rub cooked rhubarb purée through a sieve or work it smooth in a blender, sweeten it, and you have a fruit sauce. Try pouring it hot over ice-cream or over steamed puddings; or make the same basic purée into a light pink sorbet. If you are a pickling and bottling addict, then there are jams and chutneys and spicy sauces to be made, and if your palate is savoury rather than sweet try putting it with the richer meats and fish in the same way as apples.

Rhubarb sauces, unsweetened could be rather sharp, but here the flavour is mellowed by the juniper berries.

Pork Chops and Rhubarb

4 loin pork chops
225g (½ lb) rhubarb
8 juniper berries
1 clove garlic, finely chopped
pinch fine sea salt
freshly ground black pepper

30ml (2 tablespoons) pork fat or
    15g (½ oz) butter
1 medium onion, finely chopped
150ml (¼ pt) dry red wine
150ml (¼ pt) stock

Trim any excess fat from the chops. Chop the rhubarb. Crush the juniper berries, garlic, salt and pepper together with a pestle and mortar. Heat the fat in a frying pan or sauté pan on a moderate heat. Put in the chops and brown them on both sides. Remove them and set them aside. Lower the heat, put in the onion and cook it until it is soft. Mix in the rhubarb. Pour in the wine and stock and bring them to the boil. Stir in the crushed spices and garlic and replace the chops. Cover the pan and set it on a low heat for 25 minutes.

Serve the chops with the pulpy rhubarb sauce spooned over the top. Accompany them with potatoes, boiled in their skins, sliced and tossed with butter and parsley and a fresh-tasting green vegetable such as spring cabbage.

When I first made this pie I got a surprise. I was expecting the filling to turn out pink, but instead the cooked rhubarb was green and looked like leeks. There was no trace of sharpness, but the pie was tasty and savoury, and the dripping in the pastry, combined with the long, slow cooking, made it light and crisp.

270

Pork and Rhubarb Pie

For the pastry:

225g (8 oz) wholemeal flour
pinch sea salt
freshly ground black pepper
50g (2 oz) pork dripping or lard
75g (2 oz) butter
water to mix
beaten egg for glaze

900g (2 lb) lean end of the belly
*   of pork or lean pork rashers*

225g (8 oz) rhubarb
2 medium onions
1 large clove garlic
10ml (2 teaspoons) soft brown
*   sugar*
pinch sea salt
freshly ground black pepper
6 crushed allspice berries (or
*   pinch ground allspice)*

Preheat the oven to 180°C (350°F)/Gas 4.

Make the pastry and set it aside to chill. Remove the rind from the pork and cut it into 2cm (¾ in) dice. Finely chop the rhubarb, onions and garlic. Mix the pork, rhubarb, onions, garlic, sugar and seasonings in a pie dish. Roll out the pastry and cover the pie. Brush it with the beaten egg. Bake it for 1¼ hours.

The richness of mackerel contrasts well with most sharp sauces. Serve this dish with a bright green vegetable for contrast. Spinach and purple sprouting broccoli are both in season at rhubarb time and both these are excellent.

Mackerel and Rhubarb

4 small to medium mackerel

For the marinade:

1 medium onion, finely chopped
150ml (¼ pt) dry red wine
2.5ml (½ teaspoon) ground
*   cinnamon*
15ml (1 tablespoon) chopped
*   thyme*

450g (1 lb) rhubarb
60ml (2 tablespoons) dry red
*   wine*

Fillet the mackerel. Mix all the ingredients for the marinade together and put them into a flat, oven-proof dish. Turn the mackerel fillets in the marinade and leave them cut-side down. Leave them for at least four hours at room temperature. Chop the rhubarb and put it into a saucepan with the remaining wine. Cover it and set it on a low heat for 15 minutes when it should be thick and pulpy. Preheat the grill to high. Lay the mackerel fillets on the hot rack, cut side up, with all the pieces from the marinade scattered over them. Grill them, close to the heat,

271

until the onions are brown and the mackerel cooked through. Remove the mackerel onto a warmed serving dish and keep them warm. Set the grill pan on a moderate heat on top of the stove. Pour in the liquid from the marinade and bring it to the boil. Mix in the cooked rhubarb. Simmer the sauce for one minute and spoon it over the mackerel.

Towards the end of the rhubarb season, the mint should be coming along in the herb garden. Use them together to pot-roast a piece of lamb. You have three contrasts here, the meat, the sharp sauce and the slight, surprising sweetness of the one or two currants dotted around in the sauce.

Pot-Roast Lamb with Rhubarb Sauce

piece best end neck of lamb weighing around 1.125kg (2½ lb) before boning, chined
2.5ml (½ teaspoon) ground cinnamon
30ml (2 tablespoons) chopped mint

30ml (2 tablespoons) lamb fat or 15g (½ oz) butter
1 small onion, finely chopped
225g (½ lb) rhubarb, chopped
150ml (¼ pt) dry white wine
6cm (2 in) piece cinnamon stick
25g (1 oz) currants

Preheat the oven to 180°C (350°F)/Gas 4.
    Bone the lamb and trim away any excess fat. Scatter the cinnamon and mint over the cut surface. Roll up the joint and tie it with strong thread or fine cotton string. Heat the fat or butter in a flameproof casserole on a high heat. Put in the lamb and brown it all over, ends as well. Remove it and set it aside. Lower the heat and cool the pan a little. Put in the onion and cook it until it is soft. Stir in the rhubarb. Pour in the wine and bring it to the boil. Replace the lamb, tuck in the cinnamon stick, cover the casserole and put it into the oven for one hour. Take out the lamb and keep it warm. Rub all the rhubarb and pan juices through a sieve into a small saucepan. Put in the currants and simmer the sauce on a low heat while you carve the lamb into fairly thick slices. Arrange the lamb on a warm serving dish and pour the sauce over the top.

This next recipe makes a perfect spring salad. The sauce has a creamy texture and during cooking picks up a slight, chickeny flavour. It can easily be prepared in advance for a lunch-time meal. Cook the chicken the day before and let it and the sauce cool separately. Add the final orange the next day.

Chicken Salad with Rhubarb and Orange

1.5kg (3-3½ lb) roasting chicken
2 large oranges

1 onion, peeled and stuck with 2 cloves

2 sprigs thyme
225g (½ lb) rhubarb
30ml (2 tablespoons) chicken fat
* or 15g (½ oz) butter*

150ml (¼ pt) dry white wine
2 boxes mustard and cress

Preheat the oven to 180°C (350°F)/Gas 4.

Slice half of one of the oranges and put the slices inside the chicken with one sprig of thyme. Truss the chicken. Squeeze the juice from the other half. Chop the rhubarb. Heat the fat in a large, flameproof casserole on a high heat. Put in the chicken and brown it all over. Pour in the wine and orange juice and bring them to the boil. Put in the rhubarb, onion, and remaining thyme. Cover the casserole and put it into the oven for one hour. Remove the chicken and let it cool completely. Discard the onion and the thyme and pour all the remaining contents of the casserole into a bowl. Let them cool and skim them. Slice half of the remaining orange thinly. Cut all the peel and pith from the other half and chop all the flesh. Mix it into the rhubarb from the casserole. Joint the chicken and lay it on a serving dish on a bed of cress. Spoon all the rhubarb and orange mixture over the top. Garnish with the orange slices.

Bibliography

Acton, Eliza *Modern Cookery for Private Families* Facsimile Reprint Elek Books Ltd., 1964 (First published 1845)

Austin, Thomas (Editor) *Two fifteenth Century Cookery Books* Published for the Early English Text Association by the Oxford University Press, Reprint 1964 (First published 1888)

Aylett, Mary *Country wines* The 'Modern Living' Series Odhams Press Ltd., 1953

Barber, Richard *Cooking and Recipes from Rome to the Renaissance* Allen Lane, 1973

Beeton, Isabella *Beeton's Book of Household Management* First Edition Facsimile Jonathan Cape Ltd., 1974 (Facsimile first published 1968) (Original first published 1861)

Bender, Arnold *The Facts of Food* Oxford University Press, 1975

Byron, May *Pot Luck or The British Home Cookery Book* Hodder and Stoughton Ltd., 6th edition Jan 1923 (First published 1914)

Culpeper, Thomas *Culpeper's Complete Herbal* Facsimile Edition W. Foulsham and Co. Ltd.

Drive Publications Ltd. (Editors) *The Book of the British Countryside* (1973)

Ernle, Lord *English Farming Past and Present* Heinemann, 6th Edition 1961

Glasse, Hannah *The Art of Cookery Made Plain and Easy* Facsimile Edition S.R. Publishers Ltd., E. Ardsley, Wakefield, Yorks., 1971 (First published 1796)

Groundes-Peace, Zara *Mrs. Groundes-Peace's Old Cookery Notebook* Edited by Robin Howe The International Food and Wine Publishing Co., David and Charles, Rainbird Books, 1971

Hartley, Dorothy *Food in England* Macdonald, 1973 (First published 1954)

Price, Rebecca *The Compleat Cook or the Secrets of a Seventeenth Century Housewife* Compiled and introduced by Madeleine Masson Routledge and Kegan Paul, 1974

Simon, André L., and Howe, Robin *A Dictionary of Gastronomy* Rainbird Reference Books Ltd., 1970 (First Published 1962)

Tannahill, Reay *Food in History* Eyre Methuen, 1973

Whitlock, Ralph *A Short History of Farming in Britain* John Baker, 1965

Wilson, C. Anne *Food and Drink in Britain* Constable, 1973

Woodward, Marcus (arranged by) *Leaves From Gerard's Herbal* Facsimile of 1597 Edition Thorson's Publishers Ltd., 1972

Young, Arthur *The Farmer's Kalendar* Facsimile of 1771 Edition E.P. Publishing Ltd., 1973

US/UK
Conversion Guide

Spoons

1 US teaspoon or tablespoon = 4/5 equivalent standard UK measure

16 US tablespoons = 1 US cup

Liquid Measures

	US	UK
1 cup =	225ml (8 fl oz)	300ml (10 fl oz)
1 pint =	450ml (16 fl oz)	600ml (20 fl oz)

In the US dry foods, such as flour, sugar and shortening, are usually measured by volume. If a recipe calls for ½ cup, pour the ingredients into a measuring cup up to the 4-oz mark, making sure that it is level.

In the UK dry foods are measured by weight. The following weights of common ingredients all equal 1 US cup.

Breadcrumbs	(fresh)	50 g	(2 oz)
	(dried)	100 g	(4 oz)
Butter		225 g	(8 oz)
Dried Fruit	(generous cup)	175 g	(6 oz)
Flour		100 g	(4 oz)
Honey	(generous cup)	350 g	(12 oz)
Rice	(uncooked)	200 g	(7 oz)
Sugar	(granulated/caster)	225 g	(8 oz)
	(congectioner's/icing)	100 g	(4 oz)

Index

288